Two Buck$
to Happiness

Based on the true story of Richard Grudzinski
by his daughter, Vicki Stanley

Published by:
Dad, Ink
717 S. Main Street
North Canton, OH 44720

First published by Dad, Ink – March 2011

Cover design and inside layout: TheBookProducer.com

Printed in the United States of America

ISBN: 978-0-9834512-1-1

Dear Dad,

Here is the book I promised you.
Turn it into a million or two!

Love, Vicki

p.s. I hope you like it.

Table of Contents

Chapter One

"Prove it to Yourself."

There was nothing left to do but cry, so I sat down at the kitchen table and did just that. All the frustration that had been building over the past eight months bubbled over and spilled onto the pages before me. I wearily pushed the papers aside, laid my head on the table and let my doubts take control. What had possessed me to volunteer for this monumental task? What was I thinking? Who did I think I was, anyway?

I cringed with embarrassment, remembering how it had all started when my dad expressed his desire to write a book about his personal history and philosophy. He never actually asked me to write it because I never gave him the chance. In eagerness, I had begged for the opportunity to tell his story. Although he had hesitantly agreed, recalling the doubt in his voice when he said "okay," made me cry a little harder. What was I going to do now?

I groaned as I lifted my head and spotted the two boxes of file notes and volumes of old seminar materials, written and collected over the last six years that Dad had been speaking publicly. Hours upon hours of transcribed interviews and piles of pages mocked me from their perch on the table. Eight months after I actually began writing the book that summarized all his material in one place, I realized my efforts culminated only in several false starts and a second-rate draft. On second thought, what I was looking at was actually a third-rate draft written in second-grade English, and I was terrified.

"Oh God, please help me," I prayed. I didn't know for sure if God was listening, but I hoped so, and I hoped He was paying attention because Dad would be arriving at any moment. As if on cue, I heard his car pull into the driveway. I wiped my eyes with shaking hands and slowly made my way to the living room. I dreaded what he would think of his book so far. Opening the front door, I was immediately chilled by the biting wind. Figures, because that's exactly how I felt – frozen with apprehension.

Dad bounced into the house full of energy despite the six-hour drive from his home in Pennsylvania to mine in Ohio. "Hello, Daughter!" he exclaimed, and immediately folded me into a bear hug so tight that I was having trouble drawing a breath.

"What's wrong?" he asked after planting a kiss on my cheek.

"Nothing," I lied. "How was the drive?"

"Great! The sun was shining and the mountains are beautiful this time of year," he enthused, "and there was a nice breeze blowing." He handed me six boxes of donuts, "We come bearing gifts!" he exclaimed.

I wondered how he could find the monotonous drive so enjoyable but didn't say anything. I took the boxes of donuts that he always brings when he visits and put them on the kitchen counter. The kids must have smelled snacks because Dad's six youngest grandsons came running down the stairs as a pack of one, squealing, "Grandfather's here!" and threw themselves into his arms.

Dad eagerly responded with hugs and kisses for everyone. "Here, I have something for you." He reached into his pocket and handed over a twenty-dollar bill to each of his grandsons. The grandsons are affectionately referred to as The Cousins, because it's easier to remember than each of their names, The Butter Brothers, because it's my sister's last name and she has the most boys, and The Six-Pack, because they move as one pack of six.

"Go to Toys R Us and get yourself something," he offered. I frowned as he was rewarded with more squeals of delight.

Dad noticed and asked, "What's wrong kiddo?"

"Nothing," I lied again.

He shrugged and turned back to the kids, who were scrambling for his attention. For the next hour I watched him joking and laughing his way around the room.

First, he showered attention on my younger sister, Sandi Butter, and her family. She and her husband Mark are the parents of four of the grandsons, all under the age of thirteen. We have been next-door neighbors for thirteen years, allowing her boys and my boys to grow up as brothers, hence Gage, my youngest son at ten, is often referred to as "the other Butter brother."

Grandfather doled out hugs to Gage and Tyler, my oldest at twenty, who was Velcroed to his fiancée, Tiffany, as it was their custom to never be more than three inches apart. Rounding out the group was Mitchell, my nephew, thirteen, also known as "the honorary Butter brother," who had traveled with Dad to Ohio for a mini vacation with his cousins.

Around the table he went, delighting in jokes and funny stories. Dad's enthusiasm for life literally oozes from his pores. From the top of his grey ponytail down to his toes he exudes a passion and energy that on most days inspires, but at this particular moment only left me feeling colder.

After a while, my sister headed home across the driveway, and the kids left in a giggling group to find a new adventure. Dad sat down with me at the table and pushing aside donut crumbs, asked gently, "What's wrong?"

"Why do you keep asking me that?" I snapped back.

"Because it's obvious. Everything in this universe is obvious," he replied softly. "I felt the frustration coming off of you in waves as soon as I walked into the room." I looked up at him and watched with amazement as he magically transformed into *The Preacher. The*

Preacher is the persona that inhabits Dad whenever he gets excited, which is often.

> *"In truth, all is energy,"* he started. *"Everything in our universe consists of energy, and those energies interact with each other. We expend energy with every thought we think, every word we speak, and every deed that we do."*

> He continued, *"Those energies are either positive or negative, constructive or destructive. If we spend our energy constructively, then the outcomes that we experience will be constructive. If we spend our energy destructively, then the outcomes that we experience will be destructive."*

He was getting more excited now. His eyes shone, and he was leaning forward, half out of his chair. One hand was flat on the arm of the chair, and he used his other hand to make his point on his knee. Bouncing in his seat, he was fueled and ready for takeoff.

Our family is a living witness to the stunning transformation that occurs when Dad steps up on his soapbox to preach. From the first word he passionately utters, the evangelist in him engages and captivates his listeners, whether it's an audience of one or a full room. He can't stop moving and gesturing, as his entire being is involved in the process. His voice fluctuates from soft to booming, and his emotional experience plays out on his face from sorrow to triumph. He giggles with a wink, and laughs with his whole body. There are some that don't agree with Dad, but many are rendered spellbound by his presence.

> He expounded, *"The good news is that our lives reflect how we spend our energy. Of course, the bad news is that our lives also reflect how we spend our energy. But, I have*

*learned that as we become more responsible and account-
able for how we spend our energy, we become more aware
of ourselves.*

*As we become more aware of ourselves, we begin to re-
alize the power we possess in this universe. Through the
awareness, the acceptance, and the expression of our
greater Selves, we can literally co-create our own reality
and transform our lives!"*

I wanted to transform my life, really I did. But, all I could see in
the moment were my own shortcomings. I took a deep breath, pointed to my notes, and ventured, "Dad, I don't know if I can do this."

As if I had waved my magic wand, *The Preacher* disappeared
and Dad was in his place.

"What you are suffering from is doubt, daughter, and doubt
comes from fear. All energy comes from only two sources, love or
fear. Have you already forgotten about LightBuck$?" asked Dad
incredulously.

Years ago, Dad had been intent on finding a way to explain these
seemingly complicated positive and negative energy structures of the
universe, and how they interacted with other, in a way that was easy
for his grandsons to understand. One morning, he woke up with the
idea of LightBuck$.

Roughly the size and shape of dollar bills, LightBuck$ represent
all the constructive or positive energy that exists in the universe. They
encompass the most valuable substances on earth: the love a mother
feels for her children, the joy of a child's spontaneous laughter, the
tranquility of a nighttime snowfall. Think of every positive experience you have ever had throughout your life. The emotions you felt
at that moment were LightBuck$.

Other LightBuck$ include peace, wisdom, gratitude, respect, trust, compassion, confidence, happiness, caring, gratitude, compassion, patience, peace, kindness, humor, mercy, ecstasy, respect, enthusiasm, humility, vitality, liveliness, helpfulness, and love. They are all LightBuck$. There are an infinite number of LightBuck$ in the universe, and you can always get more. Dad even created a website, www.lightbucks.com, where you can log on and print as many as you wish. There is no limit per customer!

DarkBuck$ are the opposite.

Dad continued, "Whenever you endeavor to accomplish something, your mind flips back and forth between doubt and certainty. Sometimes you believe you can write a bestseller, other times you doubt your abilities to connect two words together. The only way to overcome those doubts is to be aware of your thoughts in the moment and transform the negative ones, the Darkbuck$ into positive ones, like LightBuck$, " he concluded confidently.

"But how do I do that?" I whined.

"Easy. Your mind can only focus on one thing at a time, so think of something else. Tell me, why do you want to write this book?"

I responded instantly, "Because I love doing it!"

He laughed again and challenged, "You don't act like you love it."

"But it's so hard." I sound just like my kids whining about their math homework. OMG.

"Of course it's hard. If it were easy, everyone would do it. But I learned this a long time ago: When you set out toward something, you must do everything important and necessary to bring it about, or it will never be real. You seem to be doing everything important and necessary to bring this book about, so you are on the right track." He sat back contentedly.

"Then why do I feel so bad?" I wasn't willing to give up.

"I don't know. Let's start at the beginning. " He smiled. "The first step to co-creation is intention. *Why* you do something is more important that *what* you do. We already know that you want to write a book. But more importantly, we know your intention for writing the book."

"We do?" He might know, but I was clueless.

He laughed out loud, "Sure, we do! You told me."

"I did?" By now I was starting to feel my Polish ancestry.

"You told me you wanted to write this book because you love doing it. That's a great reason, a great intention, because your intention is rooted in love. The energy you expend, when based in love, will return to you in love."

"It seems so easy for you. You're always happy," I whined again.

He chuckled, proving my point. "I've been living this philosophy a long time."

And it was true, I realized with sudden clarity. For as long as I could remember, Dad had insisted that we were the architects of our own reality and solely responsible for creating our own happiness. Over the years, he parlayed that steadfast belief into successful multi-million dollar businesses, a career-consulting practice and a public speaking passion.

I listened with fondness as Dad continued, "I learned a long time ago, when Mom and I moved into our dream house, that we co-created our own reality with our thoughts, words and deeds. But it takes practice, lots of practice."

He went on, "Remember, the average person thinks 60,000 thoughts a day, and 45,000 of those are negative. When I feel those negative feelings, or think those destructive thoughts, I catch myself and replace those negative thoughts with positive ones. I want to expend my energy from a place of love."

I hardly had time to consider his words before *The Preacher* was back.

"We create our own reality according to our thoughts, our words, and our deeds. Everything that exists in our universe was created first from a thought. That thought grew into words, and those words grew into deeds. You want to change your reality? Start with changing your thoughts."

I made a last-ditch attempt to bring Dad back to my world. "So, that's it? That's all you have to do?"

"That's what I did. That's what I do," he said confidently, "And I do it every day. That's why I create happiness for my grandsons. Because in watching their excitement, I get to experience happiness. I love my life!"

"Sounds too easy. Is it really true?"

"Who knows? I've taught you to question everything, so prove it to yourself. I have to keep proving it to myself. In your case, it either is true or it isn't. But tell me this, what do you have to lose?"

My pride, I thought, but didn't dare utter. Instead, I asked the next logical question, "So what do I do next?"

"Write it down," he responded instantly. "Here, take this piece of paper, it's blank."

I ignored the stab of his words and dutifully took the page he offered. "What do I write? Do I start at the beginning?"

"No," he smiled, "You write the end of the story. Write this down: 'I am a writer because I love writing.'"

"That's it?" I was skeptical to say the least, but I wrote.

"That's it!" he exclaimed, "Now it's real! It's right there." He pointed to the page.

"But that isn't a book," I complained, "It's a sentence."

"For now," he replied, "But are you going to cry about what you don't have, a finished book, or are you going to appreciate what you have in this moment, a beginning?" He stood up and yawned. Walking over, he wrapped me in a bear hug, "I love you and I believe in you. Now, go to bed and think about all the other things in your life that you love, write them down, and then we'll talk again tomorrow."

I wasn't sure what to believe, but he was right about one thing: What did I have to lose? Despite wanting to be the person to write Dad's book so much that my teeth hurt, I knew in my heart that I was approaching the task with absolutely no experience in creative writing, and if I failed to deliver, he would merely hire another writer to complete the project with him. His message was too important *not* to be written by *someone*.

"Okay, Dad, I'll try," I said, cautiously agreeing to the task.

"Don't try. Do," he giggled back.

I couldn't help but smile as I said my goodnights, hugs included, and headed off to bed. I knew I had to rise early the next morning, and I was mentally exhausted.

Chapter Two

"Pay Attention!"

"I knew it!" I muttered under my breath as I quickly made my way down the stairs, the sound of one of the kids crying quickening both my step and my pulse.

"What happened?" I demanded of Gage and his five cousins, who were seated around him quietly but guiltily on the sofa. The source of the crying, now reduced to a whimper and salty tears, belonged to Benji, the youngest.

"It was an accident," Gage insisted. "We were just playing and Benji got hit by the ball. It was an accident, I promise," he pleaded.

I knew this would happen. It's always the same story, I thought to myself and then turned to face Dad, who was seated at the kitchen table with his mug of hot tea, and the four newspapers he buys every morning to read throughout the day spread out in piles around him. Ignoring me, he kept reading.

I crossed my arms and shot him my best angry-mom glare and tightly asked, "Dad?" drawing his name out into two syllables. That always works.

He looked up at me over his bifocals and laughed, "Ugh, it's always fun and games until someone gets hurt." He giggled again and continued, "They're kids. They're having fun. Listen to them," he implored, "I love that sound!"

I turned to look at the kids and was stunned at what I saw; he was right. They were already giggling together over the newest Nintendo DS game, bought at yesterday's Grandfather-sponsored trip to Toys R Us, the latest injury long forgotten and filed away.

"I give up," I thought to myself, and sat down with Dad at the table. The truth was, I was ready to give up on the book as well. We had been working together all morning going over our material and refining his story, adding in more details about Dad's younger years growing up in near poverty in Camden, New Jersey. We talked about his and Mom's brave move to Allentown soon after they were married, to pursue their dream of opening their own business, and then the early years of starting and growing their employment agency together.

Documenting his history was fascinating, sure, but I took more comfort knowing that every fact was easily verifiable. Even if we made an innocuous mistake on the exact year their dream house was built, for example, a simple Google search of property tax records would quickly yield the truth that we sought. It was important to me to get it right.

But the other stuff? I had my doubts. Attempting to capture the essence of Dad's beliefs and philosophies was proving to be far more difficult than I originally anticipated. How could I describe, in a compelling way, what he believes about God, The Creator, spirituality, and creation within our universe when I wasn't even sure what I believed myself? Honestly, if I believed that I had the power to co-create my own reality, I would have co-created the winning lottery ticket a long time ago. What was the truth? I wanted some proof.

I didn't speak my doubts aloud, but rather took a deep breath and instead asked, "Are you ready to go to lunch? I'm starving."

"Absolutely!" he jumped up and started gathering up the newspapers.

"I'll go get my purse and meet you at the car. I'll drive."

"Sure thing," he responded happily. Ha! I scoffed inside. Nothing is a sure thing. But, I went to retrieve the car keys anyway.

Belted and settled, I pointed the car toward Belden Village, the shopping and restaurant district five minutes from the house. I was in the mood for Italian, but apparently Dad and The Preacher were both in the mood to talk, and each struggled for my attention.

"I'm sorry, what did you say? I was distracted." I asked everyone in the car.

The Preacher spoke first.

"Paying attention to every thought allows you to drive your consciousness. You are co-creating your own reality whether you are aware of it or not. You are either conscious of it, or you aren't. If you pay attention to your thoughts, you can drive your consciousness and drive your thinking, much like you drive your car."

Dad started laughing out loud and interrupted with, "But, most people don't even realize it! Can you imagine if you piled your whole family into the RV to go on vacation, but instead of paying attention to the road when you are flying down the highway at 65, you set the cruise control, and then climbed into the back to take a nap? That's what it's like to *not* drive your consciousness. If you don't pay attention, you could go off the road, or worse."

Dad was laughing and bouncing in his seat just thinking about the RV careening down the highway with the driver napping. He truly delighted in the telling. "Remember when I was teaching you and your sisters to drive?" he giggled, "What's the first rule of driving? *Pay Attention!*"

I shook my head and smiled, pulling into the Macaroni Grill parking lot.

"I knew it!" Dad yelled and slapped his knee. I jumped as he exclaimed again, "I knew it! I knew I should have brought the coupon for Macaroni Grill from the newspaper. I knew it, but I didn't listen to my intuition."

He continued his discourse as we got out of the car, the force of the wind making it hard to shut the car door. He raised his voice to be heard as we headed for the front door. "There was a coupon in one of the papers today for three dollars off two lunch entrees. I almost put it in my pocket, but then said to myself, 'Richard, that's dumb. I shouldn't bring a coupon because I don't know what restaurant we are going to for lunch.' So, I left it on the table. I didn't trust my intuition." He laughed at his minor misfortune.

I laughed, too, but then grew serious. "How do you know it's your intuition and not just one of those random 60,000 thoughts you think a day?" I challenged.

"You have to listen to your inner knowing," Dad responded as we sat down and accepted menus, but as he grew more animated, was dangerously close to giving way to *The Preacher*.

"Yehuda Berg, a rabbi from California wrote this, and I believe he described it well: 'Intuition is a direct and foolproof perception of something true. It brings immediate pure productive and unerring insight. It is inner knowing without reasoning. Intuition is frequently confused with imagination, which in turn is a creation of the mind. Imagination is human; intuition is divine.'"

The Preacher broke in with,

> *"Intuition is your soul talking to you. It is a knowing without thinking, and it exists beyond logic and understanding. Intuition is a hunch, a gut feeling, an insight into your greater self. It is a knowing without reasoning. We are connected to the energy that is a part of everything through our intuition; and through our intuition we experience wisdom."*

At that moment, the server appeared to take our order, causing *The Preacher* to pause and Dad to scan quickly over the menu, while

I stuck with my perennial favorite, caprese salad and chicken parmesan. After Dad ordered up lasagna with extra cheese, I responded to *The Preacher.*

"But you can't prove it – intuition. It's not fool-proof." I was daring him to make a claim he couldn't prove. Sometimes I'm not a very nice person.

Dad didn't take the bait, but instead thoughtfully replied, "No, of course not. Not everything we believe in this universe can be explained by science. Take religion, for example. Every organized religion requires its believers to take a leap of faith at some point in their doctrine.

"I believe there are universal laws and truths that are happening whether you are aware of them or not. Gravity works whether we are aware of it or not. You can't see it or touch it, but it's there nonetheless. Try taking a walk off of a three-story building and you'll see what I'm talking about," he laughed.

He paused, a distant memory surfacing, then continued quietly, "My best friend, Robbie, was killed when we were five, and my life was spared only because of my mother's intuition. Every single day we would play together, Robbie and I, and one of our favorite places to play was the railroad track that ran behind the school. Climbing over the fence was a challenge, but we did it and we would play alongside the tracks." Dad paused for a moment then nearly whispered, "On that day, my mom refused to let me outside to play, and I still have no idea why. I threw a fuss at the time, as kids do," Dad smiled, "but she was adamant."

I sighed as Dad paused, knowing how his sad story ends. "We'll never know what really happened that afternoon, whether Robbie slipped and fell, or was just too close to the track, but in the end, we know that he was killed instantly from the impact of the train. I'll never forget hearing the news, or the look on my mother's face when she learned of his death."

"I didn't understand *what* had happened or *why*. But, I knew something *did* happen that day; something that made my mother go against what was normal and rational and beyond my understanding, and it saved my life."

We were both quiet while we graciously accepted our steaming plates and began feasting. Then Dad came back to the Macaroni Grill. "So, it benefits me to pay attention to my intuition because I believe it makes my life easier. I trust my intuition. You will have to prove it to yourself that it even exists, let alone works," he concluded.

"Some people call that feeling ESP, but in our house, we call it ESPN, for the ESP Network," I said just as quietly. "You know, when I'm thinking about someone, and the phone rings, and it's that person? Doesn't happen all the time," I pointed out, " But, when it does happen, we call it ESPN." I laughed, and he laughed with me.

"So it does happen to you, sometimes. In the end, daughter, don't just believe what I say, you have to make up your own mind about what you believe and prove it to yourself."

That was my opening, and I took it. "I don't know what I believe, Dad. I'm having trouble writing anything for this book that I don't one hundred percent believe to my core. I want to write the truth, but I don't know for sure what that is. I don't even know if any of us can ever really know for sure; and, even if we think we know what the truth might be, we certainly can't prove it," I paused, out of breath.

"I taught you well, Daughter," he chuckled.

"Don't give yourself too much credit there, buddy, I don't know anything," I retorted.

"You know more than you think. I taught you to question everything, and you do. I taught you well," he repeated, then continued.

"Most people accept other people's beliefs as their own without ever stopping to examine whether they are a good fit. They listen to their parents, teachers, and friends and believe every word that comes out of their mouths. They internalize their comments, and believe what they are told about themselves by others." He got quiet for a moment, which is very rare, and therefore, it didn't last long.

"Which is great if kids are being told by their parents that they are brilliant and gifted, and not so great if they are being told they are useless and worthless. It pains me to hear those types of offhand remarks from parents who don't realize the power and responsibility they have in forming their children's belief system. The first step to co-creation is intention; the second step is beliefs. So question your beliefs."

"But my beliefs change as I get more information. There was a time when I thought Pittsburgh was in Ohio. Then I got new information, namely a map, and discovered that it was actually located in Pennsylvania. Duh."

"Beliefs do change as you learn more about yourself, your values, your geography." He smirked. I smirked back.

"When Mom was young, around thirteen, she decided to set out on a journey she referred to as her "church search," he recalled fondly. She had been raised in a Protestant church, and while she loved her church and her religion, she wanted to explore other belief systems.

"I remember her telling me about this," I smiled, encouraging my Dad to go on.

"She had fun! She loved it!" he said, laughing softly.

"Yep. She did!" I joined him.

"She visited the Catholic and Baptist churches, Jewish synagogues, Episcopalian, Methodist. Gosh, I don't even remember how many she went to, but I know it lasted for years. And what she found was this." Dad immediately sat up in his chair and pointed his finger at me, not accusingly, but emphatically. "She learned that their core beliefs were all about the same thing. Love. Love one another. That's it!" he exclaimed. "Despite all the doctrine, all the rules, and all the ways to exclude people, everyone is really saying the same thing. Love one another."

He continued, "When we got married, Mom converted to Catholocism and we had you girls baptized, and you attended St. Catherine's Cathedral."

"But you didn't believe in it. We didn't go to church often," I accused.

"It's not that we didn't believe in it," he explained. "It's that we didn't believe *everything* about the doctrine."

"Every single organized religion uses different words, enacts different rules and protocols, and practices their own rituals. But, the underlying belief they all share is *Love*. Don't get me wrong, Mom and I wanted you girls to have a religious foundation, and the Catholic education you received was top-notch. But, we also wanted you girls to learn to question your beliefs, to explore other beliefs and ultimately make up your own minds about what *you* believe."

He grew excited, "Every single one of us has the inalienable right to choose what we believe, and to practice that belief!" he patriotically proclaimed.

He grew quiet, and said, "In the end, it's all about what you believe."

The Preacher took over for a moment.

"All energy is either positive or negative. All energy is either constructive or destructive. All energy starts from love or fear."

We were quiet for a few moments, each lost in thought, when I asked for more clarification. "How do you know what to believe? How do you know it's right?" I recalled long- ago worries of making the wrong choice, thereby guaranteeing an eternity of Hell and/ or Purgatory.

"First of all, for every single person in our universe, there are equally as many different perceptions of reality." He started chuckling, "Imagine this: You are standing at the street corner, and suddenly out of nowhere, two men run out of a bank, waving guns and yelling.

"The Bank Robbers jump in their car and pull away, squealing their tires. At the same time that the bank alarm goes off, there is a car accident in the middle of the intersection when the bank robbers ran the red light and hit a dynamite truck." By now he was laughing out loud, and I couldn't help but laugh, too.

"When the police interview all thirty-two witnesses, do you know what they will find?" he demanded, laughing.

I already knew the answer, but kept quiet, letting him have the floor.

"They'll have thirty-two different versions of what happened! Oh, some of the reports will be similar at some points, and some witnesses will agree with others on other points, but no two versions will be exactly the same! And that's because we all have different perceptions of reality."

"So how do you know which one is the right one?" I challenged.

"Who says there is any right or wrong?" he shot back. "It is what it is. The case for religion is the same – it's all a matter of what you believe," he finished with a flourish.

"Then how do you know what to trust, or more importantly, *who* to trust?"

He answered instantly, "Be still and listen. You'll know. Signs will come to you. All energy starts from love or fear, so listen and you'll hear it in a person's tone of voice, or you'll feel it in the energy of the room, or you'll see it in their body language, but you must pay attention! If you feel positive energy, stay; if you feel negative energy, get the heck outta there!"

He grew more animated, "Your intuition is a sign telling you what to believe, or sadly in some cases, what *not* to believe. But you have to Pay Attention!"

Just then, the server approached our table with the check. Dad, as is his custom, reached into his pocket for his wallet and immediately offered, "I'll take that bill right here."

She turned to Dad and said, "Do you have a coupon, sir? The register automatically rang up your check with our special of three dollars off two entrees, but I would need the coupon to staple to the bill."

Dad instantly burst out laughing, holding his sides, stunning the server. I cringed as she took a frightened step backwards. "No," he roared, "I don't have the coupon. I didn't listen to my intuition." He kept giggling as she threw us a puzzled look, clearly doubting our sanity, and left to correct the check.

"You have to write this down, Daughter. Write this in the book! Write about intuition," he demanded.

"I can only write what I believe, Dad." I was firm in that belief, at the very least.

"Write that down, too. Write down everything you believe, and write down every time your intuition has either served you well, or it didn't."

"And you think that will help make a book?" I doubted it.

"Who knows? Have a little faith. Anything is possible."

With Dad still laughing and murmuring joyful praises of thanks for the laughter we had just shared, we headed for home.

I didn't say anything about my doubts, but offered up a silent prayer of my own. I didn't know what to believe, but I hoped it was true because I was running out of time.

Chapter Three

"Do it Now."

An hour later, I could feel my annoyance rising to dangerous levels as I waited impatiently for Dad to finish wasting time playing with the kids. Honestly, I fumed, he's the biggest kid of them all, never having outgrown the capacity for numerous daily bouts of play time. With mere hours left before Dad needed to head for home, we would have to hurry to cover so much ground in such a short period of time.

I waited for a break in the action before I cut in with, "Dad, are you ready to get started?"

"Huh?" He returned my pointed look with a blank one of his own.

"Uh, sure," he replied distractedly. "Carry on without me, kids." He commanded, getting up from his place on the sofa where he had been winning the latest X Box tournament against his grandsons. He must get a lot of practice time, I thought wryly.

I skillfully hid my irritation while he moved about the kitchen preparing his ritual mug of hot tea with honey. After he had settled himself at the kitchen table and had consumed a loud slurp, he looked up and asked, "Where are we?"

I responded instantly with a question of my own, "Do you know what time it is?" I knew that by requiring him to look at his iPhone, I would reinforce my eagerness to get back on task. Instead, I watched with puzzlement as Dad lifted up his arm and starting shaking it.

"First of all, we have all the time in the world," he said laughing, and then posed a question of his own. "Do you know what this is?" he continued with amusement, pointing to the red string tied around his shaking wrist. "This is my Polish watch. Whenever somebody asks me for the time, I raise my arm and shake it."

"That does two things. The first is that it reminds me that I am a spiritual being living in a physical world. The second is that it tells me the time. And the time is NOW." He concluded triumphantly smiling.

"Now" I repeated woodenly.

"Yes, now." He leaned forward as if to impart a secret and when he spoke, *The Preacher* had taken over.

"The only time is now, this moment. Time as you experience it is not real; it is man-made. Built into the human consciousness is a dynamic that allows us to remember the past as a sequence of events. Those memories stabilize our reality with a sense of continuity. The passing of time is simply an illusion and all we really experience is this Moment.

There is a new co-creation happening every single moment. The past is simply a memory and the future a thought; the only thing that exists in any given moment is the present. The NOW.

The Preacher took a deep breath and flew right on over my head.

"The perception of time is what separates the spiritual world from the physical one. It divides 'what is' from 'what is not' in the universe. Time does not exist in the spiritual world or God-consciousness. Time is actually fluid and flexible, and one moment can last a lifetime and a lifetime can pass in a moment."

"I don't understand that at all, it doesn't make sense," I blurted.

"Sure you do, you just don't remember." Dad countered, taking over for *The Preacher.* "What about the car accident?"

"The one with the bank robbers and the dynamite truck?" I asked, confused.

"No! No!" he laughed. "The one near your office."

"Oh, my God, you're right, I remember," I acknowledged, the memory flooding back to the surface.

Leaving work last week to grab lunch, I was stopped at the corner behind a little red car, the two of us waiting for the light to turn green. When it did, we both started to move. As the car in front of me reached the middle of the intersection, a dark SUV came hurtling down the road from the north. The moment the SUV entered my peripheral vision, time literally stopped.

While in reality, it actually only took three seconds for the SUV to broadside the little red car and send both cars spinning, it seemed to have taken two hours time in my mind. Time slowed down for so long that I could have easily climbed into the back of my car for a nap and still have had plenty of time to climb back up front to witness the actual impact.

"You're right, it's true," I admitted, nodding my head. "Weird and amazing at the same time, but true."

"It works the other way too, you know." He was nodding his head vigorously and pointing at me. "You can't comprehend why I love the long drive out here to see you. But, when I plug in my iTunes and let my mind just wander where it wants to take me, the time goes by instantly. The six-hour drive seems to go by in one hour! I call that *Zip Time*! I love it!" he cried gleefully.

"Okay, maybe you are right. Maybe not," I replied. "But we need to get busy. We have a lot of work to do and not much time left before your one-hour *Zip* drive home," I finished, smiling.

He smiled broadly back, "There's no time like the present!"

"Okay, then," I grabbed a pile of papers and held them up. "I'm confused about the timeline of the plot," I began, once again serious.

"We have everything we need regarding your background, the family, the businesses you opened, your philosophies and such, but, I'm stuck on the timing of when to introduce each component. Do I write the last sixty-three years of your life in chronological order? Do I write from the perspective of flashbacks and memories? Does the whole book only span one week's period of time? I'm so confused," I groaned, out of breath.

Dad smiled at my bafflement and offered, "Let's go look at the outline again."

I nodded and stood up tiredly; meanwhile Dad sprang from his chair and bounced down the two stairs that lead from the kitchen to my home office. There, we stood gazing silently at the hundred plus colorful post-it notes tacked to the wall above my desk, separated in groups of ten.

I suddenly realized that we were staring at a sea of sticky-notes instead of reviewing a professionally organized and neatly typewritten outline, complete with lettered sections and Roman numerals. "I'm sorry, Dad. I'm sorry that I can't write an outline like I imagine you're supposed to when you set out to write a book. The best I could do was this," I lamented, sweeping my arm across the wall. I suddenly wished I had gone to college, or at the very least, taken a creative writing class or two. I groaned inwardly.

"Don't be sorry. I love your outline. Here, let me take a picture," he laughed, whipping out his iPhone and capturing the moment for posterity and iPhoto. He put his phone in his pocket and walked over to the French doors that lead to the backyard deck. "You're right. Some people see the forest and some see the trees. What do you see when you look out here?"

I worried that there was so much to do and so little time. At first, it was an inkling, but by now I was certain we were not going to accomplish much in the way of the book, so I walked over to the doors resignedly to join my dad. Despite the clouds building in the distance and the shadows growing longer by the minute, I still loved what I saw. "What do I see? I see all the beautiful trees."

I stood and gazed at all the majestic trees that form a protective green-screen around the backyard I share with my sister and her family, and breathed deeply. I truly love our backyard sanctuary. I admired the towering pines scattered in the back, along the sides, and overlooking the creek that divides our house from Sandi's. I smiled at the climbing rope Tyler had tied to a high branch of the maple that sits square in the middle of the yard. Boys will be boys.

I recalled with dismay how a handyman once suggested I remove the old gnarled Maple that had grown over the years clear through the side of the kid's playhouse, originally home to a chicken coop eighty years ago when the house was built. Was he crazy? I love that tree, I thought tenderly. I loved all the trees. The tranquil backyard setting is the reason we bought the house the moment we spotted it thirteen years ago, and I still fall in love with the view every time I look outside.

Dad snatched me from my memory and brought me back to the present, exclaiming, "You are exactly right, daughter! You see all the trees. You see each and every one of them. Why, I'm willing to bet that you see every branch, leaf and twig as well!" He sounded very sure of himself, so I looked again.

"You're right, I do. I also see the squirrels and the birds and all the toys the kids left outside, and the weeds threatening to overtake the trampoline!" I laughed.

"Do you know why you see the backyard that way? Because of your personality, that's why. You're a Sensor. When you look outside you see the millions of details that make up your backyard; the trees, the leaves, the twigs and so forth. When you look at your business, you see the millions of details that go into each component: clients, employees, payroll. And, when you look at your book, you see the millions of details that populate a good story: the characters, the setting, the tone of the funny stories, even the exact words to describe each."

Dad was starting to get warmed up. "Now, I'm an intuitive thinker. I see the big picture, where you see the details. When I look outside, I see the whole back yard. When I look at our book, I see the main themes. You see all the trees, where I see the forest."

By now he was on a roll. "Neither way is right or wrong, it just is. How you take in information, orient yourself to the outside world, make decisions, and energize yourself all define your personality type. There is no right or wrong personality type, as we all exist at some point on the same scale.

Elvis had left the building and *The Preacher* was in his place.

"The third part of co-creation is understanding. Understanding your personality leads to a better understanding of your greater self. Each of us perceives reality from a different perspective, and our individual personality type contributes to that perception which is uniquely ours. Understanding your personality leads to a greater understanding of yourself. Once you understand yourself, then you can be yourself."

Dad settled down and giggled, "Every person wakes up in the morning and puts on his or her personality glasses. Some people are outgoing, and others prefer a measure of solitude; that's their personality preference. One teenager works well in advance of a history project, while her sibling prefers to leave everything to a last-minute rush; that's their personality preference. Understanding what makes you tick, understanding your personality preferences leads to a greater awareness and understanding of you, your Self." Dad turned to me suddenly and commanded, "Don't forget to put the website in the book. www.humanmetrics.com offers an online version of a personality assessment similar to the Meyers Briggs Type Indicator®."

"Okay, I will."

"Here, write it down. Now." He laughed, handing me a pen.

I did what I was told as I listened to Dad's enthusiasm for the subject with fondness. Despite having heard the merits of personality preferences approximately 3,756 times over the past twenty years, I understood my parents' passion for the subject.

For ten years after they made the decision to close their business and start an executive recruiting firm from home, they steadily built their client and industry base while enjoying their new roles as taxi drivers, shuttling their daughters to and from school and various activities.

But, while they were building their business and reveling in their family, something bigger was pulling at them, urging them in a different direction. Over the course of several years and several hundred interviews, a distinct pattern had emerged. Many people my parents talked to were unhappy in their careers, but they didn't know why.

Their desire to help those they had met led them to research personality profiles and ultimately to the Myers Briggs Type Indicator™. After becoming certified to deliver the instrument on a professional basis, they launched their newest business, American Career Center, assisting and guiding those in the midst of career or life changes.

They worked side-by-side in career counseling – Dad as the employment coach, while Mom went back to college to become a psychologist, a dream she had delayed while raising us girls. Helping others to understand more about their careers led their clients to discover truths about themselves as individuals as well. The enjoyment they felt when they were able to help people understand about themselves only added to their mutual fulfillment.

So, while Dad's enthusiasm was completely logical, I wondered with tenderness how much of his passion actually comes from helping people, or instead, the altruistic vision he shared with my mother. I interrupted with, "Mom loved being a psychologist. She loved helping people."

Dad instantly forgave my intrusion into his monologue and agreed, "Yes, she did. She waited a long time to go back to school, but when the time was right, she did it! Timing is everything."

"I agree, Dad, timing is everything. So what should I do about the timing of the plot?"

He turned and looked once again at the wall of stickies. "Time to line up the trees!" he laughed and continued, "Plan your work and work your plan." He looked at me and demanded, "What are the next five things we need to do? Write them down."

I grabbed the nearest pen from the desk and whipped a sheet of paper out of the printer tray, while blurting out my worries in quick succession, "We need to answer the timeline question. We need to fill in the blanks in units eight and ten. We need to verify some dates in question."

He laughed out loud, "Good. Good. Keep going."

"I still have difficulty with some of the philosophies. I also need to get an outside opinion on what we've written so far, to make sure I'm on the right track." I continued for about fifteen minutes filling most of the page, emptying my brain of every detail, question, problem, or issue I could muster. Exhausted, I set the pen down, both of us looking at the page I had filled with tasks.

"Great!" Dad said, "Now we have a plan! Plan your work and work your plan, that's what I always say!" he commanded in his booming CEO voice.

"This isn't a plan, it's a to-do list," I muttered ruefully. "So what do I do first?"

"Do something. Do anything. Just pick something off the list and do it." He started giggling, "What does that commercial say? Just do it!" his face was turning red from his mirth.

"How do I know it's the right thing?"

"Because there is no wrong thing. There are no mistakes. There are only opportunities to make a new plan and do something different. Pay attention and watch for the signs to show you the way. They're everywhere. Pay attention to your intuition," he finished.

"I don't know, Dad." I hated to complain, but I was looking at a very long list. "It's a lot to do. It's going to take a long time." *The Preacher* got a quick word in,

> *"Doubt Not. Remember who and what you are.*
> *Fear Not. For you are blessed.*
> *Work on. Do what is important and necessary.*
> *Wait. Have faith in your creation."*

Then Dad jumped up and ran over to the doors waving his arms, "How long do you think it took for that maple tree in your yard to get that big? It didn't happen overnight; it took about fifty years. You can't just throw a seed out the window and have it sprout up to be sixty feet tall while you are sleeping, you know." He laughed at me as if I should already know this, but I still couldn't help the feeling of impatience.

"Remember, the passing of time is simply an illusion, so don't worry about the progress. All you have is the moment, so just do something *now*, in this moment."

"Okay," I yawned. My head was swimming. I stood up, stretched, and grabbed my iPhone. "Oh my God! It's only been an hour! I thought for sure it was midnight!"

"*Zip Time!*" Dad said emphatically, "I love it!"

"I guess it's true – time flies when you're having fun," I commented wryly.

The Preacher got the last word. *"When you experience Truth in one moment, you exist outside Time for that moment."*

"You have to plan your work, work your plan, and set a deadline." Dad grabbed his phone and swung to the calendar app. "Let's set a time to get together again, and that will be your deadline for completing the next phase of the book, agreed?"

"Okay." I yawned again.

We agreed to meet several weeks later, this time in Allentown. I was feeling fairly productive about our meeting, despite my earlier misgivings, and was hopeful as I headed up the stairs to bed. Suddenly, I was assailed by regret as I recalled the disrespectful way I had treated Dad when he was playing with the kids. I had rushed him from his fun and now that we were finished working early, the kids were already sleeping. Mournfully, I prepared for bed and fell asleep wishing I could turn back the clock to allow him more time with his grandsons.

Chapter Four

"Apologize!"

I woke the next morning feeling good about the day's prospects, but then remembered Dad sleeping in the guest bedroom and instantly felt tired and full of remorse for the way I had treated him last evening. I listened to the rain pelting the house, and with fifteen minutes remaining before the alarm made the morning official, crawled out of bed and sat heavily in the armchair. Wishing for a cup of coffee, but not wanting to expend energy on the task, I lit a cigarette and considered my plight.

Another three-day marathon in my home-office with Dad working on the book would come to a close within two hours, when Dad and my nephew, after rounds of hugs and kisses, would pile into the car for the long drive home. What did I have to show for our efforts this time?

According to Dad, I should focus on what I have rather than what I don't have, so I quickly took inventory and made a mental list: I have some more research; a few sentences of text; a crink in my neck from my worn-out pillow; a lengthy to-do list; and last but not least, hardly any time left to enjoy the weekend. That should sum it up, I thought miserably. Oh, let's not forget the pit in my stomach clearly labeled 'regret' for the manner in which I treated my father yesterday.

My blue funk continued as I obsessed over my shortcomings while I showered and dressed. Dad was at the table with his tea and papers, and he looked up at me over his bifocals as I walked in.

"Good morning!" he offered cheerfully.

"It's morning." I ignored the good part of it and plunged right in. "Dad, I apologize for rushing you yesterday when you were playing with the kids."

"No apology necessary," he countered immediately.

"Yes, there is. I was rude. I rushed you, and we didn't have to hurry. We had enough time and I feel terrible about how I acted."

"You're not rude, so don't feel terrible." He quickly turned serious and *The Preacher* jumped in with,

"Remember, you are co-creating your reality according to your thoughts, words and deeds. Thoughts are things. If the thoughts you think and the words you speak are destructive, then those feeling energies will grow and will lead to destructive deeds. Don't go there.

Be aware of every word you speak and it's meaning in the moment. Say what you mean and mean what you say. Every. Single. Word."

"But, I can't control how I feel."

"No, you can't. But you can control how you respond or react to the feeling. Recognize the feeling. Express it constructively. Dismiss it. Remember?" Dad explained as he wrapped me in a tight hug.

"I know better. I'll let it go," I responded quietly. After all, he was right.

"So, do you forgive me?" I asked, laughing.

"You need to forgive yourself, I already did," he said, but seeing the crestfallen look on my face, quickly added, "I don't believe there is anything to forgive, but for your sake, yes, I forgive you." He laughed back, squeezing me tighter. I smiled, absolved.

Just then, the cousins rushed through the door, a chattering six-pack of testosterone. Only this time, their ramblings held a nasty tone. Dad and I caught the tail end of the conversation.

"I beat you in points," one cousin boasted to another.

"Yeah, well, you're stupid!" the other retorted.

"Whoa, buddy, Respect The People!" Grandfather demanded with loving firmness.

"As a matter of fact, sit down right here, kids." His tone was firm, but he was smiling as he ran around the table, pulling out chairs, encouraging the kids to sit. They did, joining Tyler and Tiff who were already seated.

After everyone had slowed their fidgeting, Dad looked at each person in the room individually and began.

"I have a question for you: If your neighbor rang your doorbell and wanted to borrow some milk, what would you do?"

They all answered at once, nodding and laughing, that they would give their neighbor some milk if he asked for some.

"Of course you would!" Grandfather exclaimed, laughing. "You're nice neighbors!" When they had quieted some (relatively speaking, that is), he continued.

"Well, what if the neighbor came back the next day and wanted to borrow some more milk, what would you do?" Raising one eyebrow, he tilted his head expectantly.

"Uh, sure." They were slower to respond this time. Still, they all agreed that they would give their neighbor more milk. I stood back, amused, wondering where this was going.

He posed the question a third time, walking around the table, but by now, the kids were seriously re-thinking the question, wondering if it had a punch line. One by one, they all agreed, albeit slowly, to give more milk to the obviously thirsty neighbor.

"Okay, then. Wow, you guys are *really* nice neighbors!" He folded his arms over his chest, hardly holding back his laughter and queried, "What would you do if he came back the fourth day and wanted to borrow some *more* milk? What would you say?"

Tyler, who up to now had been silent, but nodding, immediately piped up with, "Uh, we're out of milk?"

The kids burst into gales of laughter, and Dad bent over with his arms grasped around his sides, feebly attempting to hold in his guffaws. It took a while for everyone to calm down, and when Dad finally stood up, his laughter sounded more like wheezing, and there were tears streaming down his cheeks.

"That was so funny!" he giggled again, his chest heaving. "The point I'm trying to make though, kids, is that every time you give your neighbor milk, you are showing him compassion. Am I right?"

They all nodded, and Dad went for the zinger.

"So, if you are willing to show compassion to your neighbor over and over again, who obviously takes advantage of your hospitality, why wouldn't you want to show compassion to your cousins?" He stopped and waited for a response, but only received guilty silence in return. At least they are listening, I thought.

Point made, Dad broke the ice, laughing, "We're out of milk. Too funny!"

That eased the tension and gave the kids implicit permission to start laughing and giggling anew. A few minutes later, he stepped back and told the kids, "All right, troops, let's go! Wheels to the ground in fifteen!"

And, just like that, after rounds of hugs and kisses, they were gone and I was left alone among piles of newspapers, donut crumbs, and a lingering headache. I barely had time to catch my breath, when suddenly the front door slammed and Gage stomped in, soaking wet from the rain, and plopped down on the couch, folding his arms and giving a ferocious scowl.

His theatrical portrayal of an annoyed ten year old had me smiling inside. Before I could comment, the front door slammed again, this time with a sodden Tyler stomping sullenly up the stairs to his room, followed by an equally wet Tiffany, with moist red eyes to match. Oh, boy. I ignored the teenage love drama for the moment and instead focused on Gage.

"What's wrong, kiddo?" I asked. No reply. I repeated the question, already knowing the answer.

"It makes me so mad!" Gage wailed. "Just listen to what he did this time." With that, Gage launched into another plaintive explanation of the newest grievance bestowed upon him by his next-door-neighbor-cousin, who had recently turned thirteen, and was exercising his newly acquired teenage rite of passage to torment younger kids on the social food chain.

I played my part in the latest episode of *How the Neighborhood Turns*. "So how did it make you feel when he took the game controller when it wasn't his turn?" I asked Gage, who had mercifully paused to breathe.

"It made me mad!" He griped. "We all know the rules. We all take turns. And then he comes along and changes the rules!" he pleaded, his eyes desperate.

"So what did you do?"

"I left."

"Well, you did the right thing by not getting mad in return. You know he will apologize before the day is over, so make sure you accept it, okay?"

He mumbled his agreement.

"Okay. But, I'm so bored!"

"That didn't last long." I laughed. "Play your own video game for a little while and we'll see what happens." I said, possessing a mother's wisdom and knowing full well that the cousins would be ringing the doorbell within thirty minutes, their spat long forgotten.

I gave Gage a hug that, at ten years old and too cool for hugs, made him stiffen. He shuffled up the stairs, and I started to clean up the kitchen. I could hear rumblings of Tyler and Tiff having a heated conversation upstairs, but I blocked it out. I had a lot to do.

I cleaned the kitchen and straightened up the downstairs, picking up random toys, newspapers, and socks as the rain pelted the house so hard I felled compelled to duck my head. I could hear the creek rushing outside and knew we were in for a long night. The creek, while calm during sunshine, takes a dramatic turn even in the slightest rain, transforming into a raging torrent that threatens to overtake its banks. I shivered.

Gage went next door to play with his cousins again, and the house was quiet except for Tyler and Tiff, moving about upstairs. Despite their attempts to hide their obvious displeasure with each other, the unmistakable sounds of forcefully closing doors and hushed arguments floated downstairs and into my consciousness. It was getting worse. Again, I ignored them and carried on with my tasks. They had to work out their own problems, I reasoned.

The rest of the day brought more rain, and when I ventured to the basement to put the laundry in the dryer, I stepped in a puddle in the middle of the floor. Oh God, I hope that's a leak and not Bear, our sixteen year old chow-lab mix, who at her advanced age, sometimes leaves us presents.

I looked up and spotted the leak in the ceiling. Thank God. I thought. I turned on the dryer, toweled up the puddle and made a mental note to call the handyman. It's always something, I muttered as I walked upstairs. You know it's pretty bad when you are grateful for an unplanned repair bill.

Dad called after dinner to let us know that everyone was home safely.

"I had a great time!" he enthused. "I love getting together like this, working on the book, visiting with the grandsons. I have so much fun!"

"Me, too, Dad," I agreed. "But everyone is just so down since you left." I relayed the dramas involving Gage and Tyler, and the leak in the basement. I wrapped up my litany of complaints with, "Gage's feeling are hurt, Tyler is mad and probably hurt Tiff's feelings, judging by her tears, and I just feel like I want to curl up and cry."

"Welcome to reality, daughter, the fourth and final part of co-creation. Part of our reality is an emotional journey, and sometimes you're riding an emotional roller-coaster." He commanded, handing the phone to *The Preacher.*

"There is an emotional price to pay in the journey of co-creation. After traveling through the first three steps of co-creation – intention, beliefs and understanding – you arrive at your perception of reality.

These emotions you feel are real and must be recognized as so. Thoughts are things. The thoughts you think and the words you speak create energies that grow. Negative thoughts and destructive words grow if you allow them.

Recognize the emotion as real, Express it constructively, and then, Dismiss the negative emotion. Remember, your mind can only focus on one thing at a time."

Dad rejoined the conversation with, "You know, Daughter, people are not taught to deal with their emotions. You can get a PhD for intellectual pursuits, but rarely will you see a class on emotions. It's a social taboo, a touchy-feely thing that nobody wants to be part of."

He paused and chuckled softly, "I'll never forget the day one of you girls knocked over a glass of milk, and I just lost it." He laughed at the memory. "I was running a little overboard, ranting and raving like a madman, and all the while, you girls and Mom just looked at me like I was crazy, because I was! I had let something that was bothering me grow and grow until I exploded. I was riding an emotional tidal wave that threatened to sweep me away."

"Suddenly, looking at you girls I was instantly aware that my feelings of rage had nothing to do with you, all it did was release a tremendous amount of anger within me. But, I had no idea why, and I was embarrassed." He finished softly.

"I don't even remember that, Dad, so I hope you still don't feel bad," I said quickly, eager to impart forgiveness for something of which I had no memory.

"Mmm," he said absently, his mind elsewhere. "So, I set out on a journey to understand these emotions that I was feeling, and what to do with them. Mom helped by getting books from the library that we would read together. Then, she found a class for me that taught the intellectual components of emotions, and it started to click. Examining the intellectual aspects of each emotion helped me to understand what I was feeling. I started with my most negative feelings first because, obviously, they were the most dangerous to myself and those around me. Through that process of self-examination, I learned to recognize each feeling for what it was, because anger is different than rage and resentment."

"Once I recognized the emotion, I learned to express it constructively. For some, that might mean writing, or painting, or walking in the woods, but for me, I expressed my feelings best screaming in the closet." He laughed, and I joined him.

"You laugh, but it worked for me and didn't hurt anyone around me," he giggled.

"Except for our pronounced hearing loss!" I laughed out loud.

He laughed as well and went on, "Once I got the feeling worked out in the closet, I could dismiss it and let it go. It didn't have control over me any longer, and it wasn't threatening to sweep me away."

He repeated, "Recognize that what you are feeling is true. Express the emotion constructively. Dismiss it."

"Yeah, but how many times do you have to do that?" I questioned, realizing that I have felt these emotions before, many times.

"I know the answer to that!" he suddenly shouted into the phone. "I just saw the directions here somewhere, now where did I put that?" I could hear him walking about his house all the way in Pennsylvania and moving various items.

"Here it is! You have to read the instructions. It says right here on my shampoo bottle: Rinse and Repeat." He was laughing hysterically. "Basically, you have to Recognize, Express and Dismiss as many times as necessary to transcend the emotion." He finished with another giggle.

I shook my head and laughed at his goofiness. I love my Dad, I thought. Now, that feeling I could easily understand.

"I love you, Dad, and thank you."

"I love you too, Daughter, now get some sleep."

"I will," I replied, knowing full well what he would say next.

"And Daughter?" he continued, "Write. It. Down."

"I will." I smiled. I knew it.

We said our goodbyes and hung up as Gage came running in the door. "Did you have fun, cutie? Did everyone get along?" I asked hopefully.

"Yup," he responded absently, and flopped on the sofa.

Whew, I thought, one down and two to go. Tyler and Tiff were quiet upstairs, but it was an uneasy silence, and I had a feeling it wouldn't last.

"Let's get a snack and get ready for bed, kiddo."

"I don't wanna go to bed," he whined.

Aaaahhh, the joys of motherhood, I smiled to myself as I herded him into the kitchen.

"Snack. Brush teeth. Bed. In that order," I said, giving him another hug, but leaving no room for argument.

As a single mom for the past six years since my divorce from Dave, Gage's father, I have relished each and every bed-time ritual with Gage for the precious gift to motherhood it is. I said a quick prayer of thanks to God for personally mediating the dissolution of my marriage to Dave. For despite being divorced and living separately on paper, we are fiercely and respectfully joined in our commitment to build a life that benefits our son.

It's my job and my pleasure to provide daily consistency for Gage, whether it's supervising homework, enforcing our 9 pm school night bed-time, or kissing him as he leaves for the school bus. And it's Dave's job to inject the fun into Gage's life, which Dave pursues with relentless passion. Gage's abilities in soccer, basketball, football, hockey, and every other sport are a direct result of Dave's devoted hours of play time. You can't phone in that kind of parenting, I thought gratefully.

After the divorce, Dave made a heartfelt vow to be an active and loving part of Gage's life, and he lived up to the promise. I smiled remembering how Dave will drive to our house every morning to walk with Gage up to the bus stop to wait for the school bus. I said another quick prayer of thanks for my good fortune. It's funny, I thought, we couldn't agree on anything while we were married, but now that it just comes down to just one big important issue, Gage, we agree unanimously! *Thank you, God.*

After Gage was settled, I retreated to my bedroom and crawled under the covers with my notebook. The rain was still coming down in buckets, but I ignored the leak in the basement as I reviewed the written material and margin notes about Mom and Dad's early years.

Born Richard Grudzinski in 1947 in Philadelphia to Elizabeth and Stanley Grudzinski, second-generation Polish immigrants, Dad lived his early years in a small apartment with his parents and younger sister, Miriam, affectionately referred to in our family as "MurMur."

He and his best friend, Robbie, attended the public school located four blocks from their apartment building, alongside the railroad tracks that killed his best friend when he was five. A few years after his parents divorced and his mother remarried, they moved to Marlton, New Jersey to live with his new grandparents, who owned and operated a pig slaughter farm and farmer's market, as they had done in Poland.

After a few years, Dad and his family, which now included three younger brothers – Jimmy, Jerry, and Petey – moved to Westfield Acres, a low-income housing project known as "The Acres" in Camden, New Jersey. Dirt poor, (*Dad's words*) Dad devoted his middle school years to perfecting career trades which included breaking and entering, and theft, which precipitated his spending his thirteenth birthday in the New Jersey State Home for Boys, near Jamesburg.

During his stay, he realized poignantly that many of his fellow students continued to return to the home not because they couldn't be rehabilitated but because it was a better life than outside. Three meals a day and relative security are rare commodities in places like *The Acres*. Despite his young age, Dad held an unshakable belief that he would somehow do better for himself in the world, and he was rewarded with affirmation for that belief from an unlikely source.

Popeye, a huge bulging-muscled, bug-eyed guard who was feared throughout the home for his ferocity, was charged with escorting Dad to his counseling appointments across the grounds. He nonetheless struck up a friendship with Dad during their walks, and stopping him one day, Popeye declared, "Richard, you have a wisdom beyond your years. I listen to the things you say and learn from you every single day. I'm certain that you will never, ever return here," and Dad believed him.

Shortly after his thirteenth birthday, Dad was released and he returned to the family's third-floor apartment on Dudley Street at *The Acres,* where he promptly met his future wife, my mother, on the stairs of the apartment building where she was moving in with her family. Returning to her second floor apartment, located directly beneath Dad's, she confidently declared to her father, as only a teenager can do, "I just met the man I'm going to marry."

Born Helen Marie Hull four months after Dad, Mom was the oldest of seven brothers and sisters, and had lived on numerous navy bases before moving to *The Acres.* Mom, a petite blonde pixie, and Dad, dark haired and bursting with energy, spent their teenage years jitterbugging to 45's, dropping eggs from Dad's third-floor window to Mom's second floor window, and dreaming.

Taking long walks together holding hands, they dreamed about their future together, and what it would look like. They talked about where they would live, how many children they would have, and most of all, they talked of their future dream house – a large home, not an apartment, with enough bedrooms for everyone, more than one bathroom, and a swimming pool!

After Dad graduated from high school, they were married in a tiny ceremony at a small Catholic church, attended by their parents. Afterwards, Dad treated everyone to dinner and when they were finished, he and Mom had just two dollars in their pocket with which to start their new life together.

Dad worked as a sales closer for a company selling magazines, and they rented a small, furnished apartment in nearby Gloucester. I came along fourteen months later, and my sister, Sandi, two years after that. When the owner of the magazine company suddenly decided to close the business and become a stockbroker, taking back the car he had sold Dad on payments, they were frantic. It was little consolation that the guy went to jail for fraud a few years later.

Without a job or a car, mom moved us girls in with my grandmother while Dad went to Allentown, Pennsylvania to work for another friend, Harvey, selling magazines, sleeping on his desk during the week, and driving home to spend time with his new family on weekends in a used VW Beetle. Given to him by his father-in-law, William Senefeld, a three-tour-of-duty Vietnam Vet who later died of Agent Orange poisoning, the Beetle was a Miracle that came along at just the right time.

Later, Dad and Harvey opened a collection agency together, and when the opportunity came along to open an employment agency with a third partner, the three of them did just that. Less than a year later, when the other two partners forced Dad out of the business, he used the opportunity to launch his own employment agency, American Personnel.

For the next eleven years, Dad and Mom worked at building the business and their family. They bought their first house, a small Cape Cod, in a quiet neighborhood in West Allentown, and when I was eight years old, my youngest sister, Tawni, was born.

I put down the notebook and smiled. As a young girl, I adored traveling downtown to the office on Hamilton Street and pretending to be an employee. Dad would occasionally indulge my fantasies by allowing me menial tasks such as sitting at the desk or filing applications.

The one thing I despised was the collections. Unlike today, people in the 1970s paid employment agencies a fee to find them a job, and I was often with Dad when we went "collecting." One day, we parked near a house outside of Allentown that was badly in need of paint. The man who answered Dad's knock was extremely polite, but equally short on cash. After some negotiating back and forth, Dad happily accepted what the man pulled from his pocket, all of forty dollars. Dad came back to the station wagon feeling successful, and pulling out of the driveway, turned to me and boasted, "Someday, you will be doing this, working in the business, collecting."

Hah! There is absolutely no way will I ever take money from people who can't afford it, I thought now, as I did that day. I murmured a little prayer of gratitude that the employment industry had gone through a transformation, and now all the fees are paid by the hiring companies, as it should be. I picked up the notebook, but didn't continue reading. I already knew the rest of the story by heart and was starting to get tired.

After eleven years, Mom and Dad closed their business on Hamilton Street. I made a mental note to ask Dad why they closed the agency, choosing to work from home first as executive recruiters and later as career consultants. At any rate, I remember that time as being happy and secure as my parents worked together living their dream, I thought, yawning again.

And then Mom died. Or, so I believed.

The day I learned the truth of Mom's passing was sunny and warm, as it always seems to be at the beach, no matter the season. My extended family was convened in the brightly decorated great room of the beach house that served as an open dining area, with my dad and sisters comfortably lounging at the table while other relatives milled about the kitchen. Aunt Sally, one of Mom's younger sisters whom we all adored, was sitting at the breakfast bar, and everyone was talking quietly in groups of two or three.

I wasn't really paying attention, preferring to let my mind wander to the sand and surf outside. But I instantly tuned in when I heard a sad whisper, "She doesn't know that yet." I didn't catch who said it, but the meaning was instantly clear, and I was immediately alert, every fiber of my being tuned into the vibrations in the room. They were all talking about me. I just knew it.

Despite the undercurrent of awkwardness, the subject was changed and nobody said anything else. I listened for hours for somebody to deliver a clue as to what the mystery might be. I had almost forgotten my earlier fears when it happened again, and I almost missed it for the second time. But this time I knew I wasn't crazy. Aunt Sally was talking about Mom. Whatever it was that I didn't know was about my mom. "Oops. I guess I shouldn't have said that," she giggled to the room. Everyone else smiled and nodded in agreement but me.

"*What?*" I asked everyone. "What shouldn't you say about Mom?" By this time I was becoming alarmed. Was it something bad? A residue of an idea came to me, and then just as quickly retreated. Did I hear her correctly or make it up in my mind? I needed somebody to say it aloud for it to be real. I needed to hear the words.

"Tell me!" I demanded of anyone, everyone. My gaze flew from person to person, eyes pleading, but what they wouldn't say out loud, they screamed with their expressions. One by one, each person looked patiently back at me, mercifully, and with complete compassion for my obvious anguish, but also with an utter knowing. They all knew! Everyone knew something about Mom except me! My shaking voice betrayed my desperation, "Tell me! *Please!*"

Finally, Aunt Sally blurted out, "It's true. I'm telling you what you already know, that your mom is here. In fact, she has always been here; she never really left. She just, shall we say, *moved*." And with that, she giggled again with sheer delight.

I wanted to scream. I have always cherished my Aunt Sally, who was always old enough to babysit for my sisters and me, but was still young enough to be our friend. However, more recently I was starting to harbor feelings of dislike for her as she threw out her crazy words so casually.

Mom didn't just *move*, I reasoned. It defied all logic that my mother would choose to be separated from us. For fourteen years I have mourned her passing, missing her, crying over memories, and trying to convince myself that one day we would be together again.

There was no way that she would choose to create that horrifying reality for herself or for us. She loved us, and we loved her. I could never forgive her if she had chosen to leave us.

"What do you mean she just *moved*?" I was hanging onto my sanity by a thread.

"She moved," Sally answered slowly, as if addressing a preschooler. "She always wanted to move into her own place, and she did!"

Oh, my God. The memories came flooding back. Was it true?

I remembered my mom standing in the middle of the living room among colorfully scattered toys, dolls, and dress-up clothes when I was five with her hands on her hips declaring, "Look at this mess. Someday I'm going to get a place of my own, and *it will always be clean!*" On another day she laughed, "Someday I'm going to get my own place and decorate it the way *I want.*"

Of course, that was not her intention, I thought, she was just kidding. Looking around the room, I realized that every person held the same expression.

"How long have you all known?" By now my whole body was shaking so violently I was in danger of rattling the glasses off the table. I continued to sit, quaking, not bothering to disguise the depths of my despair.

Again, Aunt Sally was the first to jump in. I was really starting to not like her. "Oh, we each discovered it for ourselves in our own time, but your dad knew almost from the beginning."

I verbally launched at my father, who sat quietly smiling through my tirade, "How could you believe this, Dad? I was there with you when Dr. Connelly gave us the news." I demanded incredulously.

Dr. Connelly had been our family doctor for over twenty years, practicing from his home not five blocks from Mom and Dad's house in West Allentown. He had bandaged our boo-boo's, stitched our cuts, and delivered my sister, Tawni. But that day, he was unable to give us many details about Mom's terminal cancer or her life expectancy because of the sobs that racked his body while handing down her death sentence.

"I was there with you, Dad. I saw you. I watched you suffer. We watched her suffer. We *all* suffered," I cried. It wasn't logical. His expression didn't change.

I targeted my sister, Sandi, with equal amounts trepidation and bravado and challenged, "I was with you that year that Mom was sick. I drove with you the four hundred miles from Ohio to see her almost every weekend. I cried with you when we realized she wouldn't live to see the baby you were carrying."

I had cried every day for that entire lost year. Nothing could diminish the painful nightmare facing us and nothing could pull me out of my own personal black hole – not sleeping all day ignoring the world, not self-medicating with copious amounts of alcohol, nor enduring various anti-depressants prescribed for my "situational anxiety." Situational, no shit.

"We watched her die together. " I whispered, pleading with Sandi to no avail. Her expression mirrored Dad's.

I lowered my head and just let the tears flow, reliving the moment, my whole body shaking with waves of despair that threatened to sweep me away. Nobody said a word; they merely let me cry it out. It just couldn't be.

"I want to see her, then." Looking up, I declared confidently, despite my trembling voice and the doubt on the inside. "I want to talk to her and see for myself." Everyone nodded enthusiastically which only made me worry more. Oh, God.

We stood outside the front door of an ocean apartment, arriving much quicker than I had expected. I fretted that in all the years we lived so close to each other, I had never casually encountered her in passing. I took a deep breath and rang the bell. The door was opened almost instantly by a woman I didn't recognize.

My gaze passed quickly around her to the tidy room beyond, searching for my mom. Three young deeply tanned children played happily in the middle of the small room, which was overflowing with green plants and books. I turned and searched over her other shoulder and spied a group of people sitting expectantly at the table just off the living room, but no Mom.

I turned back to the woman at the door with a questioning glance. She was older than Mom had been, and slightly heavier than my mother's slight frame, with long blonde hair where Mom's had always been trimmed short. She looked, well, radiant. Smiling back at me she silently handed me a colorful children's book.

My entire body broke out in goose bumps. And right then, I knew it was Mom.

Are You My Mother? Oh, my God. Written by P.D. Eastman, *Are You My Mother* was the first book I had ever read by myself. Actually, at four years old, I had memorized the short story and recited it back repeatedly to my family, firmly believing I could read. I treasured the story of a newly hatched baby bird that falls from his nest and sets off to find his mother, who had left to look for food. Everything he encounters in his little world, from a rock, to a cow, to a backhoe, is plaintively asked the same question, "Are you my mother?" as he searches for her.

The tragic part of the story in my mind occurs near the mid-point, when the baby bird and mother bird find themselves on the opposites sides of a large boulder, neither knowing that the other is so close. It tormented me to think of the little lost bird, scared and missing his mom, and I shuddered. Eventually, they reunite and live happily ever after. I started to cry as she took me in her arms and held me tight. Oh, Mom, I cried to myself, I miss you so much. Why did you ever leave?

Suddenly, I was gripped by the sensation that she had *never* really gone away; that I had *never* been alone. I realized at that moment that she had *always* been with me, celebrating my happiest moments with me, and holding me close when I cried. She must have been the one to nudge Dad to hand me his hankie as I sobbed through Tyler's high school graduation two years ago; I smiled at the memory.

She slowly walked me over to the sofa, and we sat together.

I was hurt and angry when Mom got sick, yes, but now holding this book, I suddenly realized that while the baby bird might have been terrified to be separated from his mother, it was *nothing* compared to the feeling a mother would have if separated from her child. I was going to be okay. I sobbed with relief at the realization. I knew it. I knew she wouldn't choose to leave us.

We sat for many hours, holding each other close on the sofa while the kids played happily around us. I tried to bring Mom up to date on everything that had happened in my life over the last fourteen years we were apart, but oddly, she already knew. I thought about sharing my doubts with her about writing the book, but before I could speak my fears aloud, she grasped my arm and said, "I love you, and I believe in you." Giving me goose bumps again.

Suddenly the doorbell was broadcasting its bongo drumbeat through the small apartment, and I was being cheerfully invited to return any time.

I slid the power bar off on my iPhone to silence the alarm and sat up. Oh. My. God.

I climbed out of bed and collapsed in my oversized reading chair, dazed, not bothering with the light. Shivering in the semi darkness of early morning, I glimpsed the pack of Marlboro Lights and half full glass of iced tea left over from last night, resting on the table near me, and stared in awe. Mom had never been without iced tea or cigarettes when she would climb into her favorite reading chair.

Oh, my God, I realized with a start. *I am my mother!* As the rain grew louder, I reached for my pen and tablet and frantically started to write down everything I could remember.

Chapter Five

"Use Protection!"

An explosive blast of thunder made me jump. I looked out the window to the backyard, my heart pounding. That scared me, and I laughed at myself. The storm that had been building for days had finally arrived. I smiled and rose to open the window wider, allowing the crashing sounds of the creek, which now sounded like a raging river, course through my bedroom. I sat and let my mind wander as the creek faded soothingly into a background white noise.

The Preacher's words came back to me:

It is what it is.

Yep, I thought, nodding my head, that about sums up reality; it is what it is.

You can't choose what comes to you.

No, I can't, but I sure wish I could sometimes. I don't possess the power to change my mom's *moving* any more than I have the ability to change the weather.

You can only choose how you respond or react.

But, I realize now that I possess the power to change my perception of what is happening to me. If my feelings about the creek could change from a fear of flooding to music to my ears, then the anger and despair over Mom's suffering and death could be transformed into ones of love and acceptance. Maybe Dad was on to something, I thought to myself as tears of tenderness welled in my eyes. *Thanks, Mom.*

I stood and stretched, closed the window, and headed for the shower. Time to get a move on. I turned on the hot water and stood under the soothing spray recalling all the feelings from the dream. I could almost feel all the emotions I had experienced in the past few hours/years/lifetimes running off my body, and I watched idly as the water chased them down the drain.

I washed my hair and laughed out loud when right there on my shampoo bottle I spotted the instructions: Rinse and Repeat. Before turning off the water, I repeated my daily ritual prayer of thanks to Tyler for buying the massage showerhead at a garage sale for four dollars. I love that kid. And I love this shower, I thought, it feels like heaven, only wet.

Tyler came into the kitchen while I was making coffee, looking tired and annoyed and muttered, "It's raining. Again."

I looked at my son, to whom I had just finished paying homage, and thought with sudden clarity: Oh, my God, he learned this from me. Please God, give me strength.

"Yes, but this is Ohio weather. Give it fifteen minutes and it will change," I said, opening the fridge, repeating a common local phrase.

He grunted a response.

"Oh, crap," I said, "We're out of milk."

For an instant I was annoyed, but then I remembered – I turned to him and burst out laughing, "Uh, we're out of milk!" I sputtered.

It took him a moment, but then he caught on and a hesitant smile tugged at the corners of his mouth.

I continued to erupt into giggles at the amusing memory as I prepared my coffee, minus the moo juice.

"You're face is turning red," he said, smiling wider.

"You know what, kiddo?" I asked, forgetting that he hates to be called that, "I love you. I *still* love that showerhead, and I love your creative wit. You should write commercials."

He beamed at the compliment, and I seized the moment. "What's really bothering you?"

"Nothing."

That sounds familiar, I thought. "Not true," I smiled, "It's all over your body language, not to mention the door slamming."

He looked down sheepishly and replied, "Sorry."

"Don't be sorry," I said automatically, sensing a pronounced feeling of deja vu. "Just tell me what's wrong."

"We're broke!" he exploded, wailing. "Both of our cars are running on fumes and we can barely make it to payday."

Apparently, his well of anxiety ran deep, for he continued to rant, waving his arms, "It's just so unfair. This whole capitalistic society brainwashes you into commercialism slavery. You work. You buy. You die. It's all just so pointless!" He raged.

"You do have a choice," I offered.

"Yeah? What?" he demanded.

"Well, one option is that you don't have to work. You could live in poverty off of society for the rest of your life. Another option is that you could get a part-time job to help with unexpected repair bills. Or, you could cut back on your expenses. Another option is to rob a bank," I finished triumphantly.

He looked at me and smiled, and I returned the favor.

"At any rate," I continued, always the mom, "You have a choice. You can respond to your budgetary crisis with creativity and ingenuity, which you possess in spades, or you can react by slamming doors. Or worse, you could overreact, in which case our home life will get louder and markedly more unpleasant. Your choice."

He looked at me, wise beyond his years, and said, "You're right. I'm sorry."

"Don't be sorry," I said like a broken record, "Just think about it." I went to hug him, and he hugged me back, gingerly, as if I might break.

Gage, always the bouncing ball of happiness, skipped through the kitchen singing, stopped to show us his muscles, saying, "Look at me, I'm strong!" then helped himself to a drink of water before depositing the half-full glass on the counter.

"Can I go to Benji's?" he asked, referring to his next-door neighbor cousin. Has there ever been a question posed more times in the universe than that one? I wondered.

"Of course. Give me a hug."

He groaned and stood defensive with his head turned as if I might spread cooties, or worse, kiss him. "Get used to it buddy, our family hugs," I said laughing. He refused to acknowledge me and ran to the door.

"Wow. It's really raining. Where's the umbrella?" he yelled.

"You know what Grandfather always says," I yelled back from the kitchen, "You don't need an umbrella if you know how to run in between the raindrops."

"Mo-om," he whined, clearly exasperated. He decided to run for it, and made a dash out the door.

My cell started ringing, and Sandi's picture popped up on the iPhone. "Hellooooo?" I chirped.

She laughed and asked, "Is the Mini Market open?"

I laughed with her at our shared joke. Any time one of us runs out of a kitchen staple, we call the other to inquire if the item is in stock. "What do you need?"

"Parmesan cheese. I thought I had some."

"I'll check," I said opening the fridge. "Yep," I said, pulling it from the fridge.

"Thanks. I'll send one of the kids over," as was our ritual.

I walked to the front door and waited while Sandi commented, "That was fun, everyone coming out. My kids are tired, but it was worth it. Did you get anything done on the book?"

"We worked on the book some, but I had fun too," I replied, opening the front door and handing the condiment to Joseph who had been assigned to delivery duty. "Thanks, kiddo," I called as he ran down the steps and across the driveway.

"I have to finish dinner, but we should set a date to go out to lunch soon." She was right. Although we live not sixty-five feet from each other, our schedules rarely allowed us the opportunity to be in the same room together.

"I can't this week, but next Tuesday or Wednesday are good."

"Wednesday works, but I have to be back by 12:30 for a doctor's appointment."

"No problem, I'm starving by eleven anyway."

She laughed, and we hung up.

Sandi and I grew up as close friends, always confiding in one another, forever teasing. I'm the eldest by two years, and she never seems to miss an opportunity to remind me, "You'll always be *older* than me!" followed by insane cackling.

As pre-teenagers, I retaliated by rinsing the dishes with cold water when it was her turn to dry, making her task nearly impossible. Hah! Sweet revenge. It was always in good fun, though, and we would laugh hysterically until we were in danger of wetting our pants, or we were threatened with punishment for making too much noise in the kitchen.

Our bedrooms were located directly across the hall from each other, and we strategically placed our beds so that we could whisper to each other across the hall after lights out. Every night one of us would start the ritual with, "Night Maw," and the other would reply, "Night Paw," making fun of *The Waltons*, a show we hated, but Dad unfortunately loved to watch.

We would continue the giggling goodnights with made up names like "Billy Bobby" and "Sally Sue" until, of course, we were in danger of wetting the bed, or threatened with punishment for making too much noise when we were supposed to be sleeping.

From time to time, we actually did get into trouble, *(Author's note: I'm innocent. That's my story and I'm sticking to it)* and our punishment was doled out in the form of having to stand silently in the corner for twenty minutes. Standing in the corner is similar to a modern day time-out, but tiring, and given our attention spans, tortuous.

We solved the problem by choosing our corners to be the two sides of the piano in the living room, affording us ample opportunity to continue our fun by whispering and using improvised sign language. You guessed it; we were inevitably in danger of wetting our pants or threatened with more severe forms of punishment for making too much noise when we were supposed to be in trouble.

We were rarely apart growing up, and we would often dream of living next door to each other after we left home. Several blocks from our house were two identical ranch homes that belonged to two twin sisters. The sisters trimmed their shrubbery exactly alike, planted the same flowers in their yards every spring, decorated with identical Christmas lights, and even had the same curtains hanging in their windows. We wanted to be just like them when we grew up.

We stayed close with numerous phone calls and visits when she went away to college to Virginia Tech to become an architect. A driven student, she was tearfully terrified of failing every single flippin' test that was approaching, and patient sister that I am, I let her cry on my long-distance shoulder hundreds of times. After approximately the hundredth time she got an A or an A+, I got smart. She might have believed she was going to fail every test, but I no longer did. Apparently, she needed to prove it to herself, over and over again.

At VT, she met her soon-to-be-husband, Mark, a fellow honors architecture student, who mercifully never called me to cry about a test. After the graduation and wedding ceremonies, they moved into my house in Ohio while they pursued their first professional job search, their goals set on architecture firms in Pittsburgh, an hour and a half from my home.

After three months of fruitless job searching, despite hands-on help from Mom and Dad, our family career counselors, their efforts were for naught. They re-directed their search to the northeast Ohio area (yippee!), and with Dad coaching from the long-distance sidelines, they were both professionally employed in their fields within a month. Some things are just meant to be, I thought with a thankful smile. *It was a Miracle! Thank you, God.*

Buying a home close to their employers meant that they were still a half hour's drive and a long distance phone call away, but still we stayed close, laughing together and, later, crying throughout the year of Mom's illness. It was on one of those expensive long-distance phone calls, before the days of free national calling plans and anytime minutes, that the subject of moving closer together came up again.

"Wouldn't it be great if we lived closer?" Sandi inquired, "Then you could help me actually plant these impatiens instead of just telling me how to do it."

I laughed. If there was such a thing as a green thumb, Sandi's was black.

"Yeah, it would be great," I replied and countered with, "Wouldn't it be great if we could find a house that had a piece of land attached to it? That way I could live in the house, you could design and build your own house, and we could be neighbors!" I enthused.

"Yeah!" she laughed back. "In North Canton!"

Hey, as long as we were dreaming, we might as well go all the way! I thought. North Canton was a bedroom community of about 16,000 people that suspiciously resembled Mayberry. With a quaint town square, home to the famed Hoover Company, an excellently rated school district, and a five minute drive from fabulous Belden Village, our favorite dining and shopping mecca, it was our Dream Town.

"Yeah, that would be great," I agreed, picturing us sitting together on our front porches. It's fun to dream. Coming back to reality, we said our goodbyes before we blew the phone budget, and I put the conversation out of my mind.

A week later, I almost spilled my coffee when I spotted the classified ad that read: *For Sale By Owner: Single-family home in North Canton with an attached lot!* Up to that point, I didn't believe an open building lot even existed in North Canton. I called Sandi excitedly and read her the ad. She immediately conferred with Mark, and the three of us agreed to make an appointment to view the house as soon as possible.

Several days later, the two of them picked me up, and we carpooled to the house. As Mark parked the car during a torrential downpour, we all looked apprehensively at the BMW already parked in the driveway with another couple inside. Were we too late? We worried, and ran to ring the doorbell.

We were greeted by Mr. and Mrs. Cooper, owners of the home they had raised their family in for the past thirty-five years. "Oh, don't mind them," she greeted us warmly as we looked apprehensively at the BMW. "They wanted to see the house, but we told them we already had an appointment with you."

Relaxing, we started on a tour of their home. When we reached the back door and stepped onto the deck (despite the rain), it was love at first sight. The backyard looked like a beautiful green oasis smack dab in the middle of this quaint city. I stared at the little footbridge that spanned the creek to the empty lot beyond, and I could picture myself walking across that bridge to my sister's future house that had yet to be conceived or built.

After a quick private conference in which we could hardly contain our excitement, and propelled by a sense of urgency precipitated by the

BMW couple, we made an offer to the Cooper's on the spot. They accepted, we signed the papers at the kitchen table, and then we celebrated. Despite the financial risk we were undertaking by having to quickly sell our own homes, we were unanimously ecstatic. We were going to be neighbors! Sandi and Mark were going to design and build their own house! We were going to live in North Canton! We were going to be like the twins! It was a Miracle! We laughed and laughed. *Thank you, God.*

Since that day over thirteen years ago, we've added a few more boys and plenty of toys to the neighborhood. Between my two sisters and I, we have ten boys, with six of them living next door to each other. Sandi's oldest, Nick is followed by Joseph and Jacob, both eleven, and Benji, the youngest of all the cousins at ten.

Nick, a newly minted teenager and budding entrepreneur, has a bright future in any career that involves negotiating or debating, as he faithfully hones his skills with his mother on a daily basis. Over the years, Sandi has grown wise to his well-practiced moves, so now he involves his cousins in his hands-on education.

Joseph, a mild mannered Super Hero masquerading as an eleven year old often accidentally leaks his Superpowers in public when he picks up a golf club. Shunning the Bat Cave for the Video Game Cave, he is continually tethered to electronic media and rarely even emerges for meals.

Jacob, quiet, inquisitive, and wicked smart, is still experiencing "orientation" with his new family, and immersing himself in toys, boys, and video games. He often hangs out with Gage and I watching movies, and his unfailing politeness always causes me to smile when he asks, "can you please pass the popcorn?" And then there's Benji.

Ah, Benji, I thought. Life comes at you fast. With his mop of blond curls, dimpled cheeks, contagious smile and boundless enthusiasm, he is a joyful example of how to live your life enthusiastically despite limitations. Benji was born with Eosinophilic Gastroenteritis, which in its simplest terms means that he cannot eat anything without experiencing excruciating pain. No food. Not ever.

For many years, Sandi has had to contend with perplexed doctors, countless trials, ineffective treatments, and unsympathetic insurance companies, all while merely attempting to relieve her young son's daily suffering. The emotional toll of their medical journey was far more devastating to Sandi's belief in a healthcare system that continued to fail her, and to her faith in a God that seemed to have forgotten her.

But her strength is amazing, I thought admirably. Eventually, she traveled to a place in her heart, accepting that although she was in a situation no mother would ever choose for her child, it was up to her how she would respond. *It is what it is. It is what you make it.*

She definitely has her priorities straight, creating a home life that focuses on the responsibilities of treating the illness, combined with the creativity and adaptability that make their family joyful. It is what it is, I believe. But, it is also what you make it, and Sandi and the kids make it fun. Despite living in a house overflowing with toys, games and puzzles, the boys are ingenious inventors of fun ways to play with the various medical supplies that permeate their home.

Empty syringes (minus needles) become instant squirt guns. Crutches flipped upside down magically transform into stilts. They giggle as they put balloons on the end of the nebulizer tube to let the flowing air blow them up. Boys being boys, Benji will entertain the kids by making belly farts when he pulls out his feeding tube, and they giggle and laugh as only "tweens" can do at fart humor.

Of all the toys, the most surprising favorite is the wheelchair. Not Benji's motorized wheelchair, which he needs because he tires easily, but the used mechanical wheelchair that Tyler had bought for fifty dollars over eight years ago. I sighed as I recalled Tyler begging for permission to purchase "The Greatest Thing Ever" from the classified ads. "I always wondered what it would be like to ride in a wheelchair," he pleaded. I was appalled! What would people think? I never had it so wrong. That weekend, after Tyler won fifty dollars in the family poker game, I relented. Maybe it was meant to be. *Thank you, God.* The wheelchair has served as the neighborhood's all-time favorite toy ever since. From wheelchair races to wheelies, the cousins, and all their friends alike, take impatient turns riding the wheelchair throughout the neighborhood, and it is rarely unoccupied.

While I had thought playing with such a somber piece of medical equipment would be tasteless and disrespectful, instead, I have been rewarded over the years with watching our kids develop an appreciation and respect for the disabled from their hands-on experience. Instead of displaying pity for another child in a wheelchair, I have watched with amazement as they greet the child with, "You're lucky. You get a motorized wheelchair." Out of the mouths of babes. I will confess, though, to an occasional pang of guilt when I catch the look of horror on a random passerby staring at one of the kids who just happened to "fall" from the wheelchair onto the ground. Fully aware of their actions, they jump up and run away, laughing. It is what it is, sure, but it is also what you make it, I thought, with a growing respect for my sister's strength dealing with Benji's disease.

If I could go back and re-create a relationship with a sister, I wouldn't change a thing. We have laughed our way through childhood, the gawky teenage years, through the raising of our kids, and every year since. Every once in awhile, I still get a late night text from the house across the driveway that reads, "Night Maw."

Happily married with four kids, this was a couple who did things the right way, or "by the book." Mark worked his way up to partner of his architectural firm, and built it into a $40 million dollar company. Sandi home-schools all the boys, devotes her spare (?) time to volunteering for APFED, the non-profit seeking a cure for Benji's disease, and they're active in their church. She even bakes.

Living next to the Cleavers can be daunting when you're the black sheep of the family. With "Dos Equis" (or two X's) under my belt, no formal education, no savings to speak of as I rapidly approach middle age, and last but not least, a tattoo! OMG! Miniscule and discreet, but nevertheless a permanent mark on my body – I am the poster child for "Don't try this at home, kids."

I sighed as I considered my present circumstances. Although I own my own business, it's currently headed precipitously toward a status of red ink, and I couldn't help but give in to a feeling of resentment. Are you kidding me? Eleven years in business and it feels, depressingly, much like the first year. I know I'm not alone; I read the papers. The biggest recession since The Great Depression is wrecking havoc upon many businesses, and despite feeling fortunate that we were still operating, I'm growing weary of the never-ending cycle of taking only one step forward for every two steps back.

I allowed the sour feeling some room to grow as I looked over at Dad's book, or the start of the book, if you will. After my breakthrough, all I wanted to do was immerse myself in the story and continue to write. But, nooooooo, I thought bitterly, I have too many responsibilities I couldn't ignore, like work, I thought miserably, the other four-letter word that ends in "k."

Enough. The words of *The Preacher* came flooding back to me.

You create your own reality according to your thoughts, words, and deeds. Negative thoughts grow. Your mind can only focus on one thing at a time.

Stop it, I commanded myself, cut it out. Sometimes I'm my own worst enemy. Mindful of my thoughts, I went about my day, until it all blew up again.

Oh, my God! *He* wants to cut off all ties with *me?* What about the son we are raising? I thought incredulously, walking purposefully back to my own house after chatting with Mark in his driveway during a break in the rain, where he politely relayed that my ex-husband's intention was to cut off all ties with me.

The nerve of him, I fumed. I was so angry I was ready to explode. I stomped into the house and furiously paced the first-floor rooms, wandering from the kitchen to the living room and on to my office, opening doors and cabinets for no reason other than to give my hands something to do.

'Cause if I didn't do something constructive, my hands were liable to wrap themselves around his neck and…wait a minute, calm down, I scolded myself. It is what it is. I can't change what comes to me, I thought. This is my ex-husband after all, and there is a reason we were divorced six years ago.

Alas, logic did not prevail, and I continued my raging for the rest of the evening. How dare he? I muttered to myself over and over. I finally gave up and retreated to bed where I tossed from side to side, dreaming of ancient torture devices and increasingly creative methods for delivering pain.

I woke on the wrong side of the bed the next morning, still seeing red. Rushing through my morning, I forgot to praise Tyler for my heavenly shower, and in my haste tripped and went flying over Bear sleeping peacefully on the living room floor. Grrrrr. "You stupid dog," I muttered.

By the time Dad called around eleven, as was his daily custom, I was fully capable of maiming any person who was brave enough to venture close. Dad listened quietly, although he most likely had to hold the phone away from his ear, and when I was empty, he said quietly, "Recognize, Express, Dismiss."

"I *am* expressing, quite loudly I might add. Sorry 'bout that." I apologized, lowering my voice.

'Don't be sorry." He replied instantly. I knew that was coming.

"Listen, Daughter, you need to *Recognize* these feelings for what they are, and then *Express* them constructively, and yelling is not constructive," he admonished.

He's right, I though sheepishly, while Dad put *The Preacher* on speaker.

> *It is what it is. You can't change what comes to you. You can only choose to respond or react.*

"Grrrrrr..." I couldn't help it, it leaked out.

Dad interrupted with, "You're spending DarkBuck$. Go grab the DarkBuck$ and read the words on the back to me," he commanded, leaving me feeling like I was twelve years old, and I scrambled to remember where I had left the file for LightBuck$ and DarkBuck$.

"Here it is, Dad," I said hurriedly, not wanting to incur any further recriminations.

"Read me the words on the back of the DarkBuck$." He still sounded irritated.

I silently hoped he wasn't mad at me for my outburst, while I picked up the DarkBuck$ and flipped it over. DarkBuck$ are shaped like dollar bills, but that's where the resemblance ends. Constructed from dirty brown paper bags, they are not attractive. Sometimes, I imagine they even smell. On the reverse side of DarkBuck$ are listed approximately thirty different negative emotions. I started reading randomly:

"Anger, resentment, hostility, hatred, stress, frustration, melancholy, apprehension, fear, guilt, shame, jealousy, racism, and rage."

"That's it. Stop right there," he said, and I obeyed.

"You were raging, that's the right word."

"Yes, I was," I defended myself. "But I have a right to feel this way! Anybody else would feel the same way in my situation."

"They might or they might not," he replied. "That's not what's important. What is important is that *you* feel that way. *Recognize* that feeling for what it is and then *Express* it constructively. That means no yelling, unless you're in the closet. If you can come to terms with how you feel, then you can short-circuit those thoughts when then come to you, and dismiss that negative emotion."

"How do I do that, come to terms with it? It makes me so angry!"

"But you can't change it, can you? Just as you can't change the weather, you can't change what other people say *to* you or *about* you. The quicker you examine the reasons for why you feel the way you do, the faster you can transcend those negative emotions."

"But why do people have to act that way? I don't understand."

"Who knows why people act the way they do? People attack for many reasons, sometimes for no reason. Hey, listen to this," he began chuckling, before starting his story. "The other night I was out with a bunch of friends at the dance club. I was sitting at a table, just minding my own business, when this gentleman, who I didn't know, came up to me and said, 'What are you doing here? You're too old to be in a place like this.'"

"Are you serious?" I questioned, stunned at the audacity of some people.

"Yeah, yeah, I'm serious," he replied, laughing.

"That's so rude." I laughed along with him.

"I know. But, I didn't get mad, I smiled and said 'thank you,' then got up to dance."

For as long as I can remember, my parents have loved to dance. Mom would always dance to the radio while she was vacuuming, and Dad would habitually lock himself downstairs to blast the stereo. They would often go on dancing dates to the clubs, and now, after Mom's gone, Dad still goes to the clubs with his friends at least three nights a week. He's the type of person who can dance in public, blissfully unaware of other people or what they think. He claims it's his therapy, and I would have to agree that the experience is transformational for him.

I laughed. Of course that's what Dad would do, I thought. On the other hand, I often want to get even.

"How do you do that? How do you not let other people bother you, and why does it bother me so much?" I whined, recalling a quote by Buddha, *"If our minds are filled with sympathy and compassion, they will be resistant to the negative words we hear."*

"Because you let it bother you, that's why," he said matter of factly. "I don't. I put up my shields."

Dad, a devout Trekkie, engages his mental shields any time an enemy approaches.

"People are fearful and hostile, and they attack because they believe themselves to be evil and worthless. So to boost their confidence, they attack others by shooting flaming arrows of insults. So before I go out in public, I engage my shields, just like Captain Kirk on the *Enterprise.*

"Now, I don't want to block out the whole world, so I leave a teeny, tiny little opening, the size of a pinhole. When an attack comes, which it *will*, I put the pin in the pinhole! When the danger passes, I take the pin out of the pinhole," he concluded happily.

I laughed along with him, easily picturing flaming arrows bouncing harmlessly off Dad's invisible shields.

"Is that why you love the drive out to Ohio? Because Scotty just beams you up?" I blurted.

Dad laughed harder.

"Did you really say thank-you to that rude guy?" I was incredulous.

"I sure did! I don't have the power to change what comes to me, but I do have the power to choose how to respond or react. So I responded by smiling, and saying "thank you."

"Did he say 'you're welcome'?

"No. He didn't say anything. But do you know what happened next?"

"What?"

"He turned around to walk away, and when he did, he bumped into the server and spilled all her drinks," he exclaimed.

"I call that *Sideways*," he practically shouted. "When people attack and you react, it feeds their negativity. They want to push your buttons; they want to get a reaction from you. If you attack back, then you have absorbed their negative energy and added some of your own as well, and that negativity grows. But if you respond rather than attack, then that negative energy bounces off of you and goes back to the other person. Since it has to go somewhere, it comes out *Sideways*, he giggled and added, "If you spend Light-Buck$, you get LightBuck$ back. If you spend DarkBuck$, you get DarkBuck$ back."

"Is that true?" I asked, skeptical.

"I don't know. Prove it to yourself," he laughed. "I'm telling you what I have experienced. You need to experience it for yourself to believe it. Tell you what, if you see it happen, write it down!"

"Okay." But I wasn't entirely convinced.

"What about when bad things happen to good people? Is it because they put out negative energy?" I debated.

"Absolutely not!" He was adamant. "You can't change what comes to you. It just is what it is. Your only power is in how you choose to perceive the events. That's where you have the power to choose how you spend your energy. If there is chaos around you, are you going to add to it? If there is Love around you, are you going to add to it? Are you going to spend LightBuck$, or are you going to spend DarkBuck$?"

"Dad," I interrupted quietly.

"Yes, Daughter?"

"I'm more hurt than angry. I was just venting."

"I know you are. I love you. Look, you're strong. You'll get through this. Sleep on it tonight and you might find that you have a different perspective in the morning."

"I love you too, and thank-you. Again." I smiled.

"You're welcome. I love talking like this," he exclaimed.

Honestly, I thought, that man finds joy in everything. I wondered idly if it was in my DNA to feel joy in everything too, or, if it's not something I was born with, maybe it was something I could learn.

I hung up and went about my day considerably less fired up than an hour ago. I felt chastened by Dad's words, and the last thing I wanted was to fuel my ex's fire. No DarkBuck$ for me.

The next several weeks passed in a blur of work and extinguishing minor fires that included both cars going in for repairs, and the deaths of both our refrigerator of five years and our dishwasher of twenty years. I could handle the dishwasher's passing, it had lived a good life.

But the 'fridge? I was of the generation that expected major appliances to last twenty years, and I was hot. When I wasn't on the phone with repairmen, I snatched time in the evenings and weekends to write. But, it was slow going, and that only added to my frustration.

Outside, the forecast was calling for the rain to start tapering off. But, judging by the sounds coming from Tyler and Tiff's room, the interior forecast was predicting a storm front that would build throughout the day, with a strong likelihood of hail and another round of hushed arguments to arrive by evening.

We were advised to stay tuned for further updates and warnings, and to take cover in the basement in the event of a tornado. Even Gage seemed out of sorts. Uh-oh.

The tornado touched ground at our house at 5:05 pm. Slam! The sound was deafening as Tyler's bedroom door nearly flew off its hinges from the force of impact. I jumped up from my reading/writing chair in my room and flew up the few remaining stairs to the hall where the kid's bedrooms were located. Running, my heart racing, I was terrified something would happen to the kids before I could reach them.

"Gage! Tyler! Tiff!" I yelled, reaching the hallway, "Where are you? What happened?" I screamed, searching frantically for my children. I spotted Gage first, standing alone in the center of his room, unharmed, but a look of sheer terror on his face, and tears streaming down his dimpled cheeks.

I ran to him, throwing my arms around him, squeezing his shuddering form. "It's okay, it's okay," I kept repeating, soothing him. I could feel his heart pounding, matching mine, beat for staccato beat.

Suddenly, a high-pitched cry pierced the air, causing a moan to escape from Gage. "It's okay," I kept repeating as I shuffled him toward Tyler and Tiff's room, afraid to let him escape my grasp. I reached their closed door and shouted, "Are you guys alright? Open the door!"

"Open the door!" I commanded again when my only response was Tiff crying.

The door opened and Tiff ran into the hall, crying. "Oh my God, Sweetie, what happened?" I cried with her, including her in my hug with Gage. I imagined the worst while she took deep gulping breaths of air while struggling to calm herself, the tears still flowing from the three of us.

"Tyler is mad." She cried. Well, that's certainly an understatement, I thought.

"He slammed the door and threw the table over." Oh, my God.

"Okay, it's over. It's okay now," I said repeatedly, the three of us holding each other. Oh, my God, Oh, my God, Oh, my God, I prayed fervently. Please help me, God. What do I do?

Just then, Tyler blew past us in a rage, pointing, "That's it! She's your daughter now! You don't love *me* any more, you love her!" he accused, the pain in his voice cutting me.

Immediately, I recalled the day over ten years ago that Tyler, my beautiful little tow-head, had been savagely bitten in the face by the neighbor's dog, requiring twenty-seven stitches.

I had remained eerily calm holding him on the endless drive to the emergency room, despite being terrified for my young son's fate, even when he whispered, "Mom, am I gonna die?" I swallowed hard and drew on that strength.

No, absolutely not. This is *Not* going to happen in *MY* house!

"Come with me," I said firmly, and they followed me down the stairs.

"Sit down," I said to the three of them, and amazingly, they did.

I was taking deep breaths, attempting to control the shaking that had taken control of my body. Time slowed down, and the air hummed as I looked at each one of my kids, who looked equally shaken, and settling on Tyler said softly, "I loved you first because I met you first. I knew the moment that I looked into your eyes when you were born that I loved you completely. Nothing you ever do will ever change that feeling, or take away from it."

Drawing another deep breath, I turned and fixed my gaze on Gage. "I loved you next because I met you next." I laughed, and he laughed back.

"And an amazing thing happened when you were born, Gage," I continued, touching him gently, "The love I felt for you didn't take away one ounce of the love I felt for Tyler." I nodded my head, incredulous, still. "Instead, the love grew; in fact, it *doubled*."

Finally, turning to Tiff, I repeated, "I loved you next because I met you next." By now we were all smiling. "I love you like a daughter, Tiff, and when I met you, the same amazing thing happened! The love grew!"

Everyone was laughing and looking at me as my words danced in the vibrating room, their attention riveted. Cool. I took another deep breath and realized that my tremors had ceased. The air was still electric, but the energy buzzing around the room and bouncing off the walls wasn't from anger, it was something else, something good.

"Now, in this house, we only operate from the feeling of love, not anger," I said quietly but firmly, asserting my power as the mother of the household, while turning to stare at Tyler.

When I had his compete attention, I continued, "If we start from love, that love will grow. If we start from anger, that anger will grow. I will not allow anger in this house."

"Our home is a safe place, a sanctuary, and a refuge from the outside world. The world is scary and the people in it are scary. But, this is the *one* place that you can *always* come back to escape from that world, to feel loved and to be safe. And, I will not allow chaos to live here. This will *never, ever* happen again. It scares the shit out of me. Do you understand?"

"Yes, I do," Tyler responded, and he meant it. "I'm sorry."

"Don't be sorry," I repeated my mantra. "Just don't ever let it grow to that point again." I looked at everyone. "I love you guys. I love our family and I love our life. Let's keep it that way," I said happily.

They agreed, and Gage, nodding his head, his eyes big and round, was the first one to break the spell, "Good speech, Mom."

Wow. Thank you, God.

"Now, let's talk about the root cause of the problem. What happened?"

Tyler and Tiff's guilty looks almost made me giggle, but I held strong.

"We overdrew the checking account again," they admitted after a few moments.

"That's it?" I couldn't help it, I laughed out loud.

"It's so *unfair*, Mom," Tyler ignored my mirth and debated, "Banks do it on purpose to screw us over and take our money. I bought a cup of coffee with my debit card and now it's gonna cost me $189 in fees; that's my *whole* paycheck! If I had kids, I wouldn't be able to feed them this week. It's so unfair."

Gage stared in awe at Tyler's rant, his round eyes learning, I hoped, by osmosis from Tyler's hard-earned experience.

When he paused to breathe, I cut in with, "You're absolutely right. The banks do it on purpose."

"*What?*" he asked incredulously.

"It's a business, kiddo, and banks make money when you forget your balance and overdraw your account. As a matter of fact, it's big business. Billions of dollars in fees a year! They even have this little trick where they'll clear your largest transaction first, so it drains your account faster and you have to pay more fees," I informed my stunned son.

"You may think it's wrong, or that it's not fair, but you know what? You can't change it. It is what it is. Banks charge fees when you overdraft, pure and simple. Now, the question you have to ask yourself is, what are you going to do about it?" I paused, giving him time to form his own conclusions.

When he didn't answer, I prompted, "Are you going to keep letting them take your money, or are you going to protect your-self from the greedy coyotes that feed on your checking account? Maybe you should consider watching your balance more closely, or maybe carrying cash – then you'll always know when you're low on money? Or, maybe, you could rob a bank to pay your fees!" I finished triumphantly.

We were all laughing, when I heard Tyler mutter under his breath, "I wish I was the CEO of a bank."

"Well, kiddo, you *are* the CEO. You're the *CEO of Your Own Life!*"

"And if you want to live with your mother forever, *never* own your own home, and *never* have enough money to buy a new car, well then buddy, you're on the right track. As a matter of fact, don't change a thing," I admonished playfully.

"But your life is just like a business, and you have to run your life like a business so you don't go out of business," I continued.

"Let's start at the beginning. A business has a mission, and I know you guys have a mission."

"We do?" Ty and Tiff asked in stereo.

"Sure you do!" I laughed. "You told me hundreds of times! Let's see," I pretended to ponder for a moment, and then ticking the points off one by one on my fingers, recited "You want to finish college, get good jobs in your career field, get married, buy a house, and then have children, in that order. And, you want to do all that because you love each other. Do I have it right?"

"Yes!" they said in unison, looking at each other with stars in their young eyes. Love was definitely creeping back into the air, I thought smugly.

"Okay," I said, whipping out a blank sheet of paper, "Let's write it down." I wrote:

1. Tyler's and Tiff's Mission Statement:
   Our mission is to finish college, get good jobs in our career fields, get married, buy a house, and then have children, in that order, because we love each other.

"That's a great reason, a great intention, by the way," I commented as they soaked up the praise.

I continued, "Now a business has income. Banks charge fees; that is their income. You have income too, from your part-time jobs." I wrote it down.

"Businesses have expenses, like payroll and rent. You have expenses, like car insurance and cell phone bills." I added their expenses to the growing list.

"Now, most business owners I know want to have a profit at the end of the month. So do you. You don't want your expenses to be larger than your income, or you'll go out of business!"

I quickly made a list of everything I could think of that Tyler spends his money on from KFC to coffee, to more KFC, and wrote it all down. I added up the figures and pushed the paper across the table toward him.

"Do you want to go out of business?" I asked, knowing the answer.

"No," they agreed sheepishly. "We'll watch our expenses," Tyler said, and then added confidently and just a little wistfully, "Maybe I'll start my own business and sell it for a million dollars."

"Good goal," I agreed, "but first, you need to learn to live within your means. Otherwise, the business you sell for a million bucks will have a debt of two million," I said laughing. Standing up, I was relieved to see that nobody complained when I put out my arms for hugs.

Whew, I thought, what a day. I brought Dad up to speed on the current events of our household the next morning when he called.

"Do you know what the worst part is?" I lamented, recalling Tyler's fury.

"Hmmm. What?"

"He learned it from me."

Dad said nothing and the weight of the silence caused my shoulders to sag.

"Well," he finally replied, "It doesn't *have* to be that way."

"How do I change it?" I said remorsefully. "How do I teach him to control his emotions?"

Dad responded instantly, "How did you *already* teach him?"

When I said nothing, he answered his own question, "By example."

Ouch. The truth hurts, I thought, feeling a little queasy knowing he was right.

"You know, Daughter, you can say all you want about *Recognizing, Expressing,* and *Dismissing,* why, you can even write about it in your book, but if you don't actually *do* it, then it isn't real."

Apparently, *The Preacher* was disappointed in me as well, for he added,

> *"To be a kind person, you must do the things that a kind person does, then you will experience the reality of kindness.*
>
> *To be a generous person, you must do the things that a generous person does, then you will experience the reality of generosity."*

Dad interrupted with, "It's the same thing with being calm, or being professional, or learning to speak *Spanish.* In order to be those things, you must *do* those things." Dad was on a roll.

"I listen to the things that you say, the words that you say, and it sounds like this: 'I'm angry at my ex-husband. I'm resentful that I have to work harder in this economy. I'm frustrated because I don't have more time to do the things that I love." He paused, but not for long.

"People speak anywhere between two and seven *thousand* words a day. That's *seven thousand* opportunities for you to pay attention to your words."

"And what you don't realize is that you are the only person who has the power and the strength to change it. But power is not force."

The Preacher agreed.

> *"Power is not Force."*
>
> *"With Power comes Strength. Strength is the mental power to withstand pressure or stress from outside sources."*

"Like your ex," Dad commented, as if I needed reminding. *The Preacher* continued,

> *"Strength allows you to set and maintain personal boundaries and to maintain internal calm and external control when those boundaries are breached by others. But Power is not Force."*

Dad started chuckling, "You use your shields, right?"

"Yeah, when I remember to engage them," I admitted.

"Well, you also have a sword."

Ooohhh, I thought maliciously, a weapon!

"But your sword is not a weapon with which to stab people or chop off their heads." He corrected, reading my mind, "That would be force."

Darn. I was imagining the enemy peeking in my pinhole, and then using my pin to stick him in the eye.

"Instead, you use this sword to cut out the things in your life that don't move you forward. Use your sword to draw some lines in the sand. Set some boundaries for yourself. If engaging in battles with your ex- doesn't move you forward, cut it out! You make the rules for how you live your life, so don't be afraid to hand out some red cards, and eject players from the game!" He laughed, and I laughed with him.

It was easy to picture my invisible shields in place while I wielded my sword against the enemy (so easy to picture I could name him), gallantly defending my family's peace of mind.

"You're right," I admitted quietly. "Only I can change it."

"Yes, only you."

"Or, I could wait and see what happens. He could change. The economy could change."

Dad laughed. "Waiting is definitely one option," he agreed. "Anything is possible, but not everything is probable."

"What do you mean?" I asked.

He responded, "Well, it's like this: suppose you called me up one day and said you wanted to be a quarterback for the Cleveland Browns. Do you know what I would say?"

"You'd say, somebody has to do it!" I cried. "They suck."

"No," he laughed, "I would say, "That's great, Daughter. Anything is possible, but being a quarterback isn't very probable given your five-foot, hundred and ten pound frame. (*Author's note: I weigh more than that, but who's counting?*) So, don't quit your day job!" he giggled, and I laughed along with him.

"If you called me and told me you wanted to be a ballerina, or a runway model or an NBA star, I would say the same thing."

No need to get carried away, I thought, thinking of my short stature.

"Anything is possible, but not everything is probable. Watch for the detour signs in your life; they urge you in different directions."

After he calmed himself, he commented, "Sometimes I'm amazed that you don't even see what is right in front of you."

"*What?*" I demanded, hating the thought that I might be missing something valuable.

"You're the *CEO of Your Own Life*, too," he stated the obvious.

"You already have the start of a plan, use it! Take the advice you gave Tyler and apply it to yourself!" I could picture *The Preacher* trying to grab the phone from Dad.

"Have the strength to be the CEO of Your Own Life – don't just talk about it."

Dad won the wrestling match and added, "I love you, Daughter. I can't wait to see you guys tomorrow. What time are you leaving?"

We chatted for a few minutes about my travel plans for the next day. Gage and I were driving out together to spend a few days in Allentown so Dad and I could work on the book, and Gage could invest in some quality play-time with his cousin Mitchell.

We said our 'goodbyes' and our 'love you's, and hung up. I texted Gage to come home from his cousins' house to pack his suitcase, and then started on the same task. He came bouncing into the house, and his excitement for our upcoming "mini vacation" had me worried he wouldn't be able to fall asleep.

After about an hour of packing and repacking, non-stop chatter and intermittent bouncing, Gage eventually managed to brush his teeth and climb into bed for a goodnight kiss. Finally, the house grew quiet and I could think. What am I going to do? I thought? What do I want to do? What do I have to do? Responsibilities and desires battled for my attention as I fretted about my options. Realizing that I wouldn't solve anything or come to any rational conclusions that night, I cleaned up the downstairs, lugged the kitchen trash out to the can, and went to bed. It was going to take a miracle, I thought.

Chapter Six

"Appreciate What You Have."

I woke moments before the alarm, offering up a quick prayer of thanks for the break in the rain. The alarm startled Gage awake at 4:55, and he eagerly jumped out of bed. Although I followed a little more slowly, I was equally excited.

After showering, loading the car, and making a quick pit stop for gas and supplies – an extra-large coffee for me, and Gatorade for Gage – we were headed north on Interstate 77, the first leg of our journey from Ohio back to my hometown of Allentown, Pennsylvania, and watching the sun come up by six.

I yawned as I remembered how Gage had pleaded to leave for the six-hour drive to Allentown at 4:00 am. Absolutely not! I had insisted.

"Mom, it will be fine! I'll sleep all the way there!" he had reasoned with the logic of a ten-year old. I laughed out loud, and after some back and forth negotiating, settled on a 5:00 a.m. wake up call.

"Oops." He had looked at me slyly last night, as I smiled knowingly back. "I set the alarm on your phone for 4:55 by accident. Oh well!" he exclaimed happily, jumping onto his bed.

"Wow, Mom, look at that!" Gage said urgently from the backseat. I came out of my reverie and stared at the rays of sun streaming brilliantly down from the sky in front of us.

I was reminded of a story Tyler once told me about driving to California in the dark.

"You can't see all the roads to California when you drive in the dark. All you can see is the forty feet in front of your headlights. But you don't need to see the whole way to California, you only need to follow what is right in front of you, and eventually, you'll get there." Out of the mouths of babes.

"Wow," I said reverently, instantly overcome by a feeling of calm protection, as if God knew we were traveling and bestowed His approval by painting the morning with strokes of His light to guide us safely on our journey. *Thank you, God.*

I immediately voiced a quiet prayer of thanks for the G.P.S. (God's Protection System). Gage laughed and agreed, and within ten minutes was fast asleep, just as he had predicted last evening. We merged onto Interstate 76, which would take us east toward Pennsylvania.

I let my mind wander, and it bounced wildly from shields and swords, to sales and expenses, and from exes and anger, to responsibilities and choices. I took inventory of my thoughts and made a mental list of everything that was on my mind.

I blinked as we started to cross the long bridge over Lake Milton already thirty minutes into our drive., and then had to squint to see clearly with the sunlight sparkling off the water. Wow, *Zip Time*, I thought, smiling. With Dad and *The Preacher* looking over my shoulder, I took out an imaginary sheet of paper and poised my invisible pen to write as everyone's words came flooding back, one after another.

It is what it is. You can't control it. You can only choose how you perceive it.

I stuck with what I knew best and made a list.

1. The economy sucks for everyone.
2. The book will either get written or it won't, with or without me.
3. People will attack.

I suddenly saw the futility of the question, why do people attack? Who cares why? It is what it is, I scolded myself. But, it doesn't have to be that way, I thought smiling secretively.

We crossed the border from Ohio to Pennsylvania an hour into our journey, with Gage still sleeping and the sun bouncing brilliantly off the windshield.

All is energy. Thoughts are things. Constructive thoughts grow into constructive words, which then grow into constructive deeds. Love multiplies exponentially.

Interstate 76 merged into Interstate 80 as I turned up the radio to *Aretha Franklin's "Respect"* and added to my list:

1. I believe it will get better for everyone, and I am grateful that I still have a company to go to and a job to do.
2. I believe I can write this story, and I love doing it.
3. I believe people attack because they don't know another way, and maybe I should forgive them.

I was on a roll, look out!

4. I believe that I am capable of cooking a healthy delicious meal for my family every weeknight, and I could learn to love it. (*Okay, maybe I'm getting carried away with the delirium that the monotony of the highway brings.*)
5. I believe that I could learn to speak Spanish fluently, and that way, when I retreat to write books on the beaches of Mexico, I'll be prepared to commune with the locals. (*Maybe it's time to stop and stretch my legs, give my imagination a rest.*)

Gage woke in time to reach the summit, and I took a moment to reflect peacefully that I was high up on top of a mountain in God's country, as he read the sign aloud:

"Highest point on Interstate 80 east of the Mississippi
Elevation 2,250 feet"

"Wow," we said in stereo.

Time is an illusion. The only time is Now.

Gage started singing along with Kesha to the radio, "*...The party don't start 'til I walk in.*" I laughed and tried to join in, but he knew more words than I did. I retrieved my invisible pen and made another list:

1. What can I do about it *Now*? Nothing!
2. What *can* I do *Now*? Enjoy the view!
3. What can I do when I get home? Enjoy the *Now*!

I looked at the clock on the dash and was startled to see that we were half way through our journey. We re-fueled the car with gas, and our bodies with Mickey D's drive-thru breakfast at the exit for Dad's hunting cabin, 158 miles into Pennsylvania.

You can't change anyone else but yourself.
Only you can change you.

As we pulled back onto the highway, I was suddenly assailed by all the mistakes I've made in the past. I've made so many errors of judgment in my business that I could list them either alphabetically, or by the amount of money they've cost my company. I'm surprised they still let me work there, sometimes. As for mistakes in my personal life? Too many to mention.

I put up my shields, protecting me from myself, and dictated out loud to my imaginary tape recorder. After I get home, I'll give the tape to my imaginary assistant, who will magically transcribe my conversation while I sleep. By now, the lists were coming faster and easier.

1. Can I change the past? No. I accept that.
2. Can I change what comes to me? No. I accept that.
3. Can I change other people? No. I accept that a little more slowly. No wait, I accept it, yes, yes, I accept it, okay? That's my final answer. I accept it. Sheesh!

272 miles into Pennsylvania, we were heading south on the northeast extension of the Pennsylvania turnpike, Gage eagerly anticipating The Lehigh Valley Tunnel, just as you pass the Pocono Mountains.

Allentown is a city of over 100,000 people that lies in the middle of the Lehigh Valley, which swells to over six hundred thousand residents when you add in Bethlehem, Easton, and numerous other small towns. Just south of the Pocono Mountains, it is conveniently located one hour north of Philadelphia, 2.5 hours from Ocean City, New Jersey, our favorite beach town, and 1.5 hours from New York City, provided there isn't another car on the road on the way into the Big Apple.

When I respond "Allentown" to the question, "where are you from?" It is immediately recognized as the Billy Joel song made infamous with the words, *"We're living here in Allentown, where they're shutting all the factories down."* Yippee.

Power is not Force. Who needs a tape recorder or an assistant? I'll just transmit my growing list telepathically to my Mac for instant transcription. I hit Send.

1. What lines do I need to draw in the sand? The property lines for my new Beach House! LOL.

2. What do I need to cut out that is not moving me forward? Procrastination? Self-Pity? Sleeping late? Corona?
3. Who gets a red card? Hee hee. I could see another list looming.

Okay, so I don't have all the answers, who does? But *The Preacher* is right; *Power is not Force*. I don't need to force any conclusions, I merely need to stand back and wait; the answers will come to me, I'm sure. After all, a watched pot never boils.

We reached Allentown, me feeling strangely Zen and Gage scrambling and impatient to be out of the car and in the joyful presence of his cousin, Mitchell. While I was no closer to a resolution than when I had set out before sunrise, I was thankful for the time to spend on such a beautiful drive considering my options.

After the fastest check-in in memory at the hotel, we set out toward my sister Tawni's house, Gage chattering non-stop about the fun activities he had planned on his visit. We passed Dorney Park, the local amusement park, and deja vu gripped me as it did every time I visited my hometown.

I reminded Gage for the hundredth time of how when I was his age, Dorney Park was a tiny family-owned amusement park that only had one rickety wooden roller coaster and didn't even charge admission! Now owned by a giant corporation, it was a sprawling mega facility that included world-class roller coasters and a water park. He ignored me and begged, "Can we get Yocco's?"

"Of course!" I responded eagerly. "Text the family and see if they want anything." I said, handing my phone to Gage. *Yoccos, the Hot Dog King*, was a family favorite. We drove down Hamilton Street past Cedar Crest College, where Mom had graduated, and past Muhlenburg Lake, referred to locally back then as "duck-shit pond."

I pointed out Cedar Beach, the local swimming pool, to Gage, and remarked, "This is where my sisters and I went swimming every summer!"

Gage rolled his eyes and corrected, "Before you moved into the house with the pool, you mean, right?"

"Right, kiddo," I replied, smiling at the laser precision of his memory. We picked up our bag of hotdogs and pierogies at Yocco's, and I took a roundabout way to Tawni's house, driving Gage past The Terraces and the Union Terrace pond, where we had ice-skated every winter as kids.

"I'm glad I don't have to walk to a pond to ice-skate," Gage said graciously.

"Yep, you're lucky," I replied, thinking about the sixty-foot ice rink frame that Mark constructs in our backyards every winter with 2 x 4's and a tarp. After filling the rink frame with water pumped from the creek, we all wait impatiently for the temperature to sink low enough to freeze the water, transforming the homemade frame into an instant ice rink and the cousins into an instant hockey team.

I turned onto my sister's street, pointing out where all my child-hood friends had lived, now grown up and moved away. But, Gage was not listening in the least, his mind too focused on the fun he would soon have with his cousin. He was out of the car before it had fully stopped, and I laughed as I walked, and he ran, up the steps to Tawni's front porch.

I giggled as I told Gage about the time several years ago that Sandi and I had driven out to Allentown to surprise Tawni for her birthday, and when she had answered the doorbell, discovered the two of us on her front porch, wrapped head-to-toe in birthday wrapping paper, complete with bows.

I knocked my familiar refrain and opened the door to dogs barking, people yelling, "they're here!" and Dad running down the stairs to get a head start on the hugs. Mitchell immediately latched onto Gage, and they headed off for the first round of fun together.

I held up the Yocco's and declared, "We come bearing gifts!" After rounds of hugs and kisses, and a much-needed bathroom break, I asked the obvious, "Where is she?"

"Sleeping, for now." Tawni replied instantly, for we all knew who "she" was.

Born Mia Helene barely three months ago to my sister and her husband, Ron, Mia wears the Triple Crown of being Dad's eleventh grandchild, the *only* granddaughter, and the Family Miracle.

Tawni had suffered from "unexplained infertility" for their entire marriage, undergoing endless tests, misdiagnosis, and treatments. Despite raising Darnell, Ron's biological son and three more adopted boys, Tawni and Ron had yet to have a biological child together. I knew the excerpt from her blog by heart, and it still gives me goosebumps. She wrote:

> *"After fourteen years of marriage, and twenty-one failed Assisted Reproductive Technique cycles, our doctor kindly pointed out that producing a viable offspring was "well over a million to one." Thanks, Doc, I always knew I was one in a million!*
>
> *At that point, we had done all we could emotionally, physically, and financially. I was scared as heck to "try" again. Not because of the physical pain, or even the emotional devastation...I couldn't lose my last hope... If we tried again, and it didn't work... what hope would I have left?*
>
> *The tears are streaming now, as I write this. It's so hard to admit our vulnerabilities...It is so hard knowing that every day you live with your failure to do the basic thing*

*all women can do... the definition of womanhood...and I
failed, over and over again."*

My heart hurt as I thought about Tawni's pain and suffering for
all those years and my powerlessness to help her. If I could re-create
a relationship with a sister, I would change a lot of things.

I would change it so that every woman in the world who desired
to be a mother could do so. I would change it so that every woman who
found herself in a position of reluctant pending motherhood could do
as she chose. I would change it so that some women wouldn't struggle
with infertility, while others just think about a penis and casually find
themselves pregnant. I would change it so that every child was enthusiastically nurtured, and every parent properly fulfilled.

I never knew the right things to say to my sister, and I regretted
that everything seemed to be the wrong thing as I struggled to lessen
her grief. I knew I would never begin to be able to understand the
depths of her despair for all those years, but every time she cried, my
heart hurt more. Nor do I believe I possess the strength it took for her
to decide to "try" to conceive *again* last year, and I looked over at my
youngest sister in awe. She gazed back at me radiantly.

When I was eight years old and Sandi six, Tawni was born and
instantaneously dubbed "Little Miss Sunshine" by Mom. With her
California-girl looks of shiny blonde hair, sparkling blue eyes, and
pearly-white teeth, she lived up to her moniker by unleashing the
most radiant smile on all passers by. She danced around the house,
delighting in her life and singing its praises to all who would listen.
One of her favorite songs was the Oscar Meyer jingle.

"My bologna has a first name," she would confidently bellow.

"It's z-k-y-t-b," she would finish, and Sandi and I would burst
into unrestrained giggles. Our lack of appreciation for her spelling
abilities didn't diminish her enthusiasm for the song in the least. She

would sing the song over and over again, always substituting new letters of the alphabet for the words.

Tawni followed us everywhere that Sandi and I went, gamely keeping up with our adventures, despite the age difference. One of our favorite games was called "walking the dog," and Sandi and I would smile maliciously as we offered her one end of the leash, "You be the dog, and we'll walk you." She loved that game until a few years later when she realized we were treating her like a *pet*. She still harbors both the memory and a slight grudge. Sorry, Sis.

When Mom, our Girl Scout troop leader, took us to overnight camp, Tawni went along, outfitted with her very own sleeping bag and flashlight; a flashlight that she promptly dropped in the "on" position down the latrine.

She was instantly transformed into a celebrity with the troop, as thirty Girl Scouts stood impatiently in line to see the monstrous mound of poop and toilet tissue that were now on radiant display in all their disgusting glory. In fact, it was on display for three days until the battery in the flashlight wore out, affording us all ample opportunity to view the ghastly scene over and over again.

Suddenly, the words of Father Hartgen flooded my senses, and I began to tremble as I had that day so long ago. "We are all born with original sin," he thundered from the pulpit. I had cowered in the pew, unable to look up, my confusion making me dizzy.

There was *absolutely* no way that my beautiful little sister, who at three years old and home with Mom, (probably singing!) was born with anything resembling sin, I thought resolutely. I firmly believed that had she ever done anything wrong in her life even remotely resembling a sin, then she must have learned it from me. Afraid to confront the priest, who after all had a direct line to God, only made me more desperate, despite my young age, to discover the truth of whether or not we were born with sin.

Tawni was only nine when I left home and sixteen when I moved to Ohio, but we still make the trek to each other's houses often to visit; it's what Mom would have wanted. Tawni met Ron, her future husband right before Mom got sick, and they were married in the backyard of the house we grew up in, now home to Ron and Tawni's growing family.

Over the past fifteen years of their marriage, they added several boys to their brood. Joining Darnell, Ron's son from his previous marriage, were Nathan, Zack and Mitchell, who was currently glued to Gage somewhere off in the house. And, now we had Mia!

Nathan, otherwise known as GWH (Great White Hunter) on Gamer Tag is the oldest at twenty-six. He busies himself with all things electronic or mechanical. If he isn't taking apart a random appliance or computer, he is tearing down and rebuilding walls in his house or playing his guitar.

Darnell, the Computer Genius, divides his time between programming, web design and partying with his college buddies. An avid player in the family poker fames since he was twelve, he is affectionately referred to as "Joker" for his finely honed skills.

Zack is the Skater Cool eighteen year-old with a killer sense of style, friends all over the world, an incredible artistic ability, and a dream since childhood of being a firefighter. Currently exploring his newfound *love* with his cute girlfriend, he has added an assortment of colorful hickies to his homeschool education.

Mitchell, the youngest, red-haired and quiet, showers so much love and attention onto his two dogs, Lola and Doodle, that I swear he can communicate with them. It's no surprise he already sees himself as a future veterinarian. Just call him Doctor Dolittle and watch the smile light up his face.

Let me assure you, these people are serial overachievers. In addition to working side-by-side running the successful nursing agency that Tawni had started before they met, my sister and brother-in-law home-school all their kids, travel around the country on educational vacations in their RV, and cook dinners from scratch.

They approached the crafting of their Home-Birth Plan with the same zeal and passion they have for everything they do, and Mia cooperated by entering the world flawlessly. Both Tawni and Ron are wicked-smart computer geniuses, and they create and program complex databases for fun. She even bakes.

As a young girl, she would often sing, "I am a Star, that's what I Are." We would laugh at her play on words, but obviously she fulfilled her own destiny. Her achievements as an über businesswoman and Mother Earth are as daunting as having the Cleavers for neighbors, and it only reinforced my black-sheep status in the family.

Suddenly, a tiny squeal erupted from the dining room table. Tawni and Ron both jumped up, running from the room to attend to their baby as I stared in amazement at the contraption, no larger than an iPod, that was emitting the quiet squeaking.

"What is that?" I asked everyone.

"Oh that!" Dad responded. "That's their baby monitor. It has video so they can watch Mia sleeping, not just hear her cry."

"No kidding, " I responded, amazed at the levels our world had grown to. I love technology.

Tawni and Ron came back into the room, my sister holding her newborn close.

"Can I hold her?" I asked to no avail.

"Later. I have to nurse her," Tawni responded happily.

Yeah, right, I thought. Tawni won't put that baby down until she turns sixteen! I thought tenderly, and I wouldn't either if I were her. After my pierogies were a distant memory, we all headed outside to the back deck overlooking the pool and trampoline.

The kids were swimming happily and making joyful noises when Dad suddenly jumped up, exclaiming, "Listen to that! I love that sound!"

I nodded and smiled my agreement. He was right; kids' giggles tickle your ears, causing spontaneous laughter in return.

"Did you know that the average child laughs three hundred times a day?" he asked everyone. Nobody did.

"And adults only laugh fifteen times a day," He added.

Really? I thought, smirking, Dad probably laughs fifteen times in fifteen minutes!

"It's true," He stated, though nobody was doubting his word. Not out loud, anyway.

"This is such a Happy House! It has always been a Fun House, and it still is!" he gleefully cried to his audience, bouncing around the deck. "It's a dream come true, a Miracle." He thundered happily.

"Mom and I had dreamed about this house since we were teenagers," he mused, "walking around while holding hands and dreaming about what it would look like. In our minds, our dream house was huge with enough bedrooms for everyone; but we never imagined the house would have four bedrooms, four bathrooms and an in-ground pool!"

Suddenly, I was ten years old and hiding outside the fence that surrounded the pool in the back yard. My family lived two houses down the street in our first house, referred to as the "Little Cape Cod," and my best friend, Denny, lived another five houses beyond ours. Day after day, walking home from St. Catherine's together, we would be curiously drawn to the big house on the corner with the pool.

Tall and imposing on the top of a hill, the large house always seemed eerily vacant and mysterious and we were continually creating numerous scenarios that required us to sneak around the property. Grabbing apples that had fallen from the nearby trees, we would hurl them over the fence, competing to make the biggest splash until our fear of getting caught made us run quickly home, laughing 'til our sides hurt.

And then suddenly, Dad spontaneously bought the very house that we kids in the neighborhood had been secretly coveting and publicly destructing for years. Oh, my God! We were going to live in a mansion! Well, it was certainly a mansion from our prepubescent perspective.

My sisters and I were ecstatic! Upstairs, a large open living area joined up with an airy dining room and spacious kitchen. Down the short hall two bedrooms were facing each other (mine and Sandi's), each with it's own bathroom, and a sliding door to the outdoor deck. From the deck, you could walk down the stairs to the back yard, or you could choose our favorite route: Down the sliding board into the pool!

The downstairs of the house was exactly the same as above, except my parents' and Tawni's bedroom sliding doors opened onto a patio with a hot tub. It was like living in a vacation resort.

Dad had purchased the house fully furnished, so not only did we girls each have a new bedroom of our own, which was more a like mini-apartment, we were now able to decorate them with the "new" furniture as well. It was like winning the House Lottery.

The downstairs "living area" became our "rec room," and Dad wasted no time filling it with toys. Joining his state-of-the-art sound system, which he danced to religiously, were pinball machines, a ping-pong table, and games galore. I love my Dad!

And then there was the back yard. Between the pool, the sliding board, the hot tub, the diving board, and the trampoline we had carried from across the street when we moved from the Little Cape Cod, we never ran out of things to do.

Dad would throw his scuba tanks in the deep-end of the pool, and we would spend hours taking turns breathing underwater with nothing to look at but dead bugs. At night, we would turn all the lights out except for the underwater light, and we would swim for several more hours in its ghostly glow. The pool was like heaven only we got to swim in it. And so did all of our friends.

We spent endless sunny days swimming, running, playing, jumping, diving, giggling, and then dozing lazily in the hot sun. In the water, we were wrinkled fish with bloodshot eyes, and out of the water, the blazing sun bronzed our bodies and bleached our hair. We were always wet, or drying in the sun until we got wet again, causing Mom to joke about checking for gills behind our ears.

We made our own fun too! We spent our first night in the new house before Dad had even signed the papers, and with only one bedroom available to us, our whole family camped out on that one bedroom floor, with blankets, pillows and snacks. We spent the evening not telling ghost stories, but dreaming out loud about the ways we would decorate and the fun we would have when we could live in the whole house!

The Happy House was constantly filled with friends and family and laughter, whether we were inside playing games, outside swimming, or relaxing by the pool with a good novel. Once a year we would host a "Splash Bash," and all our aunts and uncles from New Jersey would visit, each bringing their favorite covered dish, for a day of food, fun and sun. When it came time to clean up, after foisting take-out plates on everyone who was leaving, we were still left with more food than before the party started, prompting us all to happily give thanks for the "loaves and fishes." *Thank you, God.*

Even when we were away on summer vacations, family and friends would generously offer to house-sit, hosting a large pool party of their own. We loved it! The house was always full and always happy. It was like Christmas, only every day, over and over again!

Once, after Mom had died, I discovered a short story she had written in one of her journals about our Happy House. She had described in detail the day that she had shampooed the carpet in the living room, and she watched us girls dance barefoot to the radio in the suds before she rinsed it. She wrote, *"...and the House laughed."* Yes, I whole-heartedly agree, it was a Happy House.

And now it's Tawni and Ron's Happy House. After Mom had died, Dad moved to his South Mountain duplex, and Tawni and her family took over as Keepers of the Fun House; a responsibility they take, well, *seriously*. They have eagerly carried the "fun torch," adding more toys, computers, video games, kids, friends, relatives, cats, dogs, fish, and "Splash Bashes" to the mix, ensuring that the House will never have reason to be still or lonely. And, now we have a Mia!

Dad was still talking, and I wasn't sure what I had missed. "But more than the size of the rooms or the number of bathrooms it might have, we knew we wanted our house to be a Happy House, and it is. Listen to that!" he exclaimed again, referring to the kids playing merrily in the pool.

As if to insert an exclamation point on his words, Mia let loose a happy gurgle (or maybe it was gas). We all laughed and looked over at Tawni and Ron's sweet bundle of joy.

"And she is the biggest miracle of all," Dad said quickly, and we all agreed enthusiastically as we watched Tawni tend to her baby.

We sat for a while listening to the kids' splashing, and I brought Tawni up to date on what we had been working on recently concerning emotions and anger, when Dad jumped in with, "*Recognize. Express. Dismiss.* If you don't *Recognize* the *Feeling* as real, *Express* it constructively and *Dismiss* it, it becomes psychological baggage, and ultimately could lead to psychological suicide."

"Like emotional scars," I replied.

"Yeah!" Tawni jumped in with laughing, "like the emotional scar you guys gave me with my Cabbage Patch Doll!"

Seriously? I chuckled to myself. She still remembers this?

Dad looked confused and asked, "What doll?"

Tawni eagerly recited the whole story, complete with dramatic facial expressions, emotional body contortions and flamboyant hand gestures.

"I wanted a Cabbage Patch Doll more than anything in the world," she whimpered with puppy-dog eyes, perfectly mimicking the eight year-old she had been at the time of the tragedy. "I cried when I didn't get it for Christmas," she pouted, crossing her arms.

That, I remembered.

"Finally, I got one for my birthday in March." Hands on her hips, she still looked aggrieved at the long-ago slight.

"I named her *Josephina,*" she declared maternally. "I loved her."

I couldn't help it; I jumped in. "She carried that doll everywhere, Dad! She sang to it, tried to feed it, fixed her hair, she even dressed and re-dressed that doll twenty times a day!"

Dad was laughing out loud at my teasing memory.

"I remember that," he said laughing. "She was the happiest kid on the planet."

"Until you guys kidnapped her!" Tawni accused, eyes growing dark and pointing at me.

"That was Sandi," I claimed, raising my arms in mock self-defense and mentally engaging my shields. *(Author's note: I'm innocent. That's my story and I'm sticking to it.)*

Tawni turned urgently to Dad, "I opened my closet door and Josephina was hanging from a noose with a suicide note pinned to her dress!" she choked out the words, clearly still horrified at the twenty-five year-old memory.

That's all it took. Suddenly, we were all laughing uproariously, each of us bent over holding our sides, Tawni repeating horrifying details, me pleading my innocence while throwing Sandi under the Blame Bus, and Dad laughing and shaking so vigorously he could hardly speak.

When we had all calmed down and Tawni was certain we wouldn't scare the baby, she let me hold her. Oh, my God! I forgot babies come this small, I thought, as I held the warm, sweet-smelling bundle of softness close.

Zipping back to Tawni's pregnancy, we had all, family and friends alike, eagerly looked forward to Mia's pending arrival, celebrating every stage of fetal development with delightful anticipation, impatient to finally meet the Miracle. Dad's dancing buddies even threw him a "Grandfather Baby Shower" at the club complete with cake, gifts, and of course, lots of laughing and dancing. A good friend of Dad's, Daisy, a first-grade teacher, praised, "This just keeps getting funner and funner!" she enthused, if not grammatically correct. And, she was right.

"Wow. Babies are such a great way to start people," I said repeating a quote whose author escaped me. It's like Heaven, only with diapers.

With her shock of black hair tied in a "Pebbles" style ponytail, she looked familiar, but new enough to the world that I couldn't quite place her. Suddenly, she looked right at me, and at only three months old, the ancient yet timeless wisdom that resides behind all babies' eyes reached out and squeezed my heart, and of course, I promptly melted.

I turned to Tawni and asked, "So, when did it happen? When did you look into your baby's eyes and just '*know*' that she '*knew*' more than you?" I asked, remembering the same intimately profound experience with my own newborns as if it was only yesterday.

Tawni looked at me peacefully and replied instantly, "As soon as she was born. She was probably not even a minute old."

"Wow. She is a beautiful miracle. Congratulations."

Tawni and Ron beamed.

After a few minutes, Mia started to fuss, and I promptly handed her back to her mother, exercising my fundamental aunt's rights.

Leaving Gage to watch movies with Mitchell, Dad and I left for his house, where we intended to spend some time reviewing book materials. We drove the three miles south from Allentown to Upper Milford Township, a small rural community located halfway up South Mountain on the outskirts of Emmaus.

I loved Emmaus for its small town atmosphere combined with the profusion of family-owned businesses including eclectic shops, coffee houses, and galleries that line State Street, the main thoroughfare. Dad pulled into Mountain Spring Farms, where he rents a duplex from a kindly retired couple who spend their days tending to their overflowing flowerbeds and the exotic animals that populate their farm. I realize that some people might not consider emus, guinea hens, and peacocks to be exotic animals, but I'm a city girl, born and raised, and any animals other than standard house pets are considered exotic in my book.

Going inside, I smiled at the hundreds of photographs of family and friends that greet you immediately as you enter. I turned to shut the front door and laughed out loud at a note Dad had tacked to the door:

1. Meditate 2 X a day
2. Buy donuts
3. Pay rent

Well, Dad certainly has his priorities in order! I thought to myself. Depositing my backpack on the kitchen chair, I first had to clear a stack of newspapers from the table in order to make room for my coffee. Some things never change, I thought, remembering the piles of newspapers that perpetually littered our table growing up.

"How can you ever find anything in here, Dad?" I asked, slightly alarmed.

"I know where everything is," he replied confidently, and he was right. I remembered as a teenager looking with dismay at his office desk, which was habitually piled high with papers, files and miscellaneous toys. He had a small sign on his desk, barely visible, that stated, *"A neat desk is a sign of a sick mind."*

Dad's mind must have been the healthiest on the planet 'cause he had the ability to instantly put his hands on any piece of paper that was required of him, and I envied that sense of organized chaos.

"I love my life!" Dad exclaimed as he joined me at the table, "It's like Christmas every day." He looked skyward and added, "Thank you, God."

"I love my life, too, Dad," I responded truthfully.

"Good, because you can't just be aware of your blessings, and accept them, you must give thanks continually. I not only give thanks for my blessings, I count them as Miracles."

"Dad, I understand that your house, or rather Tawni's house, was a dream come true, but why is it a miracle?"

Dad responded enthusiastically, "Because of what we discovered in the house."

"You mean like *The Money* hidden in the floorboards?" I asked conspiratorially. In every house I had ever moved into, I searched high and low for the secret stash of cash I am certain a long-ago millionaire hid in my house before my time. I know it's there; I just have to find it!

"No, no, no, nothing like that," he smiled. "It was out on the sidewalk."

"*The Money*?" I repeated hopefully, not willing to surrender my fantasy.

"No!" He laughed. "The date they built the house. After we moved in, we were exploring the house, looking in all the closets and cabinets, testing all the faucets and such. But, while we were exploring outside, I noticed that engraved in the sidewalk on the corner was the date they built the house: 1966."

"Why is 1966 so special? I mean, other than that's the year your first daughter was born, of course," I said smugly.

He jumped up from his chair and practically danced, "Because that's the year your mom and I were walking around talking about our Dream House, that's why." He was almost teary from the memory.

"I learned two things that day, Daughter. The first is that you must do everything important and necessary in order to make your dream a reality. That means we had to work hard at our jobs, pay our bills on time, and keep saving money."

That, I could completely understand, I thought as I watched Dad dance around the room. "What was the second thing?"

"The second is that once you set out toward something, it is already there, waiting for you." Dad sang, and *The Preacher* echoed,

"It is already there, waiting for you."

That, I most definitely do *not* comprehend.

"Well, when Mom and I were walking around dreaming about the house we wanted to live in, we didn't know what city it would be in, or what style of home it would be, or how we would ever afford it. But that didn't matter, because the very house we dreamed of was being built at the very same time we were dreaming about it."

The Preacher closed his eyes, lifted his arms upward in praise and whispered,

"Doubt Not. Fear Not. Work on. Wait."

After a moment, Dad took over. "It's as if our dream was answered instantly, even though we didn't know it yet. We still had to work toward it doing everything important and necessary to bring it about, and then we had to wait eleven years to actually live there. But, it was already there, waiting for us the moment we first dreamed of it." He paused with a faraway look in his eyes and excitement trembling his voice.

"I had proven to myself that I create my own reality." Joyful tears were ready to spring from his eyes. "It was an epiphany for me, and I didn't sleep for three days! My mind was reeling with all the possibilities. It was a miracle," he gushed.

The Preacher assumed the same worshipful pose and declared,

"You create your own reality according to your thoughts, words, and deeds. Starting with a good intention, a steadfast belief, and understanding that you need to do everything important and necessary to bring it about, you create your own reality."

He summarized as an afterthought, *"Thoughts are Things."*

Dad came back to the room. "You need to write down your miracles as they happen," he intoned. "That way, when you doubt yourself, or forget who and what you are, you can read the list and remember!" He whipped out his iPhone and showed me where he records the miracles in his life.

"You write them on your phone?" I asked, as he scrolled through page after page of notations.

"Yeah, I do!" he laughed. "That way, I always have them with me."

"There should be an app for that!" I laughed back, and Dad wondered aloud, "Wouldn't it be great if there was an app on your phone that once you record your miracles, they are sent back to you as a text message randomly and automatically when you need them most?"

"That would be amazing!" I agreed, "Especially if somebody in our family designed the app and became an overnight million-aire!" We both chuckled with the dreamy looks of people holding PowerBall tickets, mentally spending the jackpot before the winning numbers were even drawn.

"Do you write your miracles down?" he looked at me sideways, knowing the answer.

"No," I admitted. "But, I remember them," I countered.

"Yeah? What are they?"

My mind drew a blank, and I was instantly chastised. He was right. Again.

"You know, Daughter, I'm not always 'up.' Sometimes I experience frustration and annoyance just like everyone else." I sincerely doubted that, since I had never seen him "down," but I didn't respond.

"But then I look at my list of miracles, and I remember how blessed I am. You could do the same thing when you are down; you could review your list of miracles, and it just might make you feel better."

I didn't want to be contrary, *but,* "The house is a once in a lifetime miracle," I challenged. "What about the rest of the *Time?*"

The Preacher jumped up from the table and shouted,

> *"Miracles don't happen once in a lifetime.*
> *Miracles happen ALL the time!"*

Dad took the mic, but stood standing,

"You just have to look for them." He was excited as he relayed, "The other day, I was giving a speech for the Boy Scouts, and on the wall in the classroom was a sign that said *'Miracles happen every day.'* I believe that!" He said emphatically and continued, "Listen to this: Once, my business partner and I had purchased a small apartment building as an investment property, but unfortunately, we didn't have the $5,000 in closing costs and the settlement was in two hours."

I looked at him curiously, attempting that one-eyebrow trick and failing miserably.

"So, then the phone rings, and on the other end of the line is an old friend of my business partner. He was in town, needed a place to stay, and by the way, could pay an entire year's rent in advance, "$5,000."

"Are you kidding?" I asked incredulously.

"Yeah, I'm kidding," And, gullible blonde me believed him.

"No, I'm not kidding!" he yelled, laughing at my cluelessness. "It was a miracle!"

"But sadly, most people don't notice the miracles around them as they are occurring, and consequently, they are still waiting for the first miracle in their life. If they looked for them, they would see them and experience them, and then they could write them down too!"

The Preacher, feeling completely left out from his most passionate subject, took the stage.

> *"Miracles don't happen once in a lifetime.*
> *Miracles happen ALL the time!"*

I sat quietly remembering a quote I read recently by Albert Einstein that said: *"There are two ways in which to live your life. One, as if nothing is a miracle. Two, as if everything is a miracle."* Dad certainly held membership in the second category, and I longed to be like that, too.

"How do you do that, Dad?" I pleaded, "How do you live your life as if everything is a miracle?"

"I give thanks continually," he replied, beaming. "That means for eve-ry-thing," he emphasized, drawing out the word slowly.

"The moment I wake up, before I even get out of bed, I give thanks for another day. I constantly give praise for the magnificence the Creator has bestowed upon us! Harmony is the peace, love, tranquility, and balance that originate in the joyful acceptance of all that is. And, I accept it joyfully!" he enthused, relishing this morning's memory.

"Come with me, I have something to show you," he commanded, jumping up and heading out the front door before I could even register what was happening. I rose to follow, fervently hoping there was a secret to this miracle stuff that he would share with me but wondering why it would be outside and not in some dusty ancient tome hidden in the bookshelves.

I found *The Preacher* standing on his front walk, head tilted back to the sunshine, smiling with his eyes closed and arms raised in supplication. But, when he spoke, it was Dad who was putting forth the quiet and sincere words of praise.

"I love my life! I live my life quietly while celebrating every moment."

Preacher/Dad continued with, *"I marvel at the incredible matrix that has been prepared for us to experience. I see the magnificence of the Creator in ev-ery-thing, and I graciously give thanks for the benevolence of God."*

"We are meant to experience who and what we are. And who and what we are are co-creators of our universe. I start with the magnificent bounty that the Creator continuously bestows upon us, and I co-create my own happiness from there."

"I enjoy my life, and I have fun. I search for ways to experience joy. And, I seek out opportunities to share that joy and create an experience of happiness for others...in everything I do!"

I was transfixed. This was the first time I had ever seen Dad, or was it *The Preacher*, or both of them, like this. It's as if they were one.

Preacher/Dad laughed out loud with his whole body and cried with tears in his eyes, "Look around!"

And I did, gazing through their eyes. At first, I was aware of the utter silence, noting the absence of background highway noises, kids' playing, muted televisions, or distant car doors slamming. There was, well, nothing. I looked up at the tops of the trees and watched them sway gently in a breeze that slowly trickled down to ruffle my hair and cool my face.

I turned to gaze toward the meadow at the back of the farm, where the emus galloped awkwardly, and I could feel their determination through the grass. Slowly, small sounds grew louder and more distinct, and after a moment I could decipher the bird's song from the crickets' insistent chatter. And, all the while, the brilliant sunshine seemed to warm me from the inside out.

I don't know how long I stood soaking up the sunshine, it could have been minutes or maybe it was months, but I could have stayed there forever, in the peaceful meadow on that quiet mountain. I felt weightless, empty and full at the same time, as if the spaces of air separating the molecules that made my body whole were bigger than the molecules themselves. Instead of the gentle breeze rustling my hair, I imagined it instead flowing right through me to the other side, leaving me untouched.

I took a deep, cleansing breath, my smile growing wider, and opened my eyes, startled to see my arms lifted up toward the sky. Embarrassed, I giggled and walked over to the porch, sacrificing my ego on the way to sit down. Wow. *Thank you, God.*

The Preacher/Dad mistaking my embarrassment for rapture, joined me on the porch repeating, "Magnificent, just magnificent!"

"And I saw that there is nothing better
than for a person to rejoice."
– Ecc. 3:22

"I understand why you love this place, Dad."

"I get to live in heaven!" he exclaimed.

"But what about when you *aren't* here on this beautiful mountain? What about when you're stuck in traffic, or late for an appointment, or you get a flat tire?" I asked. "How do you see the magnificence in those things?"

"I go flying," he replied instantly.

Dad has been a private pilot for over thirty years and rarely misses an opportunity to take to the skies. Since I was a young girl, he has flown our entire family in the blue and white Cessna to pancake breakfast fly-in's, vacations, spur of the moment jaunts to Atlantic City, and breathtaking trips up the Hudson River at night to see the Statue of Liberty blazing in all her glory. *(Author's Note: Before 9/11).*

Even when he isn't flying, he often (actually it's every single morning) hangs out at the Queen City Airport with the other pilots, eating the boxes of donuts *(We come bearing gifts!)* that Dad provides and talking shop.

"When things go wrong, as they sometimes will…" he laughed, citing the first line from one of our favorite poems, *"Don't Quit,"* I laughed with him.

"When somebody pushes my buttons, or worrisome thoughts try to intrude on my peace of mind, I fly. I close my eyes, and within a moment I am in my airplane and flying all over the Lehigh Valley, past South Mountain, over the Lehigh and Delaware Rivers.

I fly all over the valley, witnessing from above the beauty of the Creator in everything I see. My mind can focus only on one thing at a time, so I choose what to focus on. To me, flying is life. Everthing else is waiting."

I recalled once reading that a *Yogi* was someone who lived in a permanent state of enlightened bliss. Maybe *Yogi* was *The Preacher/Dad* 's new name. No, I can't call him that, I thought smiling inside, it reminds me too much of Yogi Bear, which would make me Boo Boo.

"Everyone is different, and you must choose what to focus on. For me, it's flying. For you, maybe it's writing, or dancing, or going to the beach. Only you can decide what's right for you." He broke out in giddy song with, "Go to your Happy Place! Where life is beautiful all the time!" then continued in a significantly more sane manner,

"As you refine your thoughts, the outcomes in your life will be different. In ancient times, alchemists attempted to transform lead into gold. You are the alchemist of your mind, transforming your negative thoughts into positive ones."

He suddenly leaned forward, excited, and said, "You wonder how I experience Miracles all the time? I start from a place of miraculous wonder, and from there, it's easy!"

He sat back and quietly added, "That house was miraculous for your mother and me in another way, too. It ignited a spiritual fire in us that couldn't be quenched. We immediately set out on a journey, a search for truth that has lasted over thirty years."

Mom and Dad had been "Searching for Truth" for as long as I can remember, the word truth being a general catch all term for any thought, scripture or writing that resonates spiritually with them, and brings clarity to their beliefs. Truth to my parents is *anything* that moves them closer to the state of being their true selves.

"Where did you go?" I asked, not quite sure the direction this was taking.

"Inside. We went inside to find the truth."

"Inside the house?" I asked, revealing my blonde roots.

"Inside ourselves. The search for truth is an inside journey, it exists in each one of us. There is not one truth because there is truth in everything."

"How can there be truth in everything? Wouldn't somebody have to be right and somebody have to be wrong?"

"Who's to say who is right and who is wrong? Certainly not me," he chuckled. "We weren't judging, we were exploring different perspective of truth, and we were discovering *new* truths every single day that added to our belief system and our philosophy of how we wanted to live our lives."

"How did you want to live your lives?"

"Joyfully!" he sang.

"So where did you find these truths?" I asked skeptically.

"Ev-ery-where!" He thundered. "Everywhere we looked, we saw truth. In fact, after some time, we couldn't look anywhere and *not* see truth." He sat back and reminisced.

"We found truth in all religions; studying The Bible, The Quran, The Zohar, Rosticrucians, Bhagavad Gita, even Scientology. We explored and found more truths hidden in ancient mysticisms and broadcasted through New Age philosophies.

"We visited healers, mediums, psychics, channelers, and participated in séances and prayer groups. We devoured any written material that concerned itself with growth, maturation of consciousness, or self-help. We constructed pyramids around our beds, dabbled in crystals, and even floated in a depravation tank, all in an effort to discover more truth!"

"I remember this time, Dad. My friends thought we were weird," I said reprovingly.

I'll admit it, I thought, there were times when I was considered weird too. Maybe I still am. People thought it weird that I went to Catholic school but didn't attend their church. But, I just couldn't seem to reconcile their fire and brimstone God, and loud shouting sermons dripping with guilt, with the loving, benevolent version of my God.

Later, people thought I was weird when I began attending a charismatic church, eventually leading to my "born again-ness." But, after some time, I couldn't seem to reconcile the people who "talked the talk" but didn't "walk the walk." What church does God go to? I wondered.

People thought I was weird again when I stopped attending all churches, instead preferring solitude and meditation as my preferred method of prayer and thanksgiving.

And, later still, they thought I was weird when I adopted my own personal custom of celebrating the Sabbath on Friday night, complete with dressing up, good food, and close friends and family. Maybe it's in my DNA to be weird when it comes to spirituality. But, I know this – I have always loved God, I have always felt loved by God, and I still do. As far as I'm concerned, God is a verb, I thought as I *Zip Timed* back to the porch with Dad.

"We were weird!" he admitted, laughing. "Our search for truth consumed us," he confided, "and we loved every moment of it! Everything we read or experienced added to our knowledge; it never took away from us or harmed us.

"We started from a place of love and it grew from there. We started with our love for each other, our love for our daughters, and the desire to know more about that love and how to share it with others. We embraced every truth that led us closer to that love and discarded everything that turned us away from it. We wanted to *be* that *love* for Eve-ry-thing."

Every single day, we would experience another revelation that brought us closer and closer to the state of being we sought! It was exhilarating!" he laughed.

"So, what did you find?" I pleaded, perched on the edge of my seat, eager to hear the happy ending of how the heroes (my parents) uncovered the ancient hidden treasure (the meaning of truth) that mankind has been searching for since the beginning of time.

"We found that there is truth in everything," he shrugged. "You can find truth on a Campbell's soup can."

The music stopped. "*What?*" I demanded. Seriously? All this time truth has been hiding in plain sight on the bottom shelf of my pantry? I was understandably deflated.

"Truth is ev-ery-where, Daughter," he said smiling. "When you soaked up the sunshine a few minutes ago, you experienced truth. When Mia looked into your soul this morning, you experienced truth. When you break out in goose bumps thinking about your favorite book as a child, or the kids' laughter causes you to spontaneously giggle, you experience truth. When you are standing among throngs of people in church in the middle of joyful praise and worship, with the band playing majestically in the background, and you feel bliss-fully swept away with the spirit, you experience truth."

The Preacher/Dad stood up and proclaimed,

"When you experience Truth for a moment, you exist out-side the constraints of time and space. When you experience Truth, you are harmoniously One with everything that is, everything that ever was, and ev-ery-thing that ever shall be. You are One with the Creator. You are One with God."

He pegged me; I had goose bumps.

"So, that's it? That's the truth? That truth is everywhere?" I could hardly contain my skepticism.

He giggled and said, "Don't believe me, what do I know? You have to prove it to yourself. I'm just telling you what I experienced, and what I get to experience every single day. You have to prove to yourself what your own truth is. Like I said, it's an inside journey, but I do know this – all roads lead to Rome, so there is no wrong way."

I alternately felt peaceful and cryptically short-changed at the same time as I tried to absorb the implications of his words.

"So, basically, you're saying that whatever I believe is my truth, that whatever I choose is One way, because there is no wrong way, and that what I do from there is up to me."

"Yes! Yes, that's it, exactly!" he exclaimed, bouncing around again. *Preacher/Dad* cried,

> *"Life is God's gift to you. What you do with your life*
> *is your gift to God."*

"So what do I do?" I asked plaintively, feeling the need for more explicit instructions.

They responded instantly, as if it were basic addition, *"Live joyfully. Pray continually. Give thanks in all things."*

"Okay, Dad, I will," I sighed, feeling small and inadequate.

"'Will' is in the future. Be the change you want to see in the world *now*. Be joyful *now*. Be thankful *now*."

I was quiet for a moment and then offered, "I made a list on the way out. It's titled 'It Is What It Is,' like my problems," I said, eager to deflect the conversation away from my fears of being ill equipped to reside in a state of constant joy to something more concrete; I explained my various lists, omitting the beach house and the *Spanish* lessons.

"Great!" he responded, either not noticing my deft change of subject, or not caring. "Now that you *recognized* it for what it is, and *expressed* it constructively, now you can get on to *dismissing* it!" He was emphatic. "Time to let it go."

"Look over there at that trash can," he ordered, pointing to the side of the house. "You have one of those trash cans at your house, am I right?"

"Of course," I replied, instantly recalling the bag of trash I had lugged out to the can last night before bed.

"Well, then I have a question for you. What happens when you take out your trash?" he asked with a smile on his lips and a gleam in his eye. Uh-oh.

"What do you mean, what happens? I take the trash out to the can and then once a week the garbage men come and take it to the dump. Why?"

"Exactly!" he praised, and I felt oddly proud for delivering the right answer.

"Now I have another question for you: Do you ever go outside to the trash can and open one of the bags and look through it?"

"Well," I replied truthfully, but in a smarty-pants tone, "there was this time I threw away Gage's homework by accident," knowing full well that wasn't the answer he was looking for.

He didn't take the bait and instead continued as if I hadn't said anything. "I have another question for you. Did you ever pick through the rotted banana peels and hold them up in the air and play with them? " he quizzed, with that one-eyebrow trick I envy. I shuddered.

"Do you ever sift through the coffee grinds to see if there are any you can re-use?" he laughed while I was wrinkling my nose in distaste, but still, he went on with the visuals.

"Do you ever attempt to find leftovers that weren't green and fuzzy because you were hungry?"

I shook my head, turning greener.

"Now, imagine this: Imagine that digging around in the trash bags you threw away last week isn't good enough for you. Imagine instead that you want to re-live past hurts like something your ex did to you years ago," he looked at me reprovingly.

"Now you have to actually get in your car and drive your consciousness to the city dump and dig through the mounds and mounds of rotting garbage because you remembered a tasty argument you had a year ago."

Yuck, I was struck simultaneously by a vague feeling of nausea and a grudging respect for my Dad's ability to tell a great story.

"I get the point," I conceded.

"The point is this: Once you've identified what it is that is garbage (*Recognize*), and you throw it away (*Express*), you don't keep digging it up to play with it (*Dismiss*)."

"Get it?"

"Got it."

"Good."

We both laughed, and *The Preacher/Dad* rose for one final encore.

"It is what it is. As it is above, so it is below."

"Once you Recognize, Express and Dismiss, then you can transcend those emotions and experience the sublime feelings of the Creator including Love, Joy, Ecstasy, Bliss, and Rapture."

"Remember," they continued, *"co-creation starts exactly where you are in this moment. It meets you wherever you are in your Life at any given Moment and eagerly anticipates your intention. Every thought is a thing."*

"Eliminate expectations, desires, and judgments and allow the moment to unfold itself to you."

"Don't say, 'I want to finish this book.' because that creates an experience of wanting."

"Don't say, 'I need time to write.' because that creates an experience of needing."

"Be aware that you are co-creating in the Moment. Every

word uttered is a prayer already answered. Choose your words carefully."

"Say, 'I am a writer.' because that is a state of Being."

"Say, 'I love writing.' because that is a state of Being."

The Preacher/Dad finished with a flourish. I jumped up and clapped enthusiastically, calling "Bravo! Bravo!" and Dad, to his credit, startled at first, gamely took a bow.

The morning after next, I peeled Gage from Mitchell's embrace with promises of a return trip "soon." After rounds of hugs and kisses, Gage and I set off to fuel the car, load up on coffee and Gatorade, and make one last stop at Yocco's on our way out of town.

Honestly, that kid is going to turn into a hot dog, I thought, recalling the four times that Gage had insisted we eat at Yocco's in the past 36 hours, which means I would most certainly be morphing into a pierogie in the very near future.

"Thanks! Enjoy the weather," I called, accepting the take out bag and diet soda from the counterman.

"Yeah. You better enjoy it while it lasts. It's supposed to rain tomorrow."

Not dampening my spirits, I smiled in return, engaged my shields, and made a mental note to Self: Count how many times this happens.

The Preacher/Dad said in a disembodied voice from somewhere over my right shoulder,

"Write it down."

Gage and I were making good time north on the turnpike and west on Interstate 80 until with little warning, we were behind an endless sea of red brake lights. The freeway had transformed into a monstrous parking lot, and we were stuck in the middle of it.

Gage, who up until that moment, had quietly contented himself with his drawing book, his Nintendo DS, and his pillow, was instantly alert and popped up from the back seat. He fired off his questions in rapid succession, "What happened, Mom? Why are we all stopped? Was it an accident? Can you see it? Is that a policeman? Why are those people out of their cars? Can we get out of the car? Do we have anything to eat?"

I chuckled and settled in for the ride, or in this case, the sit-and-wait. This wasn't a new experience for me. Of the thousands of miles we had driven to visit the family over the past eighteen years since I moved to Ohio, I have endured my fair share of delays. I put the car in "park" and turned to face the back seat, still eager to impart my memories in deference to my persistent state of déjà vu.

"One time, Gage, we were driving back to Ohio, and got stuck in a snowstorm that had blown in unexpectedly from the mountains. It took us twelve hours to get home!"

"*Really?*" he asked predictably wide-eyed.

"Really. There were cars and tractor-trailers flipped over on the side of the road everywhere you looked. It was a miracle we didn't end up in a ditch."

"*Wow,*" he said, awestruck.

I suddenly realized what I had said and sent an instant message from my mind to my MacBook: *Recognize the miracle. Write it down.*

"One time, I was driving Tyler, who was only a baby, back from Allentown, when our tire had a blowout."

"What did you do?"

"I kept driving – very, very slowly, and amazingly, around the bend, there was an exit with a Sears Automotive. I pulled in very

slowly and got a new tire. It was a miracle I didn't ruin the rim."
I laughed and sent another MIM. (*That's Mental Instant Message for short*).

"Wow," he enthused, eyes still wide.

"Here's one about you," I offered.

He took the bait, hanging on every word.

"You were just a toddler, like two years old, and when we left Tawni's house to drive home to Ohio, we realized we forgot your "blankie." The "blankie" was a soft yellow square creation with ribbons of creamy yellow satin trimming the edges. Gage's constant companion since he was born, he often strokes the "blankie" lovingly across his cheek as he falls gently asleep.

"My blankie?" Gage asked, horrified at the thought of being separated from his yellow shadow.

"Yep. Your blankie," I said solemnly. "A few hours into the drive, after you woke up, we realized it was missing, and you let loose with the wails while buckets of tears poured from your big eyes. But, an amazing thing happened! Almost instantly, we came upon an exit with a WalMart. So we pulled in and bought a new yellow blankie. It was a miracle!" I laughed.

"This is a different blankie?" He asked worriedly, holding up his tattered and worn remnant of yellow cloth that he still clings to.

"Yep. You've had it since you were two!" I replied cheerfully, realizing it was another miracle that he never noticed before, and sent another *MIM* to my MacBook. The Miracles were adding up quite nicely, thank you.

"Listen to this one," I said quickly to divert Gage's attention. "One time we were driving back to Ohio after it had snowed. At one point, I got too close to the shoulder, and when my tire hit the ice, we went airborne, flying off the side of the road!"

"*You did?*" he was incredulous.

"Yeah, but the amazing thing was, we flew up in the air and then landed in the biggest, fluffiest, softest snowdrift you ever saw! It was like landing in cotton candy!" He laughed out loud, and I repeated my mantra, "It was a miracle!"

Gage was laughing out loud, probably picturing flying cars and cotton candy.

"Do you know what the funniest part was?" I asked, tears of laughter at the ready.

"As soon as we landed, everything was silent. Then Tyler, who was about six years old at the time, piped up from the back seat and exclaimed, "That was fun! Can we do it again?"

We both burst out laughing as we had that day over fifteen years ago. Truly, it was a miracle, I thought, and said a silent prayer of gratitude for our ongoing safety.

Eventually, we started to move, inching along at first, and then slowly building speed until we were cruising along at our regular rhythm, instantly lulling Gage back to sleep. I pulled into the driveway with Dad's response to my last question lingering at the back of my mind. "Dad, what did you do after your epiphany with the house, when you realized you co-created your own reality?" I had asked.

He looked over at me with a twinkle in his eye and replied merrily, "I asked myself: Could I do it again?"

Chapter Seven

"Do it Again."

"*A gain?*" I asked incredulously. Are you kidding me? "They sent the check back *again?*" I repeated, still not ready to accept the inevitable answer. I was standing in front of Ben's desk, our company's CFO of six years and my friend for over twelve years, my hands holding a letter from Workers' Comp that informed us they were kindly refunding our premium. *Again.*

Ben just sat shaking his head, his tolerance for government ineptness only a few notches above mine.

"Does the right hand *not* know what the left hand is doing?" I posed this question not just to the CFO, but to every single person in America who has ever had to deal with any maddening form of governmental bureaucracy or been subjected to endless piles of sticky red-tape. Nobody answered; they didn't have to.

For the past eighteen months, our company has been playing a fun little game we like to call Worker's Comp Sends Us a Bill. We pay the bill; Worker's Comp says we overpaid, and sends us a refund; Workers' Comp sends us a nasty bill saying we underpaid; we pay the nasty bill; Workers' Comp sends us a refund, over and over again. It would be amusing if it weren't so frightening.

I chuckled and pronounced, "Our tax dollars at work, folks. Seriously, isn't that like, seven times our money has gone to Columbus only to be returned to us? Maybe it's a *sign!*" I suddenly cried enthusiastically. "Maybe they *want* us to have the money! Maybe we are *meant* to have the money!" I was getting carried away, but I couldn't help it. "I have an idea! Let's cash the check and go to Mexico!" Ben just smiled sardonically, knowing well enough that any comment he made would only prolong my fantasy.

"It is what it is.
Recognize. Express. Dismiss."

The Preacher's words came out of nowhere and I looked around confused; the comment sounded like *The Preacher/*Dad's words, but not their voices. Fine. Once again, I thought I was *expressing* myself quite well, thank you. I must really need a vacation, I thought as I headed back to my office, located right next door to Ben's. Sadly there were no beach getaways planned in my near future, I thought wistfully, not with so much work to do. I sat down at my desk and pulled my marketing file closer, trying not to think about the manuscript begging for my attention at home. My responsibility to paying the mortgage and putting food on the table this month battled against my desire to retreat home to write. I said a quick prayer of thanks that Gage was in school today so I didn't have to contend with a fresh dose of mother's guilt on top of my other anxieties. *Thank you, God.*

Although I remained seated at my desk, my marketing file in front of me, responsibility could not quite claim victory. I had yet to pick up the phone, and I sat there, paralyzed, not from fear, I realized, but from sheer boredom. Honestly, it felt like I was cursed to relive *The Groundhog Day* nightmare over and over again.

How many times have I made cold calls in the past twenty-five years of my career? I thought, immediately *Zipping* back to the *Time* when 'work' wasn't synonymous with boredom and repetition but instead infused with the wonder of possibility and prospect of success.

I am a writer because I love writing. But what if I change my mind? Funny, I wondered ironically, ignoring the intrusion, I had always loved to work, so what happened? Why did the luster fade? Even from my first part-time job working summers at Dorney Park for $2.35 an hour (after they started charging admission), I have always savored the feeling of independence that only earning your own keep and paying your own way can bring.

I treasured working part-time in high school as a front-desk receptionist at Oakwood Medical Clinic, feeling professional, responsible, and most definitely grown up in my 'nurse's whites.' When I wasn't working at the clinic, I was begging Dad for odd jobs in his executive recruiting firm, which he and Mom had opened in our home when they closed their agency on Hamilton Street. I was willing to do anything, and he obliged by assigning me more tasks with increasing responsibility as I got older.

By the time I graduated, I was typing mailing lists on an ancient, puke-green Smith Corona, running the mimeo, preparing bulk mailings, filing, and typing resumes and correspondence. I loved every minute of it, and my parents fully supported my efforts working in their home business, our old game room downstairs having been supplanted by desks and filing cabinets.

When I was sixteen, out of the blue, Dad made a tantalizing proposal. "How would you like to earn enough money to buy your own car?"

I jumped up excitedly and demanded, "What do I have to do?" Already certain I would agree to almost anything he put forth.

He explained patiently, "All you have to do is make a placement with me. I have a job order to find a fundraiser for a non-profit, but that's not what we specialize in. We'll have to write a newspaper ad, screen applicants, arrange interviews, and hopefully negotiate the starting salary and benefits." He laughed. "If you work the job order with me, and we get somebody hired, we'll split the company's fee and you can buy your first car!"

"I'll do it," I answered instantly. I had no clue what "it" was, but I didn't care, I was in one hundred percent.

We did it. In reality, Dad did absolutely everything, while I contributed nothing of importance to the whole placement process, which took about three months' time. Reverently, I just watched Dad work his magic as he reviewed resumes and conducted numerous interviews, all in his efforts to find the right person for the job.

He coached me along while he worked the job order, and attempting to include me one day, asked my opinion on the resumes that had been submitted. I tentatively pointed out my first and second choices. Immediately discarding my picks as irrelevant, he picked up one particular resume and said, "This is the guy who's going to get the job." And, he was right.

The guy got the job, Dad collected his fee, he paid me my 'commission,' and I bought my first car, a ten year-old, bright pumpkin-orange Honda Civic. I was ecstatic! No longer did I need to borrow Mom's VW Beetle, I had my own wheels. I promptly turned into a 'gas ass' as I zipped around Allentown gloriously exploring the city and my new independence from the driver's seat. I still have a photo, standing proudly with arms wide in my 'nurse's whites' in front of that car. I was hooked. *It was a miracle! Thank you, God!*

Despite graduating from William Allen High School with honors, I had shunned the college preparatory classes to the dismay of my guidance counselors and instead focused on business. I didn't want to waste time going to college, I reasoned, I just wanted to work, and I couldn't be dissuaded.

Growing up, we had often played the board game, *Careers,* on family game nights, and early in the game every player must make the choice to either go to college, thereby increasing their future earnings potential, or to bypass college and go directly to work. I always skipped college.

In my mind, people who went to college had to work eventually anyway, so I figured I was getting a four-year head start on everyone else. I didn't know what I wanted to do after graduation, and quite frankly, with over 20,000 different job titles out there, I was having a hard time narrowing down my options.

But strangely, I wasn't worried about the future. With teenage blinders on, and the wisdom that comes from being eighteen and *knowing everything,* I was addicted to the feeling of independence and control over your future that working brings, and I craved more and more of it.

Six months after I graduated and married Jake, Dad called on a whim with another amazing opportunity, this time for a 'real job.' Of course, I immediately accepted his offer to train me as an executive recruiter (or headhunter) in his company, American Plastics Personnel.

It would be my responsibility to do the very things that Dad had miraculously done when he placed his fundraiser: interviewing, typing resumes, negotiating salaries, and relocating families across the nation. I was so excited I could hardly sit still, already indulging my fantasies of becoming a successful businessperson, imagining my future professional self with a desk, chair, and my very own business cards!

Rushing to share the news with my new husband, I was mortified at his response. "What do you need a job for? I can take care of you."

When I had remained insistent all throughout dinner, even after he had exhausted all the virtues of being a stay-at-home-wife, his words took a nasty turn with, "Are you trying to be a man?"

Doubt not. Fear not. Gratefully, the *Preacher's* words came rushing back to me. Seriously? What year do you live in? I thought as I made the obvious choice. My first day of my first real job was April 15, known as the dreaded dark *Tax Day* in our house growing up. I arrived for work bright and early in the downstairs office of my parents' house, eager to soak up everything there was to learn.

I suffered a slight hesitation when I swiveled around in my (very own!) chair and realized that my feet didn't even touch the floor. For an instant, I felt like a little girl all dressed up in Mommy's work clothes and playing 'grown up.' But my enthusiasm outpaced my fear, and I was quickly over it.

While Dad stormed around the office berating the dark governmental forces that take his hard earned money and waste it, and muttering phrases like, "You have to pay your taxes, or they'll take your shit and throw you in jail." I was dancing in my mind.

Why grumble? I thought. Only in America's melting pot can anybody with a dream hang out their shingle and start a business! As car dealership owner Bob Serpetini would later sing on his radio commercial, "I'm American and Prooooouuuuuud of it!"

I was enthralled with Dad's entrepreneurial spirit and thought smugly to myself that if I ever owned my own business, I would be *happy* to pay taxes! Hey, don't laugh, I was eighteen and *knew everything*.

But, at the end of that first year, I sat at the kitchen table and cried while my then-husband berated me from in front of the sink. "You *owe* money?" he demanded incredulously. I was paid $125 a week as a trainee, but it was a draw against my commissions, and those commissions hadn't appeared with enough frequency throughout my first year to even cover my draw. Even if I quit now, a thought I abhorred, I would still owe the company over $6,000. I was mortified at my own failure. I had let everyone down.

Unfortunately, this fact delighted Jake and he sat down at the table with me and proceeded to draw two pictures on the back of my pay envelope.

"This is my paycheck," he boasted, drawing a large rectangle.

"And, this is your paycheck," he finished off what little dignity I had left by drawing a miniscule dot inside his huge paycheck, and I withered inside.

"Doubt Not. Fear Not. Work on, and Wait."

I heard *The Preacher* in my mind but couldn't bring myself to believe the words. I refused to admit to anyone, including myself, that I wasn't even sure if I *could* do it. But, even if the numbers on the paycheck didn't show it yet, even if people close to me who loved (?) me scoffed at my efforts, even if nobody else in the whole world believed in me, I wasn't ready to give up...*yet.* So, despite hands shaking with fear as I dialed the phone to make cold-calls, I still stuck with it.

For the next year, I practiced the art of being a sponge, absorbing everything that Dad, Mom, and Cheryl, a long-time family friend and my fellow headhunter, did on a daily basis to make placements. I listened to their phone calls, mimicked the way they arranged interviews, watched them negotiate salaries and fees, and make collection calls. I was green with envy at the way they made everything look so easy and eagerly copied their every phrase and gesture. They were my teachers, my mentors, my gurus, and I idolized them, becoming a reflection for their every action and cloning their words, duplicating their habits over and over again, eventually developing my very own professional phone voice.

Let me assure you, Dad was truly amazing to watch. He bounced around with so much energy from task to task that he never actually sat in his chair; instead he stood at his desk while making phone calls, pacing back and forth while putting together deals, persuading a slow paying client to mail a check, or demanding a refund from an over charging utility. I was entranced.

Then he took that same enthusiasm and applied it to every facet of his life. When it came time for Sandi to sell hoagies to raise money for Central Catholic's band trip, Dad organized a 'phone room' staffed with all our family members, complete with the criss-cross directory, calling scripts, and tally sheets.

Dad was the head cheerleader, shouting out encouragement to us between his own sales calls. We sold over two hundred hoagies for the band in an hour. When it came time to deliver the hoagies, we would joyfully give thanks to the people who weren't home at that time, so we could purchase their hoagies 'cause those band hoagies were de-li-cious.

The business was as much a part of our family lives growing up as if it had been my parents' fourth child; they were always jumping up eagerly to tend to its needs, caring and nurturing it through its different stages of growth, and sweating through sleepless nights when it was ailing. It was difficult to *not* be aware of the business on an intimate and daily basis.

Dad lived by the credo that "*all work and no play makes Jack a dull boy*" (and everyone else too), so *fun* was the very next priority in line after *responsibility*. We started work around nine, and Mom and I would head out around eleven for an exercise class and return to Dad, flipping channels in the living room. After eating lunch while watching the requisite CNN noontime broadcast with Bobbie Batista, and a quick thirty-minute power nap on Mom and Dad's couch, it was back to work until 4, when we quit for the day.

On days that promised to be hot and sunny, I would rush through my morning responsibilities and skip our lunchtime workout so I could escape to the pool to fill my own personal prescription for happiness: sun, water, and a good book.

Dad caught me one afternoon, clad only in bikini and sunglasses, completely engrossed in a great novel while floating gently and peacefully on a raft in the pool. But, instead of ordering me back to work, his face broke into a wide grin and then he called back into the house, laughing profusely, "I found Vicki. She said to hold all her calls!" and we all laughed with him. I loved my job!

Every once in a while, Dad would jump up from his desk and enthusiastically proclaim, "I have an idea! Whoever books the most placements in the next ninety days gets an all-expense paid, three-day weekend in Atlantic City! Or a TV! Or a bonus! Whatever you want up to $500 bucks!"

We all took turns winning (not on purpose) and celebrated everybody's placements, playfully recording our sales on the chalkboard in our group office. One year, I traded my vacation prize for our company's first fax machine – a slow moving new-fangled piece of wizardry that spit out curls of waxy paper instantly and magically from across the nation. I love technology.

New Movie Fridays meant Dad and I left work by 12:30, in time to make the Friday afternoon matinee of every single action/adventure movie that debuted during the late eighties. Movies like *Aliens, Terminator* and *Die Hard* ignited my fierce and loving addiction for action flicks that lasts to this day. We'd stumble out of the dark move theatre into the bright sunlight, squinty eyed and buttery fingered, reliving the movie highlights on the drive home, with Dad finally remarking, "Great movie! We might as well quit for the day. Have a great weekend." And we laughed and laughed. I loved my life!

And I love my Dad, too. Now, he knows how to run a business the right way, I thought admirably, and I longed to emulate his joyful qualities. Despite the absence of an employee handbook or any form of written policy, Dad had created a fun and relaxing work atmosphere that catered to our individual personalities, and we all experienced not just financial success but a complete contentment with our careers – a rare feat for most Americans.

By the time we all gathered for our office Christmas party at *The Villa Richard,* our favorite French restaurant, at the end of that next year, I had set a company record for placements, earning back the $6,000 I had owed, and then some. *It was a miracle.*

"To what do you attribute your success?" Jorge, a college professor and Cheryl's long-time boyfriend, asked as I humbly accepted an engraved plaque from Dad after dinner at the end of that exciting year.

"I have great teachers," I responded sincerely. It was true. Who needs college when you can get one-on-one instruction on a daily basis from the best in the business? Why sit in a crowded auditorium when you can work side by side with your very own mentors? I loved absorbing knowledge on a real-time basis emulating the qualities of my 'professors,' learned masters in their fields of study.

I wasn't just sitting at a desk thinking about business ideas, or reading about marketing philosophies, or writing a paper on a fictitious organization, I was actually doing it, every single day! Life was my university education, and work was my curriculum, I reasoned. The cherry on my cupcake was that I was able to pocket tuition while also collecting a paycheck. To me, this was a *great* education.

So what if I didn't get a piece of paper with my name on it, or a graduation ceremony complete with plenty of pomp and an overdose of circumstance? I got a plaque! I wanted to do this forever, or so I thought at the time.

* * * * *

And, so it went, working and playing, and playing some more, for five more years until the day I woke up and didn't care if I never worked again. *Seriously*. The day Tyler was born was Friday the thirteenth, which that year also happened to correspond with Good Friday and his paternal grandmother's fiftieth birthday. Leave it to Tyler to be born under such auspicious circumstances. It was as if all the planets and all the trees had lined up to welcome him into existence.

Rushing into the world after barely three hours of labor, I held him in my arms, and when he opened his eyes only moments born, he looked right through me. All the wisdom of the ages was packed into barely six pounds and although I knew he could see nothing, in his eyes, I saw ev-ery-thing. I saw God. *Thank you, God.*

It terrified me. Seriously? The smart, educated professionals at this hospital were going to let *me* take this all-knowing creature home and care for him? Were they crazy? I was frightened to my core, and felt monumentally ill-equipped to handle this awesome responsibility.

My voice shook as I begged the nurses for another day in the hospital; enough time, I reasoned, to learn how to hold my newborn without quaking. Amazingly, they agreed. (Author's note: Try to get an extra day in the hospital approved by your insurance company in *this* day and age.)

Bringing him home from Sacred Heart Hospital on Easter Sunday, I happily (and only a little fearfully) devoted myself to my new caregiver role, eagerly anticipating Tyler's every whimper, burp or poop, no matter the hour. I was fascinated at the new discoveries he would make on a daily basis, witnessing them in awe through his eyes. I was enamored with this baby, and perfectly content to just sit and watch him all day and night. I loved my new job.

However, my responsibility to the household didn't just include child rearing. As my earnings had grown over the past five years, so had my contribution to the family budget. I now found myself in the middle of the most timeless dilemma facing women across all reaches of socio-economic backgrounds: Mother's Guilt. The responsibility of providing financially for my family versus the responsibility of nurturing my child through his ongoing development had caught me in its steely grip, and I was devastated. Wasn't I of the generation that was promised to *have it all?* I bemoaned. Maybe. Maybe not. Or maybe we just can't have it *all at the same time.* Tentatively approaching Jake and voicing my concerns netted me a ferocious scowl.

"First you said you wanted to work, now you want to quit. You keep changing your mind. You don't know what you want."

He was right, and I cringed. There was a *time* I believed I wanted to work forever, but then I got new information (namely, I gave birth), and now I believed I wanted to stay home and actively witness this gurgling, giggling miracle on a daily basis, thank you very much. Don't I have a fundamental right to change my mind? I mused as I made the obvious choice: Tyler would only be young once and I didn't want to miss it, I reasoned logically. I could always go back to my career when he goes to school.

I cut back to part-time, scaling back on both my career and financial ambitions, making do with less and not flinching when Jake would taunt me for my now scant income calling me a "welfare mother." I just kept at it.

I loved working part-time from home with Tyler playing underfoot or close by, happily engrossed with toys, a juice cup and his blankie. I didn't apologize for my toddler chattering in the background while I conducted telephone interviews. Instead, I explained that I was working from home while raising my son, and my clients accepted that, some even slightly envying my unique opportunity. It was a dream job, working from home, and I uttered a quick prayer of thanks, before jumping on the *Zip Ship* back to the present workday, where I was still seated motionless at my desk.

"Write it Down."

Again, *The Preacher's* admonishment came out of nowhere, and I sat up at attention. What would it hurt? I thought. I wondered how many pages I could write and hurriedly opened the document on my MacBook that contained the draft for Dad's book.

I set my *Zip Timer,* and amazingly, I was only interrupted three times, managing to whip out seven pages by the time Dad called.

I answered the phone breathlessly, "Hi Dad!" I exclaimed, exhilarated at my accomplishment, my excitement contagious.

"Wow. You sound great. What happened?" he asked happily, mimicking my tone.

"I got seven more pages done this morning!" I pronounced,

"Wonderful!" he agreed gleefully.

"Now, if I can just do this approximately thirty more times, we might have a book!" I commented, a little wryly. I wanted to hold on to this good feeling, truly I did, but in reality, it was only seven pages, a mere fraction of the story we still needed to record.

Dad was not deterred. "How do you eat an elephant?" he chuckled. This should be good, I thought, and giggled back, "How?"

"One bite at a time!" He burst out in loud laughter. I love that sound.

"How do you dig a hole?" he continued.

"How?" I knew my part, and was playing it well.

"One shovel full at a time!" He laughed some more and went on, "Wait, I have one more!"

"How do you write a book?" he asked, feigning a somber tone.

"One page at a time," we said in stereo.

"I know, Dad, I know."

The Preacher joined in on the party line.

"Once you have cut out everything in your life that does not move you forward, you must then apply yourself to doing all the things that are important and necessary to bring your creation about, over and over again."

"Co-creation is not just thoughts, not just words, it is also deeds. You must "Do" in order to "Be."

Dad, impersonating *The Preacher* stepped up on his soapbox and broadcast in a loud musical voice,

"Step right up, folks. Hur-ray, hur-ray, hur-ray. You won't believe your eyes. Step right up and witness a miracle! Right here in front of us we have a new discovery, which when applied correctly, and in the proper dosage, can create anything you desire in your life!"

Dad/The Preacher continued his huckster spiel with enthusiasm, playing the carny to the hilt. *"That's right, folks! This amazing discovery is the medicine for all your ills, the salve for all your boo-boo's, the answer to all your prayers. It's a miracle! Step right up folks, and I'll reveal to you the three easy steps to transform yourself from a state of 'wanting' into a joyous state of 'Being.' It's as easy as 1-2-3! And it's free!"* He rattled off the instructions in quick order.

1. **Do.** *This means you "Do" it now.*
2. **Did.** *This means you "Did" it one time.*
3. **Deed.** *This means you "Deed" it over and over again!*

Dad starting laughing hysterically, and I couldn't keep myself from joining him as he added joyfully, "**Do. Did. Deed.** It's the New English!"

You are soooooo goofy, I thought, loving it. After we calmed some, he went on, "You have to prove to yourself over and over again that it's real. First, you plant the seeds of your co-creation, then you tend to them, water them, and watch them grow."

He continued with, "You watch what happens. You planted the seed of that book and you are tending to it, now you watch it grow. I'll bet that within thirty days, you have many more pages to add to what you've accomplished today. It's a rule of business: Thirty days bears fruit."

I wondered a little giddily if that might be true as *The Preacher* added,

"Thirty days bears fruit. The efforts you make today toward your creation will bear fruit within thirty days."

"Do you know what all that other horseshit is that bothers you? Fertilizer!" He laughed, and I joined him. I wanted to believe them, I truly did. Could I really do it again? Could I write seven more pages tomorrow? I allowed myself some time to dabble in my fantasy before crashing back to earth.

I doubted I could repeat this performance tomorrow because I had to work at my real job, too; the one that pays the bills and feeds the kids. I had to go to work so I could make enough money to buy the bacon, bring it home, and then fry it up in the pan, I thought, immediately abandoning my enthusiasm and replacing it with a mild case of ennui.

"Doubt Not. Fear Not. Work on. Wait."

Maybe I could call off tomorrow and work on the book, I daydreamed guiltily. Dad, meanwhile switched to the ESPN channel, (sometimes it's creepy how tuned-in he is to my thoughts) and commanded in his booming CEO voice, "Remember, fifty percent of the job is just showing up!"

He expounded, "Remember when we had employees who were just so fed up with their jobs or their bosses that they didn't even want to show up for work? They were so desperate for a change they wanted to call it quits before they even found another job."

"Yeah, I remember," I agreed, noting that not much has changed in the forty plus years that Dad has been finding people jobs and briefly considered how similar my own situation was.

"When they would complain, and be ready to give up, we always told them the same thing. Go to work, because fifty percent of the job is just showing up, and from there it's easy!"

"How can it be easy, when you still have to give another fifty percent once you get to work?"

"No, you don't. That's a myth, an urban legend. It's not true."

"Sure it is," I argued. "In fact, some self-help gurus and even some companies require you to give not just 100%, but 110%!" I knew I had him this time.

"Well, you may believe that, and they may believe that, but in our family, we believe in something called 51%. And, it's called 51% because that's the amount of 'things' a person has to 'do' in order to prove to themselves that what they believe is real."

"The individual must do 51% of the work in order to believe that it is going to come about. 51% is the shift from *possible* to *probable*."

"Now, not everyone has to do 51% to believe it is real, some people must do 75% or 80% to believe it. Others never believe that it will be real. They *never* prove it to themselves."

He continued, laughing, "An object in motion tends to stay in motion. So, if fifty percent of the job is just showing up, you only need to give an additional one percent. Do the math; it's simple addition. Once you have 51%, do you know what else you have on your side?" he asked slyly.

I had not a clue.

"Momentum!" he answered himself happily. "An object in motion tends to stay in motion. After that, it's all down hill from there," he proffered.

"Is that true?" I asked suspiciously.

"I don't know. Prove it to yourself. In fact, you *must prove it to yourself over and over again.*" The Preacher/Dad sang in unison.

"I have one more thing," Dad took control of the conversation.

"I know," I interrupted, tuning my own receiver to pick up the ESPN channel. "Write it down."

"Exactly." He smiled and I smiled back.

"So, how's business?" he queried, bouncing to a new subject.

Grrrrr. I whined about having to make cold calls for the billionth time in my career, but instead of agreeing with me, Dad started laughing at me, leaving me feeling oddly cheated out of my grumpiness, but grateful for the redirection.

"How is business any different than the book?" he asked, and suddenly the answer seemed obvious.

"Everything in this universe is obvious, Daughter," Dad continued.

OMG. ESPN sends and receives on two channels!

"And it's obvious to me that the challenges you imagine you are going through are really all about the same thing."

"What's that?" I asked, picturing the worst while mentally engaging my shields.

"Persistence and discipline," he replied matter of factly, and I was only mildly stung because it was true.

"Right after you made your first placement as a brand new headhunter all those years ago, you looked at me and asked, 'So what do I do now?' Do you remember what I answered?"

"What?"

"Do it Again!" he laughed happily. "Look at it this way: Instead of starting from a place in your mind where you resent the work that you are doing, travel back to that place when you *loved* what you did. Go back to the day you opened your business when you craved the excitement of the unknown and ran headlong into opportunities, never doubting the outcomes. Do you remember that *time*?"

I remembered.

"Now take the feeling you felt back then, and add it to where you are right now. Start from the *now*. You're not sitting in an empty office with nothing but a cell phone and a resume. You've been in business for eleven years now. Start from *this moment* and do the same things you did then. All states of mind reproduce themselves. A sense of accomplishment breeds an additional sense of accomplishment. A feeling of success begets success. Do it again, over and over."

Could I do that? I wondered. Could I do it again?

The Preacher flew overhead in his Cessna, trailed by a long banner.

"Patience + Persistence + Discipline = Anything"

"Daughter, I have one last question for you before I let you get back to work."

I smiled inside, wondering what it could possibly be, but knowing it would probably be good, or funny, or inspiring, or all three.

"How do you make a million dollars in sales?"

I laughed out loud remembering the pep talk and envelope containing a note and check that Dad had given to me in the days right before I opened my business.

"One sale at a time." We all joined together in laughter – Dad, *The Preacher* and I.

We said our "goodbyes" and our "love you's," and I listened to another seven echos of "write it down" before I disconnected and faced the green file folder on my desk, labeled "Sales."

But, first I reached into my top drawer and withdrew the envelope that contained the stained and wrinkled note, torn on one end, and soft from years of over handling. The note had been wrapped around a check for $10,000, the seed money to start our company, both handed to me long ago by Dad. Printed on the note, in his handwriting, were the words:

> Here is the money I promised you, Daughter.
> Turn it into a million or two!
> Love, Dad

The phone rang loudly in my Ohio home that day almost twelve years ago and once again, Dad offered up the seemingly impossible opportunity. "How would you like to open your own temporary agency? Tawni and I have done really well these past two years since she opened her agency, and we want to lend you the money to open your own agency, too."

Are you kidding me? I jumped up and started pacing across my living room, firing off questions to Dad in rapid succession, my enthusiasm contagious.

"What do you mean, a temporary agency? How would I do it? Who would work it with me? Can I do it by myself? How much will it cost?" I was breathless, both from excitement and a tinge of apprehension.

Dad just laughed, and we continued talking for several hours, making plans and working out the details. I'll be honest; despite my palpable excitement, I wasn't entirely convinced that I wanted any part of opening a business. I knew first-hand what was involved, and I wasn't sure I could do it again, or even if I *wanted* to.

Within the past five years, I had said goodbye to Jake, amicably splitting after ten years of trying to be happy, goodbye to the executive recruiting business and goodbye to the freedom of working from home when I accepted the challenge to open two temporary staffing locations for a local businessman.

I had waffled over whether to explore different careers for over two years after the divorce was final. Although I treasured working from home, Tyler was now in school and I was bored to tears doing the same things every single day. I longed for a new adventure, *knowing* it was time to do something new, but terrified of stepping out of my comfort zone. The security that arises from income stability often causes one to stay stuck in the mundane, mired muck of indecision for far too long.

I ignored sign after sign that I needed a change in another direction – like my sudden lack of enthusiasm for everything I did, or my lack of motivation for working, or sleeping at all hours of the day, or stuffing Little Debbie snack cakes into my mouth, or crying in the shower. I continued in that fugue state for two years ignoring (not caring?) the fact that my lack of motivation toward making placements had caused my income stability to plummet into *instability*, my savings to run dry, and I was in danger of missing my first mortgage payment in my entire home-owning life. I was mortified. Once again, I had let everyone down. I called Mom to cry on her shoulder and when I thought I was all cried out, I lay down on my home-office floor to cry some more on the carpet. It was going to take a miracle, I thought, as I closed my eyes for another quick cat-nap.

And then the phone rang.

I answered my office line, disguising my grogginess, and listened incredulously as a long-term client, Ray, explained the chain of events. A resume I had presented to him six months before (Pete, Production Manager) had resulted in Pete's accepting an employment offer three months past. But, I didn't know anything about it, hiding as I was in my deep dark hole of self-pity, and, Ray, my client, forgot about me until Pete's ninety-day review. *Thank you, God!*

Ray had been wrapping up the performance review, praising him for his achievements, when he questioned Pete, "Where did you come from, anyway?"

Pete immediately answered, "From American Plastics Personnel."

Ray, stunned at everyone's oversight, replied, "You're absolutely right."

After he finished his amazing story, he concluded with, "By my calculations, we owe you $8,500. Will you take $7,000?"

Goose bumps dancing on my skin, I laughed out loud and instantly agreed, quaking from head to toe as I chatted for a time before disconnecting. I sat at my desk, stunned. Oh! My! God! Who, in their right mind, in this day and age, in the cut-throat world of *business* would call another person out of the blue and say, "I owe you money." I was amazed. *It truly was a miracle. Thank you, God.*

I called Mom, crying again, but this time for a different reason. *Thank you, Ray! Thank you, God!*

Later that night, I eagerly dug out the week's newspaper classifieds and starting looking for a new job. If it took a miracle to pay this month's mortgage, I wasn't going to wait around next month for another one.

Opening a new business (even if it's for somebody else), or the first day on a new job, or arriving for a blind date, or dreading a tax audit, all foster their own energy and it's called fear. Fear of failure causes your body to run continually on adrenaline as you race through the days doing the "things" that will enable you to "survive." An unanticipated and sometimes not unwelcome side effect of entrepreneurism is weight loss.

After opening two temporary staffing offices in the two and half years of working for somebody other than my Dad, my now skinny frame had learned exactly two things: One, how to open a temporary employment agency from scratch; and two, *how NOT to treat your employees.*

All this talk about family values floating around, but, when the time came for this single mom to go home and care for my sick kid, I realized it was just that: talk. After one particularly galling incident where I had to persuade the owner to let me use my accrued vacation days to care for my young son who was currently itching his way through a bout of chicken pox, I promptly handed in my thirty days notice and went home to the only two things I knew how to do well: Be a mother and a headhunter.

My fears of running the Adrenaline Race opening a new business were justified in my mind, considering Dad's latest proposal. I had concerns and was being cautious. Mindful of the mired muck, I continued asking him questions, trying to work the opportunity out in my mind.

Tawni grabbed the phone at one point and laughed as she promised, "Don't worry. I'll help you. We'll do it together." I took a deep breath, steadied my frazzled nerves. I'm ready for this, I thought and declared confidently, "Okay, I'll do it."

I rented office space in Belden Village, and when Tawni came out to visit for three weeks, we bought supplies, created documents and forms, set up the computers, organized the office, and made preparations for a grand opening celebration.

Exactly one month after marrying Dave, and one week before that very same Grand Opening, I discovered I was pregnant with my second son, Gage. Oh. My. God. *Thank you, God.*

I had promised myself that I would never have another child until I had the financial means to be a stay-at-home mom with my baby without guilt, recrimination, or the need to cut coupons. Tyler, now nine, had survived my part-time work/mothering experience without the need for medication and/or therapy, but I wasn't willing to take another chance. I held the positive pregnancy test in my hand and actually said the words aloud as I demanded of myself: "How could this happen?"

Oh, yeah, I remember. I thought, laughing. Wow. I'm going to have a baby and open a new business at the same time. Am I crazy? How am I going to do this? Each is its own painstaking twenty-four hour job, each its own tremendous emotional commitment, each its own set of overwhelming responsibilities. How am I going to do this *all at the same time*? But, I had no choice; I was already committed on both fronts.

We launched American Personnel (like father, like daughter), an industrial temporary staffing agency in September of 1999, and welcomed Gage to the world the following April. I spent my first day in my new office, empty except for my phone, my iMac, the cobwebs, and of course, the three people who shared all of the responsibility: me, myself and I, and they were all talking at once.

"Doubt Not. Fear Not. I can do it."

"Good morning. Who is the best person to speak to who hires the maintenance crew?" My voice echoed off the empty walls, and my hands shook as I fearfully completed my first cold call as a new business owner. Just like old times, I thought, as I picked up the phone to dial again.

The business grew in direct proportion to my waistline as I bravely waddled into the offices of potential clients, my swollen belly and intermittent burping notwithstanding.

We met Gage for the first time seven months later. *Thank you, God.*

I quickly searched his tiny face as I held him, new to the world for mere moments, and his large round eyes betrayed all the wisdom of the universe as I serenely wondered how babies are born *all-knowing* and I know, well, *nothing.*

This time around, I begged the nurses to go home early and impatiently waited to be discharged, knowing full well what I was getting into as the mother of a newborn, and I couldn't *wait* to get started! I love being a mom.

The next year, we followed Tawni's successful lead and opened a medical staffing division specializing in hiring nursing staff for hospitals and long-term care facilities. Running the business while mothering an infant was an emotional roller coaster ride that never stopped to rest or recharge its batteries.

If I wasn't crying in the shower because it was Friday and we didn't have enough money in the bank for Monday's payroll, then I was crying because I wanted to stay home and play on the floor with my son. My mind and life were on autopilot, the adrenalin pumping through my body made the post-baby weight loss simple, and I was along for the carnival ride, whether I was amused or not.

We kept on going; nurturing, tending, guiding, sweating it out, and the business grew in direct proportion to my toddler, who now spent his days playing happily at home with our beloved nanny, Linda, a retired grandmother we had been blessed to meet, while I dashed from sales call to sales call.

When 9/11 devastated the country's collective spirit and our industrial staffing division in one fell swoop, we hugged our families and then quickly retreated, retrenched and redirected our focus to specializing only in the medical field, and both Gage and the business kept right on growing.

And then one day, out of the blue, another miracle happened. I sat at my desk, my feet still not reaching the floor, staring at the Year-to-Date Sales statement in front of me while goose bumps battled for real estate up and down my body. Oh, My God.

One million dollars in sales and it was only July. Oh, My God. *It was a miracle! Thank you, God.* There was nothing left to do but jump up and down, scream, and celebrate, so I did just that. I ran out into the front office and just kept bouncing around, crying and hugging the staff all at the same time.

We knew we were doing well; we knew we were growing, but now here is the proof in black and white (not red all over!). Our company was now a million dollar company! It was like heaven, only with a P & L. It was more than I had ever dared to dream, and I whispered praises of gratitude to everything. After more hugs and tears, I cheerfully wrote out modest bonus checks for everyone, and happily stuffed my backpack with my laptop as I headed out the door. "I'm taking a week off."

I called Dad giggling and crying, tears of joy cascading in rivers down my cheeks, "Thank you, Dad. Thank you. Thank you so much! I love you."

"I didn't do anything, you did it," he laughed merrily back, recognizing my euphoria and matching it with his own memory from his own long-ago house epiphany.

"I can't believe it," I gushed.

"Believe it. It's real," he enthused. He was right, I thought, remembering *The Preacher's* words:

> *"When you set out toward something,*
> *it is already there, waiting for you."*

For the entire next week, I continued to leak happy tears of joy and thanksgiving, stunned at what had grown in just a few short years from nothing except cobwebs and an echo. I was in a perpetual daze as I wandered around, refusing to grant any time to responsibilities and instead only focusing on the *possibilities,* which were seemingly infinite and magical in their shared qualities.

I could hardly sleep that next week as I danced around the house delighting in my environment, cuddling my toddler, and joyfully giving praise and thanks to God for everything. If I could do this, what else could I do? I laughed. Did I want to do this again? Could I do something different? Did I want to do something different? What did Dad do?

He did it again, of course. Three months after purchasing their dream house, Dad had answered his own question, "Can I do it again" with an emphatic "Heck, yeah!" and promptly purchased the house located next door to their dream house. I remembered as he explained, "The timing couldn't have been worse. We didn't have any extra money, and people kept telling us, You're crazy! How is this going to work out?'

"But it did work out. Bridge loans, mortgage refinancing, spending months fixing up the property, all were hoops we had to jump through and obstacles to overcome. But then finally, selling the second house for a tidy profit gave us something far more valuable."

"What?"

"Another thirty feet of backyard next to the pool," he laughed. "No, really. We had proven to ourselves that we create our own reality, not just *once*, but *once again*. I had experienced another miracle, and now I wanted to do it over and over again!" he stated emphatically.

Could I do it again?

That's the question, I thought, as the Magical Bus stopped and I got off at Planet Earth. Could I do it again? I drew strength at that moment not from a long-ago achievement, or Dad's advice, or even *The Preacher,* but from all the self-help gurus who ever intoned, "Fake it 'til you make it."

Taking a deep breath, I put Dad's note on my desk where I could see it, pasted a big smile on my face, thought to myself, "here we grow again," then picked up the phone to play a nice little game I like to call *"Dialing For Dollars."*

Phone-sales is a numbers game, and to win the game you simply need to keep calling, over and over again, until you hit your numbers. "There are *always* jobs out there," Dad would often cite from behind his desk, dialing the telephone. "You just have to find them. Business is *always* happening anyway, so just put yourself in the middle of it."

The Numbers Game is the same game you would play if you were looking for a job, exercising to lose weight, or saving for a beach vacation. To play those games, you travel around the *Board Game of Life* and make a certain number of contacts, email another number of resumes, run on the treadmill for a number of minutes, count a number of calories, arrange to have a number directly deposited into your vacation savings, and count the growing balance as you race toward your goal number. Numbers. Numbers. Numbers. Over and over again.

After a fair amount of *Zip Time* had passed, I found that I had scheduled three appointments, and had several new leads for business on which to follow up over the next few weeks. Certainly not a million dollars, I smiled to myself as I meticulously recorded my calls into the database, but a beginning.

Satisfied, I grabbed my on-going "to-do" list that sits perpetually on my desk and scanned it quickly: Write a resume, finish a proposal, ad deadline in two days, tax letter. Yuck, I thought, squirming in my chair. I didn't want to write those things, I whined silently, I wanted to *write my book.*

Write. It. Down.
Now.

Ignoring *The Preacher's* long-ago summons, I instead retreated to my most trusted skill: List Making. I grabbed my calculator, did the math and wrote it all down:

Number of resumes and cover letters I've written to help people find jobs in the past twenty-five years: Thousands.

Number of letters I've written in the course of my career to obtain new clients, keep existing clients happy, apologize when we screw up, collect our money, dispute a bill, request a refund, plea for mercy from a nameless bureaucratic agency, apply for an award, or commend an employee for doing a great job: More thousands.

Number of pages of content I've written for employee hand books, safety manuals, operating procedures, forms, web site pages, database fields, marketing brochures, advertising copy, promotional flyers, Powerpoint presentations, trade show hand-outs, press releases, federal trademark applications, job search manuals and seminar materials: Many, many more thousands.

Number of books I've started, including this one, and also counting the one about Tyler and his hysterical adventures titled *Made in TyLand*, which I promised to him by his 21st birthday, barely six months from now. Then there was the half-written book about the April Fool's Day prank I played one year, when with the ink barely dry on my second divorce, I took my neighbor's positive pregnancy test into my office staff, silently presented it to each person, and then watched their priceless responses with amazement, called *Is it Yours?* Answer: Seven

Number of books I've finished: Zero. Zilch. Nada. None.

I can do it. I mentally filed thoughts of the book for further consideration that evening, and smiled as I put away the calculator and put down my pen. If writing a book were as easy as collecting the various ads, PowerPoint slides, and contracts I've written over the years, I would be done. Sitting cross-legged in my chair, I spun happily around, watching my office dance before my eyes over and over again. I love our office.

Beam me up, Scotty, I thought as I hopped on the *Zip Ship* and then landed at my kitchen table over eight years ago. "Wouldn't it be great if we could buy a commercial building in North Canton and the business could rent from us?" I had posed the question to Sandi and Mark when Dad was visiting, and we were all discussing the possibility of investment properties, as déjà vu sat down at the table with us and joined the party.

"I'll contribute the down-payment," Dad offered generously, instantly sealing the deal.

"Sweet! Thanks, Dad." We all immediately agreed and accepted his amazing offer, and promptly began looking for the "ideal" investment property for our newest venture.

It's already there, waiting for us. This time around, it took nearly a month before almost spilling my coffee driving down Main Street in North Canton and noticing the "For Sale by Owner" sign on the front lawn of a beautiful old Victorian home that had been converted to offices. I pulled into the parking lot and wrote down the phone number of the "By Owner" as I stared in awe.

The majestic two-story Victorian boasted a light colored brick at its base, was wrapped in faded green shingles on its upper floors, and topped with what looked like the original slate roof. A century home, the building was converted thirty years ago from a family residence into its current office space, but still maintained its homey comfort. A brick walkway curved around the charming house from the back parking lot to the wide front porch, which just begged for the rattan armchairs I had spotted at Pier One the week before. Standing sentry grandly in the front yard was the original thirty-foot flagpole from the Canton City Post Office, with a gently billowing American flag.

I could already picture myself working here, I thought wistfully, as goosebumps jostled for position. I wonder what the inside looks like? I thought as I hurriedly dialed my sister, bubbling over with excitement.

The inside was even more impressive. The solid oak front door with beveled glass window opened into a spacious living room and boasted an open staircase spiraling to the second floor, paneled in rich dark oak. To the left was the other half of the bright and airy living room, with expansive windows overlooking the front yard and Main Street, USA.

With two additional spacious offices, formerly the kitchen and dining room, and a bathroom downstairs, four more offices (previously bedrooms), and another bathroom on the second floor all trimmed in the original rich oak; *and* a third-floor attic, formerly a child's bedroom that just begged for more kids to jump happily around its environs, it was the perfect family building for our growing family business. It was a miracle that we had found it.

It was another dream come true, we realized as we hurriedly formed a partnership to purchase the building, and promptly and joyfully made preparations to move our business from Belden Village to Main Street USA, and into this beautiful family home, with the proud Hoover Company smokestack keeping quiet, but not yet silent vigil from down the block on North Canton's quaint town square. *It was a miracle! And it had happened again! Thank you, God.*

I love this building, and I love this business, I thought as I turned off the *Zip Timer*. But, the monotony of doing the same thing over and over again, day after day, year after year, tires my soul. I longed to set my sights on different horizons, to experience new and interesting facets of living and earning a living.

I didn't want to give up what I have; I love what I do! I just want to *add more* to what is already here. I want to keep growing the business, but, I want to also continue my hands-on education at *Life University*, and now was the time to register for a new class.

You always change your mind. You don't know what you want. Engaging my shields against myself, I packed my laptop into my backpack and got ready to head for home, where Gage would be getting off the bus at 3:30. I danced into Ben's office and sang, "I got three appointments!" knowing this would please the company bean counter.

He smiled and nodded his head vigorously, allowing me exactly three seconds to bask in my victory before he peppered me with questions.

"Are you taking the picnic basket? Are you going to visit any of our existing clients in the same area? Did you research them to see if their parent company owns any other facilities?"

I expected this from Ben; it's one of the reasons I had asked him all those years ago to come to work with us and help grow the company. I took a calming breath, turned up the power on my shields, and mindful of the pinhole, answered, "Yes, I'm taking the picnic basket."

The picnic basket is my preferred method for delivering lunch to a potential client, complete with checkered tablecloth, crusty bread and cutting board, grapes and non-alcoholic sparkling juice (*Italian vino would be perfect, but probably not politically correct*).

"And I thought I would stop by Century Oaks to see Beth while I'm in Cleveland, and no, I didn't Google the parent company. Can you do it?" I pleaded with sincerity. Two outa three ain't bad.

"Sure," he responded instantly, smiling.

"*Muchas gracias*," I smiled back, clapping my hands.

"*De nada.*"

Ben's cog in the business machine is as the money guy. He handles all the payroll, taxes, insurance, workers' comp claims, unemployment processing, accounting, and finance. He watches the company's money like a hawk, and woe be to the person who tries to add an extra fifteen minutes onto their timecard or get a reimbursement from him without a receipt. LOL. He handles all the details I used to have to scrutinize when we were a brand new company, when my job description and responsibilities as owner included, well, every-thing. Eleven years later, those very same details now cause my eyes to glaze over and urges a slight headache to form behind my eyes. I was grateful that those millions of minutiae were now his responsibility. *Thank you, God.*

"Don't you ever get tired of doing the same thing every day?" I ventured.

He shook his head no, but offered, "I did have this dream once, when I was about six, where I was driving a tiny car around and around on the inside of a Cheerio. I just kept driving around, and around, and around. I remember it was horrible for some reason, but I don't remember why" he laughed, and I joined in.

"That's not a dream, that's a nightmare, and it's exactly what I'm talking about. I feel like a hamster in a cage." I laughed some more. "Well, I'm going home to write, but I wish I had more time than just nights and weekends," I whined.

"If it's important to you, you'll do it. If it isn't, you won't," he responded logically.

"There's just so much to do, so much material to organize," I added to my list of complaints.

"Focus. Focus. Focus." He said the words tightly and I could readily detect his annoyance, but I wasn't yet empty.

"It seems like I'll never finish."

"Just write the first draft. Do what you say you're going to do," he commanded, closing off all further communication.

"You're right," I agreed, getting up to leave. *"Buenas noches. Hasta manana."*

"Adios," he smiled back, and I offered up a quick prayer of thanks that he doesn't stay annoyed for long.

I headed down the solid oak staircase to the first floor, and said my goodbye's to Doug, Ben's younger brother, and Dee-Dee, who looks uncannily like my mom – both long time employees and fondly considered to be members of my adopted family. I laughed, as I always do, at the framed email that Doug had proudly hung on the wall behind his desk: "Doug, You were right and I was wrong." The sender of the email? Me. Heading through the back office, I threw out a cheerful *hasta luego* to Tyler, who works part time in the office, when he isn't taking classes in graphic design, as I headed out the door.

I pulled out of the parking lot and headed north up Main Street, turning west onto Maple at the town square as I glanced at the old Hoover Company building on the northeast corner, whose massive size engulfed the entire block. I love this town, I thought happily as

I drove the rest of my whopping seven block commute from work to my front door taking approximately three eco-friendly minutes to drive.

Pulling into the driveway, I had to put the car in "park" and move all the kids' toys out of the way before I could pull all the way into the garage, and I as I did, I realized with relish that other than preparing dinner (hah!) or ordering take-out, I had absolutely NO responsibilities on my calendar for this evening, leaving me endless amounts of *Zip Time* to work on Dad's book.

I sat down with my laptop on the back deck overlooking the tranquil green setting that is our backyard, realizing how fortunate I was to write in this peaceful serenity. I love this time of year, I thought wistfully. The start of the new school year always beckons memories of a brand new chalkboard – a fresh, clean slate bursting with opportunities, remaining green in the background, but with each chalk stroke hinting of autumn colors and the changes the pending season will soon bring.

Gage ran outside onto the deck, immediately launching into a play-by-play account of The Best Kick Ever last Saturday at soccer. "Mom, as soon as I kicked the ball, I knew it was a goal, but it was in slow motion."

"Zip Time," I explained, smiling, and wondering what other sports account for *Zip Time* in their rulebooks.

"Did you see the Kyle Driver?" I asked Gage, and he laughed his yes. The biggest kid on Gage's team (seriously, he looks old enough to drive), Kyle can kick the ball from one end of the field clear across into the next soccer field, and he often does.

I could hear Tyler and Tiff making dinner, most definitely a happy sound (!) in the kitchen next to the deck, and I offered up a quick prayer of gratitude as Gage bounced down the deck stairs, off to find his cousins. *Thank you, God.*

The quiet park-like solitude of the back yard, rimmed with its profusion of green trees and bushes, with the creek gurgling happily in the background, is the perfect venue to diligently and faithfully practice my newest solo sport, I thought gratefully. I have spent the years since my second divorce perfecting the art of a being a hermit, and I can now say that my efforts have been generously rewarded.

Drawing an imaginary line in the sand around my house and my values, I slowly began to pay attention to exactly who was crossing my line on a regular basis with their negativity and hostility. Eventually, I handed out select Red Cards and stopped inviting them back to play. Chaos isn't allowed to live here, I reasoned, why should it be allowed to visit periodically and disrupt the Zen that is now my post-divorce environment, eat my food, and drink my beer?

I applied the same line in the sand technique when I left the house, too. How many times was I going to let this group of "friends" invite me, dis-invite me, include me, not include me, talk to me, talk about me, dish out food or dish out rude, and how many times was I going to let it bother me?

I felt like a yo-yo, a ping-pong ball. She's up. She's down. She's in. She's out. Back and forth, over and over again, I played that game until one day I handed *myself* a Red Card and stopped going to the poker game. Chaos isn't allowed to live here, in my house and mind of serenity, I reasoned. So I'd rather be here, even if it is completely by myself.

It took years for that retreat, that submission, that surrender to achieve its current turtle-in-a-shell and hermit-in-a cave status. Over and over again, I had to *recognize* that doing the same things every day, every weekend, every year, but expecting different results was clearly the definition of insanity. I trained myself to wake up from my *Groundhog Day* nightmare and change the channel, over and over again, day after day.

I formed new relationships with myself, my kids, and my DVD player. In the first three years post-divorce of hermiting at home with movies, we found that we had amassed a collection of over two hundred DVDs from every aisle and genre, prompting the kids to immediately grow dollar signs on their eyelids as they calculated how much they could sell them for on eBay.

"I have an idea!" I offered brightly. "We could donate them to the company, and our employees could 'rent' them for free," I laughed. We enjoyed watching the movies, I reasoned, others might as well enjoy them too, and *without* the threat of late fees. So, we lugged the two hundred DVDs to the office and instituted a new company policy, effective immediately. Employees now had the ability to sign out up to five movies for free, and return them to our office when the whole family had finished watching them.

I continued my completely necessary, long overdue, self induced, not at all pitiful seclusion for the next several years, turning my newly discovered solo sport into a downright art form. I shunned poker and Bud Light with the "gang," preferring Chinese delivery, Corona, and the newest release. I declined fundraiser invitations, networking events, dinner with friends and family and traded them instead for the comforting feeling of being lost in another world, immersed in a great book on the back deck.

My world, my comfort zone, my refuge, had been reduced in size to exist within just a few buildings including my house, my office, and sporadic trips to Acme. My new boundaries were populated with just my family, co-workers (who I think of as family), and a few (very few! Like two or three!) close friends – some of whom even "adopted" me into their family last year, complete with an official ceremony, a family chant, and adoption papers signed in blood (mine!), requiring plenty of alcohol.

Both my sisters had adopted boys, so my crazy reasoning was that it was perfectly natural to be adopted as an adult into another family, which gloriously came with two more sisters, a brother (my first one!) and another mom! Now I'm a little "sista" to "Queen Bitch" and "Bitchette," while they lovingly address me by my new name, "Bitchlette." Added bonus? I'm finally the youngest! (I'm going to have to practice the Sandi cackle.) It is what it is, and it is what you make it. And we make if fun!

Don't get the wrong idea – I'm not somebody to pity, to deliver casseroles to, or to host an intervention for. I don't have thirty cats, I don't hoard old newspapers and Saran Wrap, and I don't hide the toys that the neighborhood kids perpetually leave in our yard. I just happen to relish the peace and serenity that comes from inviting chaos never to return. I don't want to change a thing, I thought. I love my life.

I'm comfortable hanging out alone, reading a good book on the deck, listening to the neighborhood kids jump on the trampoline, or hiding under the blankets with Gage watching a scary movie, or hanging out with a good friend enjoying a lazy late lunch, or hanging out when I visit all my families (!), or taking off for a tropical beach. Repetitive solitude is good for the soul, and I kinda like it. All right, I like it a lot.

I lead a quiet life, mind my own business, and now I work with my hands, writing. All that time that I had spent over the years doing the same things over and over again, that had propelled me absolutely *nowhere,* had been magically transformed into chunks of free time that I used to sit quietly, travel by *Zip Line* into my imagination, and then write down what I saw.

I truly love doing this, recording Dad's story, his history, his beliefs, every single day, in this beautiful and peaceful setting with joyful background noises, over and over again. Wouldn't it be great if I could write books on the beach? I thought dreamily as I headed inside to eat with the kids. *Could it be true? It is already there, waiting for me?*

And, so it went, working and writing, over and over again. I would fall into bed exhausted at the end of each delightful day, for another great night's sleep and wake up refreshed, over and over again. Until the day I woke up and instantly forgot absolutely every-thing. I forgot that the comfort of repetitive action, if not carefully monitored, often tilts precipitously toward complacency and stagnation, thereby causing any progress enjoyed up to this point to run smack into a brick wall. I forgot last night's dream and all my other dreams. When I woke, I forgot *where I was* for a moment, but then I forgot *who I was* all day long. Before I went to sleep last night, I forgot to "save as" that which is my internal programming. Then, I forgot to make a back-up.

The next morning, I forgot to reboot my spiritual operating system, thereby wiping out every recently acquired good intention and refined belief. Erased were my intuitive insights and logical understandings. I forgot to Recognize, Express and Dismiss and neglected to Rinse and Repeat. Gone was the pool of forgiveness and mercy I had amassed throughout the years. I forgot to spend LightBuck$, and I forgot my prayer of thanks for my heavenly shower. I forgot how to operate from a feeling of gratitude and forgot my fortitude on the kitchen counter. I had no strength, no *power*, not even a spare battery. I just simply forgot.

And now I was facing the day with an empty spiritual hard drive, and no spare memory stick. With rapidly ebbing power and no reserve, I focused my attention on the green cursor light blinking over and over again, counting the repetitions:

How many times do I wake up, wake up Gage, wake up my laptop, brush my teeth, brush my hair, brush crumbs off the counter, brush off a put-down, brush off my negativity, shave my legs, shave time off getting dressed by throwing on jeans, make coffee, make an English muffin, make a decision, make a grocery list, make a mistake, pet the dog, pet a peeve, drive to work, drive home, drive myself crazy with worry, pay bills, pay taxes, pay attention, pay an emotional price, pay the piper; hold my kids, hold my temper, hold a grudge?

How many times do I lose my courage, lose my car keys, lose my inhibitions, walk the walk, talk the talk, chew gum (all at the same time), answer an email, answer a phone call, answer a question? Every day it's the same thing, over and over again. Breathe. Breathe. Breathe.

The copy machine of my life was jammed and spitting copy after identical copy onto the floor. The remote for the universe was stuck on rewind and replay, and I was forced to view the same dizzying scene over and over again. I was driving around and around on the inside of the Cheerio, heading perilously for the edge on the cliff of insanity.

Please God, please help me. Show me *A Way,* Show me *The Way,* or show me a way out of this stagnation. Show me the money or show me the door, but show me a *sign* that I'm on the right track. *Now*? Pretty please?

Chapter Eight

"Share with Your Sister."

Dad's smiling face popped up on my iPhone while I was leaving the house after lunch, and I stepped out onto the front porch to answer the call. The orange leaves and the slight hint of cooler air were tempered with the brilliant sunshine, warming my skin. A perfect October day must be a good omen.

"I blew them away!" Dad said quietly, immediately sounding my inner alarm bells. His voice was odd; his words infused with a buzzing vibrating energy, but his tone was uncharacteristically calm. It kinda scared me.

"I told them my story, and I blew them away!"

I grew goose bumps on my arms and neck as Dad told me about the deep-study conference he was attending in Oregon sponsored by Neale Donald Walsch, the bestselling author of *Conversations With God.*

At one point during the conference, Dad had the opportunity to take the microphone and share his life philosophy with the room, and he did it with all the passion and verve that is *The Preacher.* He riveted them with his story and his beliefs, holding their attention tight with every passionate word. I had goose bumps on my scalp!

After it was over, Neale, the Bestselling Author and world-traveled speaker, applauded and suggested to Dad that he write a book as a platform for public speaking, for he saw Dad as an important and extraordinary Messenger.

Can you get goose bumps on your toes? I wondered as I felt the sensation travel up and down my body. Oh. My. God.

"I have to go," he said hurriedly, and in the same sparkling combination of bursting energy and eerie calm. "I'm only on a break, and they're starting again. I'll call you later. I love you."

Dad disconnected the call and left me on the porch alone and dazed, rooted to the spot while my mind traveled a million miles in every direction, exploring the magically infinite possibilities. *Oh, my God!* Maybe this was the sign I had been seeking. *Thank you, God.*

Later, when I watched the video online that somebody in the audience had taped on their iPhone, I was astounded at his magnificent performance.

The video opens with the microphone being handed awkwardly to Dad, who is seated at a large conference table with approximately twelve others as Neal Donald Walsch extends his invitation to share. The scene wiggles blurrily as the iPhone handler gets settled and Neale, seated out of view, speaks first. "Richard, the microphone please. Richard?"

Dad and The Preacher both owned the floor and everyone's complete attention, including mine, as he began.

"I spent a lot of time listening to what Jim is saying. And I noticed that he is creating by his thoughts, words and deeds. And his words were "try this,' 'try that' and 'want this.' There is so much fear that comes out of those words."

"If he spent his time, when he gets to those worries, replacing them with something constructive, like a happy thought, he could short-circuit those negative thoughts. But, he must pay attention to what is going on in his stream-of-consciousness thinking every day. And, as he stops those things, he short-circuits them. His words won't be 'trying' anymore, he'll be 'doing.' He won't be 'wanting,' he'll be 'choosing.'

Those words add to the energy of the moment in the things that he is doing. So, by him paying attention to his 60,000 thoughts a day that he is thinking and turning them around, because for most people,

45,000 of those thoughts are destructive, so it is obvious that their life is going to be that way. So, if you pay attention to those things, you short-circuit them. It's a tremendous job when it starts out, but after a period of time, it becomes second nature and your mind becomes a lot cleaner."

Dad was rockin' and rollin,' but Neale interrupted with the most obvious question, "So, if I was Jim, I would go 'that's great, but how do you do that?'" My words exactly! I thought as I jumped up and down clapping, completely agreeing with Neale. I like this guy.

The Preacher/Dad continued in his disembodied one voice, *"For me, I started many years ago, because many years ago I learned that thoughts are things. So, what I did when I would start to worry, I would remember something that I enjoy doing. So, pilots always fly. So, when those moments would come, when the worry would come, I would close my eyes and I would go in a moment to flying. I would be flying around the Lehigh Valley and I would see the north mountain, and the south mountain, and the rivers that run through them. And, I would see the Creator in all the things around, and that would take me to a place in my mind where I would be at peace and serenity. After a period of time, my mind is focused on something else. Your mind can only focus on one thing at a time."*

Neale interrupted again with, "Wow! This is pretty powerful stuff." Indeed it is, I agreed, smiling with hands on hips. I'd like to meet this guy.

Dad took the floor again, *"This is what he needs to do. He needs to pay attention to his 60,000 thoughts a day that he is thinking. He's doing it to himself. And, if he pays attention to them, he'll be short-circuiting them. He'll be refining them, and as he refines them, then the outcomes will be different. Your mind can only focus on one thing at a time."*

Neale agreed, and giving the statement added impact, repeated, "Because your mind can only focus on one thing at a time. That was the most powerful thing you said. Your mind can only focus on one thing at a time. So if you deliberately redirect your thoughts, and refocus your mind, you almost automatically alter your thoughts, because your mind can't hold two thoughts at once. So, when is your book coming out?" he laughed. I'm working on it! I thought, suddenly terrified as I swallowed my stomach.

Dad continued, *"Everyone that I tell the story to, about the Family Circle Bank, encourages people. So, I'm going to write about it, and do something about it. I'm certainly going to do something for that. I've been doing this for a long time."* Could we cover the Family Circle Bank in the last chapter, Dad? Is that okay? I wondered as I asked the air.

Dad turned to face Neale, still seated off-camera, *"I will say that I had ninety percent of what you have said in your books, that I have been practicing for many years. What I loved about your books, is that the ten percent I didn't have, you filled in."* He addressed the rest of the table, *"So, now it's a complete philosophy that I live every day. I've been living it for a long time, that's why my life is the way it is, because I create it."* He paused for a moment, then continued, *"Now when I tell that to people, it goes right over their heads. Obviously."* I nodded my head, knowing that I was most obviously part of the population that waits helplessly as these things often soar right over my head.

"Because it's a conscious effort that you make every moment of every day. You've got to pay attention to every thought you think, every word you say, and every deed you do. It's a reflection of who and what you are. As you become better and better at it, then your life will become easier and easier.

Dad was quietly reverent for a moment, then grew increasingly animated as he espoused, *"So, I live my life quietly. I celebrate my life. I enjoy it, and I have fun. I have fun! So, it's fun every day. I get up in the morning and I walk out on my step, and I giggle and laugh. I can't help it because it's such a joy. I take that joy and that happiness to every thing that I do. It's a joy to live life. I'm creating it in my own way and I continue to do so,"* Dad promised confidently.

"My goal in life is to make sure that my family understands that. Now, I have nine grandsons (Author's note: Dad now has ten grandsons and a Mia!) *that for sure are going to live this. My three daughters already live this because they grew up with it. We did not live a typical life like most people because we created our own reality.* No, we didn't live a typical life, I agreed, but I don't regret it even though my friends thought we were weird. In fact, I kinda like it. *Thank you, Dad. Thank you, God.*

"I learned something a long time ago. And I've told this story many times, hundreds of times because of the Boy Scouts, I go around to the schools and talk about it. I met my wife in a public housing project when I was thirteen years old. We used to walk around holding hands and talk about the life we wanted and the family we wanted. But most of all, we talked about the house we wanted. We would walk around the nice neighborhoods and describe the house we wanted."

He continued, *"We got married when I was eighteen. It was a small wedding, just six people: me, Helen, my parents, and her parents. And, when I paid for the dinner when it was all said and done, we had two bucks. Eleven years later, we moved into a grand house in west Allentown. It was a big house, four bedrooms, four bathrooms, and a swimming pool. It had all the amenities. In exploring the house, I went out to the sidewalk and looked. The date on the sidewalk was the date they built the house. Well, the date they built the house was the date we walked around holding hands talking about the house we wanted."* Dad continued with his epiphany and concluded with, *"I learned two things that day. Number one: When you start out towards something, it is already there waiting for you."*

"Number two: If you do everything important and necessary to bring it about, it becomes reality." I wondered if I had mixed those two up? I worried as I took notes.

"So, I learned a long time ago that you create your own reality according to your beliefs. Imagination and feeling follow beliefs. It's not the other way around. Now with that, we have been able to start multi-million dollar businesses and do all these things, because we believed it. We have physical manifestation of conscious creation. Now what we do as a family is we write these things down." "That's the job I want! Please, please, please. I love writing!" I begged the empty room, fidgeting excitedly.

"We call them family miracles. By writing them down, when you have any doubts, you can go back and read them. As you go back and read them, it takes you back to that place. As you go back to that place it's easy to remember that energy and focus to have the ability to create who and what you are. So as you live it, you become better and better at it every day. It takes a lot of effort to begin with, but the payoff is enormous. It brings peace and tranquility to the individual. It certainly has in my life. Now I go around to the schools for the Boy Scouts and I talk to them about this. When I tell that story, I give out $2 bills to the kids." Do you still want to include $2 bills in our book? I wondered, listening raptly.

"I tell them, "Now you have as much money as I did when I started out. But, more importantly, you have a plan. This is how the plan works, and I break it down into four parts: First is intention. Everything starts with your intention. Your intention comes from either fear or from love. If it starts in fear, then the outcome is going to be destructive. If it starts in love, the outcome is going to be constructive." This is all clicking into place quite nicely, thinking gratefully of my Chapter One notes.

"The next part is beliefs. Most people accept beliefs from other people. Tear out those old beliefs that are destructive, and plug in new beliefs. Say to yourself: I am a human being of great worth and value. I am successful in the things I do.

The next is personality. You get up each morning and you put on those personality glasses. We talked about Myers-Briggs™." "I got it," I whispered to Video Dad.

"And last is reality. Reality does not happen to you, you happen to it. You create it, maintain it, and experience it according to your beliefs. Your imagination and feeling will follow your belief. It's not the other way around. So, that's how I live. I live it every day. And as I live it, I get to be it. As I get to be it, I get to see my outside world created by my hand. Everyone does it. Most people don't realize it. I do." Dad/*The Preacher*/*One* all paused at the same time, letting his words, which were floating invisibly throughout the magical room, find their predestined targets and settle in for a gentle three-point landing before his voice rose again with precise passion.

"And, I learned a long time ago from that house and that side-walk. Now, that house is still in the family and will be there, forever. It is a symbol of physical manifestation of conscious creation. Now, we've had hundreds of Miracles since then. But, everyone remembers them because it's something that focuses us and keeps us grounded. Dad paused, accepting the applause, and I leaned closer to my laptop as I tried to decipher the indistinct chatter as their clapping subsided and he continued.

"In our family we have something called 51%. You must do fif-ty-one percent of the work in order to make it become reality. We discovered that the reason you have to do fifty-one percent of the work is because that's how much it takes for the individual to believe it. After a period of time, if you believe it at one percent, you don't have to do a whole lot. So, over the years we've had to do less and

less for the creation to come into reality. Create it. Maintain it. And Experience it. We have a sign in our business. It says: Doubt not. Fear not. Work on. Wait."

"You have to do fifty-one percent of the work in order to bring it into reality. You, as the individual. Because that's how long it takes you, the individual, to believe it. The better you get at it, the more you believe it, the less you have to do. Now, I have to do very little to bring something into reality." He sat back, considered for a moment, and then continued with every person in the room thoroughly entranced.

"Here's a story that happened a couple of months ago. We were sitting on the back porch of the same (Miracle) house: myself, my daughter, and my son-in-law, and we're having a good 'ol time as we're talking about a tree we have outside that is diseased, that must come down. So, my daughter says, 'Wouldn't it be nice if the tree fell down and broke up into little bundles on the sidewalk?' We all say, "Yeah, that would great." So, my daughter gets up and calls downstairs to my grandson, 'Go move your car out of the way of the tree.' he says 'why?' She says, 'Just move the car.'" You go Girl! I sang, contorting around the room with my own special brand of hula dance to music only I could hear, admiring my sister's ability to act so boldly in the *'wouldn't it be great if'* game."

He moves the car, and three hours later a storm comes through and knocks the tree into the street. Now, the tree belongs to the city now, so the city comes along, cuts up the tree and puts it in little bundles on the sidewalk." He paused as laughter danced around the table, looking from person to person, his gaze riveted to their souls. *"Physical manifestation of conscious creation in five hours. In five hours. That's how it works."*

Dad paused for a moment, *" Now, she did something that most people wouldn't do. What did she do? She made room for it to hap-*

pen. She called downstairs to my grandson and said, "Move your car out of the way." Because she believed it. And, since she believed it, and there was energy, since the more people you have, the more energy you have. So, that's what we do. And that's how it works for me. It's real. I live it every day. And I'd like to say, "Neale, thank you." You gave me that ten percent. You filled in all the blanks and that gave me peace. Those little parts that I didn't have about creation and death kind of troubled my mind. Your books filled in all those blanks. I have peace and tranquility. If my life ends right at this moment, I'll be satisfied.

You could hear a pin drop for moments or years, depending on which *Zip Time Zone* you were in when Neale spoke quietly, softly, and passionately, "The only thing I wish, the only thing I wish, is that a way could be found to put you in front of 10,000 people a week. Television. Multi-media. Something. First, a book, a platform."

Goose bumps nested and procreated, spawning even more generations of goose bumps on top of goose bumps as I jumped up and down, thrusting my arm in the air and begging everyone, "Please, please, please let *me* write it," barely avoiding memories of Horeshack on *Welcome Back Kotter.*

"Because, Richard, in your whole family you have really placed on the ground in physical form what the world dreams of. And, you have proven that it works. And, you have an astonishing ability to articulate that not everyone has. I am thunderstruck and flabbergasted at who you are. And, I only want to now, having experienced you in this way. I mean, we all got little snippets along the way, but that last six-minute run was powerful.

"It gave me a window into who you are to the point that I am hardly going to be able to rest until I encourage you to find a way now to share that power and message with large numbers of people, if you choose. You have a way of instilling hope into the human experience again. People hear you talk and they say 'Wow! Wow, it could be that way.' And they go from that to 'It is that way. He got it. It is that way.' And, that is an unspeakable gift. So, I would invite you to seriously consider that the last quarter of your life, the last 25 years of your life, were meant to be as a very, very important and extraordinary Messenger. You don't have to accept that invitation, but take a look at it. Because that's magnificent. That's magnificent. Utterly magnificent."

Neale paused and then continued with, "And, I don't know how I let you escape from my world. If I could handcuff you and take you wherever I go, you could be opening for me. By the time I got out there, there would be nothing left to say. I could just follow him and say, 'he's right.' So, very nice, Richard, thank you for that contribution." Wow! I stood and gave Dad/*The Preacher/One* a much-deserved standing ovation in front of my MacBook. *This is a Miracle! Thank you, God!*

Just as suddenly the bone chilling, mind numbing, limb paralyzing fear began to settle in and lay eggs. Where moments ago, I had experienced an exhilarating rush of anticipation and excitement, sending my endorphins into overdrive, I was now filled with a terror so pervasive it oozed from my pores into the room in choking tentacles, releasing a rush of a adrenaline for all the wrong reasons. *Recognize. Express. Dismiss.*The movie in my mind featured *Future Dad* speaking at a conference, knowing to the ends of my chipping toenail polish that he would wow any crowd he addressed, his passion and enthusiasm for his message bursting into the room with earnest conviction.

The camera angle changed to show him in front of throngs of people – all clamoring for more insight, more funny stories, more joyful giggles. It was an easy leap to fathom his contagious excitement rippling across an auditorium infecting the audience with positive energy, elevating their moods, and levitating their sense of self worth. The focus cleared, and I watched *The Future Preacher* encouraging the crowds as they shared their stories and posed their questions. I could hear him graciously and enthusiastically inviting them to visit his website, and participate in the interactive online chats held weekly.

The scene shifted, and I could now see *Preacher*/Dad happily reaching for his Sharpie in response to a kindly grandma requesting him to sign her newly purchased copy of his yet-unpublished book. And, that's where the Disney movie disintegrates into a horror flick, fading the screen to inky black. The creepy music rose ominously in the background as Jason and Freddie both lunged for my peace of mind and threatened to beat the living confidence out of me as I raced for my sanity up the dark basement stairs, toward the safety of the upstairs light. *Engage Shields Full Power!*

I struggled to push down my fears as I sat back down in front of my Mac. Writing Dad's book is one thing, but people actually *reading* the book? What will you think? Will you snicker or snarl, criticize or condemn, appreciate or annihilate? Will you ridicule me for botching up Dad's amazing great story with a half-baked tale and flaccid plot written in un-educated blonde Polish? I mean English?

Will you laugh at the part I deem amusing, or am I the only one that thinks it's funny? What if you think the book, well, *sucks*? Will you pat me on the head as you walk away, disappointed? Will you run me out of town? Will you take away my laptop? O.M.G. I must have been crazy when I begged for this job. *It is what it is. Recognize. Express. Dismiss.*

I *Zip Timed* it back to Carrabba's and my birthday dinner last year, where, with five of my family and closest friends, I had spontaneously polled everyone at the table, "Who here thinks I'm crazy?" Four of the five simultaneously threw their arms up in the air, leaving me feeling deflated, and reaching for the *vino*. Then, somebody said loudly, "You know, one of the first symptoms of being crazy is *not thinking* you are," causing everybody to burst out laughing, even admittedly, me.

Later, when Dad and I were talking at home, he offered quietly, "I didn't raise my hand, you know, I don't think you're crazy. I believe in you."

"You don't count," I protested mournfully. "You're my Dad. You're *supposed* to believe in me. It's that whole unconditional parental love thing."

"So what's wrong with that?" he quizzed, raising one eyebrow. I answered, "Nothing and thank you for not committing me to the loony bin in a straightjacket just yet." I quickly pulled in for a *Zip Stop* in the pits, traveling further down the rabbit hole, remembering the conversation where I had confided to a close friend that I believed God had spoken to me in a dream.

"What did God say?" he demanded, somewhat irritated.

"I love you and I believe in you."

"How do you know it was God?" he challenged, eyes firing at full speed.

"I don't know, I just know," I responded truthfully, not trusting my words, *anybody's words,* to describe an unthinkable, indescribable, unbelievable feeling.

"I wouldn't tell people that if I were you," he admonished, making me feel small, insignificant, and terrified to utter a further word... to anyone.

I squealed my tires pulling out of the *Zip Stop* as Dad started singing in a loony-toon voice, "They're coming to take me away, ha ha, ho ho, hee hee."

I cringed, then laughed with him and asked, despair softening my tone, "Why do people do it Dad? Why do people keep going when all the world thinks they're crazy?"

Dad jumped up eager to relay another story, "Imagine you are in the middle of the forest in the dead of winter with five feet of snow on the ground. But, despite the blizzard raging outside, you're all toasty and warm because you're nestled in a warm cozy cabin with a big roaring fireplace." Dad giggled, getting into the scene.

"Now, you look out the window, and far away on the other side of the woods, is another cabin. Only this cabin is stuffed full of people having a party! There are people dancing and laughing in all the rooms, and you can hear the music thumping from all the way across the woods. Everyone is having a grand ol' time," Dad enthused, completely acting the part.

"You look out your window, and you see five feet of snow between you and the fun, and you think to yourself, 'I would be *crazy* to go out into all that snow and ice!' But, that doesn't deter you! So you dress warmly, pull on your boots, and set out in the snow."

Dad started laughing, holding his sides and turning red, and I had to wait a few moments before he could continue with the story, wondering how I was going to get through the snow.

"Remember," Dad chortled, "there are five feet of snow on the ground, and you're only five feet tall, so you have to *dig* your way through the snow, shoveling it to clear the path in front of you as you move *slowly* along," he continued laughing, picturing me buried in a blizzard over my head. *Great.*

"It takes you a *long, long* time." Dad laughs, and I can't keep myself from smiling. "And you're digging, and you're shoveling, and you're sweating, and your face is red, and your hair is sticking to your forehead." He burst out laughing, and so did I.

"But, eventually, you get there!" Dad beamed. "You get to your destination and you get to enjoy the party. You get to enjoy the fun!" He sat back smiling, "Of course, by now, you're too tired to party, but that's beside the point," and threw in a spot of laughter, but no special effects were needed.

"But do you know what happens next?" he asked, sitting up at attention, eyebrow saluting.

"I take a nap?" I ask logically, throwing up my left eyebrow while my right one felt compelled to join.

"No! The next person who walks into that cabin and wants to go the party across the woods will see your path, and now their journey will be *easier* for them, because you already cleared the way."

He started chuckling for emphasis, "Not much of a way, mind you, as tiny as you are, I mean, how much can you do? You're *only* one person. But, a teeny tiny path nonetheless."

Dad started pointing at me and proclaimed, "And then, an amazing thing happens! The next *twenty* people who want to get to the party have an easier and easier time on their journey. In fact, after some *Zip Time*, that teeny tiny path that you started by digging *first*, is now a superhighway and eve-ry-one can come to the party!" We laughed together.

I knew he was right…but.

"I just want somebody *else* to believe in me too, Dad. I need feedback, affirmation."

The Preacher, who had not cast a vote at dinner, jumped up with,

"Within the human consciousness there is a profound need to affirm our own reality as a reflection of our outer environment. We need these psychological reference points to prove to ourselves that we are indeed Real."

Dad interpreted, "If I sit here and say hello to you, then your response to me affirms that I am real, that I am here. But, if in response to my greeting, you just sit there and look through me, then I would question my sense of reality. If *every* person I encountered gave me the same response, I would question whether I was Real."

My point exactly, I thought, thinking of the lone tree falling in the forest with not a creature around to hear. That's why I need somebody *else* to believe in me too, I thought, otherwise, it's true – I'm crazy.

Dad offered thoughtfully, "A few months ago, I was feeling really down and discouraged, just '*bleh*' all the time, all over."

Really? You? I mused.

"At the club that night, I ran into a woman I hadn't seen in a few months. When I last saw her, she had been looking for a new job, and I had offered some advice and encouragement. This night, she threw her arms around me, hugging me tight, and gave me a big kiss on the cheek."

"'Thank you, Richard. Thank you!' She had gushed, 'I start my new job next week!'

Then she hugged me again, which was nice," Dad said, eyes crinkling in laughter.

"She was so ecstatic and sincere, I couldn't help but feel good and my sadness immediately lifted. She had affirmed my reality right when I needed it most. This woman, who I hadn't seen in months, was a messenger, and I was paying attention to the message. I was, indeed, on the right track." *The Preacher* appeared out of nowhere:

"Spread the Word. Seek out those that will support and assist you in your journey. Search for Messengers that will magically guide you and propel you forward in your journey to Self. Remember Who and What You Are."

Dad chuckled as he concluded with, "Inquiring minds want to know, and it's been posited that there are only six degrees of separation. You never can tell if the seed that you plant in somebody's ear today might not grow and bear fruit within thirty days." I laughed with him, easily imagining ears of corn.

"It's the 'telling people' part that scares me the most," I admitted. "There's so much that can go wrong from *here*" I said, pointing to my vivid and sometimes difficult to control imagination, "to *here*." I finished lamely pointing to the unfinished book.

"You're absolutely right," Dad agreed.

"I am?" Uh-oh.

"Sure you are! Communication is a great way to tell a story, to spread the word, to spread good news to others, or to warn of dangers that threaten. But, communication in itself is inherently faulty. The story changes with each telling. People say one thing, but others often hear something entirely different. It's like the Telephone Game, or *Whisper Down the Valley*."

Dad suddenly burst out laughing and raised his arm, waving and saying between giggles, "Hey! F. U. Buddy!" He continued laughing, now holding his sides.

"*What?*" I asked, spontaneously giggling just from watching his mirth.

It took a few minutes, but then Dad settled enough to explain. "Remember that song *Ride Wit' Me* by Nelly that went like this: 'Hey! Must be the money.' Do you remember that song?"

"Yeah, I remember." It's on my iPod.

"Well, for months after that song came out, I thought the words for 'Hey! Must be the money' were, 'Hey! F.U. Buddy!' he broke out into body contorting laughter as he kept repeating, "Hey! F.U. Buddy," over and over again. I couldn't help it, I joined him in laughter, and with my R rated potty mouth, substituted the real words as I mentally sang along.

Dad picked up the thread of conversation, "From the time you conceive of a thought to the time you speak it or write it down, it has already changed. You have added your own perspective to the thought. It's a new creation."

"Now, somebody else comes along and hears what you say, or reads what you wrote, and they place their own interpretation on your words, whether you intend it or not. Then, that person tells somebody else what you said or wrote, and the story changes again. And, so on and so on. Communication is inherently faulty."

"You're not making me feel *any* better, Dad," I fretted.

"I'm not trying to," he replied solemnly. "I'm telling you the way it is. Some people won't like what I have to say, or the way you write, or the way you fix your hair."

What? I thought, immediately reaching up to pat my fly-away, do-whatever-they-want locks.

Dad continued as if he hadn't noticed my fashion crisis. "For every single person that listens to me speak or who reads this book, there will be that many different perspectives. Remember the bank robbers and the dynamite truck?" he laughed.

Now, where did I put that black hole, I thought, and how fast can I crawl into it?

"But that's okay! Because that's part of the creation process. It never stops, don't you see? Every single person who reads this book *should* question it and explore his own beliefs through com-munication. They shouldn't take *our* word for it. They have to prove it to themselves that what they believe, whatever it is, is indeed true, whether it is real.

"Every single person is a messenger who will add insights to guide you on your path and assist you in refining *your* beliefs. It's an ongoing process, a perpetual cycle that never ends. It's material for the next book!"

"Who's the messenger?" I questioned, ignoring future books for the moment and immediately trying to conjure people of importance or minor fame that I've encountered recently, who might have had anything to say of value.

"Eve-ry-one!" he responded emphatically. "If you are *aware of your surroundings* you will notice messengers delivering messages of truth eve-ry-where," he giggled. "You'll gain insights from the grocery clerk, wisdom from the paper boy, a solution to a problem from a billboard, and inspiration from a stranger's kindness."

Is there another word for goose bumps? He was right, I thought, thinking of random social encounters where I've been transformed from a state of melancholy to grudging happiness with just a few friendly words. But, then I remembered other times when I cringed at the seemingly casual flaming arrows, I mean remarks, of others.

"Not everyone is out to help, some are out to harm."

"No doubt," he agreed quickly. "You have shields – use them," and then started laughing at a memory. "Some people lie. Remember the story about the peas? You should put that story in the book," he commanded, laughing.

"It wasn't peas, it was wax beans. I like peas," I corrected, giggling out loud, instantly recalling the time in fifth grade that Dad had promised me a "hookie day" from school if I would eat the whole bowl of wax beans, which I absolutely detested and was therefore struggling to swallow at the dinner table, while barely suppressing my gag reflex. (*Author's note: Some of those gags were for giggles. Sorry, Sis.*)

Immediately accepting his offer, I delightfully inhaled the bowl of detestable, colorless, odorless, and distinctly tasteless vegetables and went to bed happily, if not a little nauseated, eagerly anticipating my "Get out of Jail Free Day" tomorrow.

"I lied," Dad announced the next morning, as I stood stunned and betrayed. "People lie. It's up to you to determine to what degree. You better get used to it. Now, go get ready for school." And I did, grumpily donning my uniform and grabbing my backpack, but I didn't like it.

Dad continued, "I'm telling you the way it is. Some people lie. Others seek to deliberately construct scenarios of chaos; they like to 'stir the shit pot' to see what they can cook up. Some people tell the truth, but not the 'whole' truth, potentially leading you down a path of deception to believe things to be one way, when it's really another. It's technically lying by omission."

Hey, I know some of those people, I thought. "*Great*," I replied, drawing out the word deliberately sarcastic. "You're doing a great job cheering me up, Dad. I think I'll be going now." I smiled, making as if to leave. *The Preacher* stopped me with,

It is what it is. You can't change it.
It is what you make it.

Dad continued, "Those people are Messengers too, and their message is: *Be aware of your surroundings.* Don't let yourself get caught up in their web of falsehood, or untruth. Use your intuition to *recognize* those imposters for what they are, and remember who and what you are in the moment. Steer yourself in another direction when the need dictates.

"It is what it is. You can't change it. You only possess the power to change you and nobody else."

We sat quietly for a few moments, each lost in thought, when I asked timidly, "So, is it true? Am I crazy?"

"Who knows?" Dad laughed. "You either are, or you aren't. Maybe you have to be a little crazy to write a book. Prove it to yourself whether it's true or not."

I briefly considered the virtues of joining the Witness Protection Program while he continued nonchalantly, "Look, just tell the story; it's a great story. Write it down so we can share it with others, and we'll see what happens. If just *one* person gets *one* good thing from the book, it was worth it. Besides, we're having fun writing it, are we not?" He laughed playfully with not a care in the world, as I continued to sit quietly, wondering what kind of test you take for *crazy*.

Just tell the story, we'll see what happens, I repeated to myself as I returned from my *Zip Trip* from the state of Feeling Sorry For Myself. I moved the mouse to wake up my laptop, spied Dad's exuberant face frozen on my screen, then replayed the video *one more time*, just to make *absolutely* sure I had heard the Famous Author correctly. I did. *Oh, my God.*

Just tell the story. Write. It. Down. A teeny tiny silver lining peeked out from my cloud of doubt, and I ran with it. That's right, I thought happily, writing is *my* job. This time around, the *offer* of a lifetime didn't actually arrive in the form of a phone call with an offer from Dad, instead, I had begged for this *opportunity* of a lifetime. I had pleaded with him all those months ago to let me be the one to write the book that told his life story, and although he was hesitant in his initial agreement, it was now my job. I admit it sometimes scares the pajamas off me, but I still crave doing it. *Thank you, Dad.*

Thank you, God.

My job is cake compared to his job, public speaking, I thought gleefully as I considered Dad's enthusiastic contribution to our quasi-partnership that is half-jokingly referred to in our house as "Dad, Inc."

That's right. I mean, I write and he speaks, as in "in front of people," with all the hand trembling, voice cracking, body quaking, adrenaline spiking, nerve wracking, hair graying fear that goes with it.

Oh, wait, that's *me* who feels that way about public speaking, I thought happily, dancing a little jig in my mind. Dad, on the other hand *loves* the thrill of speaking in groups, *thrives* on the energy in a crowded roomful of people, and *embraces* the challenge of engaging and captivating an audience.

Dad's newest career incarnation combines the best qualities of Dad and *The Preacher* as *One* and they travel around together as a matching pair to schools in and around the Lehigh Valley to speak to students on behalf of the Boy Scouts. He starts the presentation with information about career counseling and employment choices, and the benefits of personality profiles. Then, he reverently turns the stage over to *The Preacher,* who electrifies the room as he shares his rags to riches, two-dollar bill to Miracle Dream House story with the kids and concludes with relish, giving each student his very own crisp two-dollar bill.

"Is this real? Can you spend it?" they ask, checking out the queerly odd currency, some never having seen a two-dollar bill before.

"Of course it's real. It's right there!" he points and laughs. "And yes, you can spend it 'cause now you have the exact same amount of money that I had when I started out. But, more importantly, you have a plan." Dad/*The Preacher* says, breaking it down into four parts. "This is how the plan works:

1. *First is your intention.* Everything starts with intention. Your intention comes from either fear or love. If it starts in fear, then the outcome is going to be destructive. If it starts in love, then the outcome will be constructive.

2. *Second are your beliefs.* Most people accept beliefs from other people. Tear out those old beliefs that are destructive, and plug in new beliefs. Say to yourself, every day, 'I am a human being of great value and worth. I am successful in the things I do."

3. *Next is personality.* Every day when you wake up, you put on your personality glasses. Understanding your personality

leads you to a greater understanding of yourself, giving you greater insights into who and what you are.

4. *The fourth part of co-creation is reality.* Reality doesn't happen to you. You happen to it. You create it, maintain it and experience it. Your imagination and feeling follow your belief, it's not the other way around."

The kids stare in awe equally at Dad/*The Preacher* and their crisp new two-dollar bills as he finishes with a flourish, the electricity bouncing off the walls for *Zip Hours.* Consequently, Dad's name is passed enthusiastically among school administrators and he is repeatedly invited to share his story, giving away thousands of two-dollar bills over the past years in the process. I love my Dad. Being around him is like heaven, only with Santa Claus.

I struggled to steer my mind off presents and onto the present, but instead *Zip Timed* back one year to the day I had fearfully agreed to give a speech for a Rotary meeting.

"Don't worry, kid, we'll do it together," Jeff, my mentor, my community guru, town newspaper publisher, Rotarian buddy, committee chair, and my friend offered, immediately quelling my anxiety.

"We will?" I asked hopefully.

"Yeah, I'll introduce you, and you speak," he laughed, and I couldn't help but giggle with him.

But, suddenly the *Zipper* turned into a chainsaw and I found myself two years prior standing at the podium of Walsh University, about to begin my presentation on Female Entrepreneurs, when suddenly, out of nowhere, the laptop ate my Powerpoint presentation. I broke out in hives just recording the memory on paper. Truly frightening stuff there, public speaking. It's not called Americas' number one fear for nothing. *Push it Down!*

The way I saw it, the only more dreadfully terrifying, more insomnia producing, more nightmare inducing form of torture than public speaking would be going door-to-door. Seriously, I feel sorry for all those tired magazine sales kids they bus in from out of state, or the thirsty siding repair guy, or the diligent Witnesses. I cringe when I see neighbors slam their doors rudely in their expectant faces, or worse yet, not even answer the doorbell as they peek from behind their curtains. Seriously? Do they thing we don't notice? It hurts *my feelings* when I hear kids referring to church outreach ministries as "Bible Thumpers." I flipped the calendar back a few *Zip Pages* and found myself staring at Gage with large fearful eyes as he whispered to me, "Mom, someone is coming to the front door."

"What do you mean?" I demanded, mistakenly interpreting his anxiety for guilt and tensely expecting a neighbor/mom to ring the doorbell with a complaint about unbecoming behavior.

"I don't know who it is," he whispered back, his tone immediately giving birth to increasingly more dire images of armed robbers or a wayward alien that had him spooked as I made my way purposefully to the front door. I swung the door wide open, having to push through the seven inches of snow on the porch that had fallen last night while we slept, *gloriously* precipitating our "snow day" from school and work, as I brightly greeted the two moms and four kids trudging through the deep snowdrifts to spread their message.

"Good morning. It's a *great* day to be out in the snow!" I called cheerfully, stepping out onto the porch to meet them.

"That's the last thing we expected you to say," they laughed back.

"I love snow, and I love snow days!" I enthused.

"It's a good thing you live in Ohio," they returned dryly.

"Look around! Look how beautiful the snow hangs on the branches over there," I said breathlessly pointing overhead. And, miraculously, they did. "Listen to how muffled and silent the neighborhood sounds with this big blanket of snow," I laughed, sweeping my arm around the neighborhood, and they did.

"Hey, do you kids like to ice skate?" I happily asked the four mini-moms hiding behind their big-moms. They peeked out and nodded hesitantly as the messengers stared back perplexed.

"Great! Before you leave, make sure you walk around to the back of the house and see the ice rink. My sister and her four kids live next door, and all of our kids and the rest of the neighborhood kids skate and play hockey every winter in the backyard," I explained with enthusiasm. They stared back at me, eyes wide.

"We wanted to invite you to our church," one mom suddenly pleaded, thrusting a pamphlet toward me, urging me to accept it. I looked down to a big yellow smiley face and the words: "God Loves You."

"I know!" I replied earnestly, "I know God loves me and I love God, and I see God eve-ry-where! Thank you for inviting me to your church, and I will definitely consider visiting," I finished sincerely.

"Don't forget to check out the ice rink, kids," I reminded them after chatting for a few more moments, and then closed the front door to find myself face to face with Gage, frozen to the living room floor, staring at me with eyes as large as pancakes and mouth open wide enough to catch flies.

"Now, *that's* how you talk to people who come to the front door," I pronounced, fervently wishing I had practiced that one eyebrow trick I envy, and then continued on to the kitchen while Gage suddenly dashed to the deck doors exclaiming, "Mom, they're going back there! They're going to the backyard!"

"I hope so, Gage," I laughed, "I invited them to."

"Why did they invite you to their church? They don't even know you," he asked perceptively, his inner radar and laser gaze honing in on the target question. I smiled my answer. "They love God, and they love their church, and they want to share that feeling with other people, especially those people they don't know yet, so they go door-to-door to spread their message of love."

"Are you going to go?" he asked.

Target in sight.

"Maybe, maybe not. Do *you* want to go?" I asked, and he parried with a question of his own.

Near miss.

"Why don't *you* go to church, Mom?"

Direct hit!

I answered sincerely without hesitation, "Because I see God everywhere, cutie, all the time. I see God in eve-ry-thing. I see God in the beautiful trees heavy with snow, I see God in the people who come to our door sharing their good news, I see God in every person and in every thing, even you!" I giggled, tickling him. "I like church, but I don't *have* to go there to see God on Sundays because I see God eve-ry-where, every day, and I give thanks to God, and all He gives us, *all the time!*"

Gage looked outside toward the snowy trees and the ice rink haphazardly littered with hockey sticks and pucks for a few *Zip Time-less* moments, then declared happily, "I see God everywhere too, Mom. I love God." Out of the mouths of babes.

"I love God too, cutie," I laughed out loud, agreeing with my ten-year old ageless wizard. "I love you, and I *love* being your Mom," I smiled, while reaching for a hug. And, for once, he let me! OMG! *It's a miracle! Thank you, God.*

He sank my battleship!

And thank you, Dad, for taking the harder of our two jobs! I danced some more in my musical mind as I remembered how many times I have had the pleasure of going to my Happy Place to record on paper what I saw, heard and felt. Not so with public speaking. There are no do-overs with public speaking, it's live mic time. And, I always seem to put my foot in my mouth.

Like the night I forgot to thank my Dad, my brother-in-law, and my best friend at a fundaiser, but managed to include every *other* member of the board (*Author's note: The former best friend doesn't talk to me anymore. Can you blame her?*) Or, the time I said "choke the chicken" at a job search seminar instead of "pluck the chicken." Or, the time I just froze.

But, with writing, there was no chance for a slip of the tongue because every error could be magically erased with the *delete* key, every awkward phrase made more melodic by editing correction; a brick wall in the plot could be remedied with a re-write, and I quickly gave thanks for my good fortune. Go for it, Dad! You can have the public speaking job; it's all yours.

I *Zip Timed* it back to the present, where I had exactly twenty-five minutes before I had to dash from the house for another fundraiser, my nervous energy already beginning to sparkle in fear, dreading the deadly *microphone*.

"I just wanted to make you cry," Jack, my mentor, my guru, my fellow board member, my friend, and unbeknownst to me in the moment, my messenger, had laughed at me later that evening after introducing me on the imposing *microphone*.

"I don't cry," I laughed back, forgetting to tune into the ESPN channel, instead flipping to the 24-hour All Embarrassment, All The Time channel. I thought, as I remembered cringing and turning beet red when it was my turn to speak. I would have paid any amount of money to hide backstage instead.

Little did I know how prophetic my messenger's words would turn out to be, as I made my way around the auditorium of the Hoover building that night, chatting and catching up with fellow business people and non-profit volunteers. Who knew I would end up crying my heart out for that entire lost weekend after discovering *The Worst News Ever* later that evening? Who would ever have predicted that I would want to run away, disappear, or retreat even further into my shell never to venture out again? Who would have guessed that within short order, I would be squealing my tires out of town headed for a five-week sabbatical/retreat/surrender at the nearest beach? Who "woulda thunk" that reality could hurt this much? Whoever said, *"Life sucks, then you die"* must have felt *exactly* like I did. God, I thought as I headed desperately for the nearest interstate, Life's a Beach.

Chapter Nine

"Life's a Beach!"

I am *finally* at the beach! I smiled as Dad's face popped up on the iPhone the minute I parked the car in the driveway of the rented beach house in Ocean City, New Jersey on that frigid February afternoon. Apparently, his ESPN broadcasts nationally. "Hi Dad. I'm just getting ready to unload the car," I answered the phone, my breath hanging in foggy clouds in the salty chilly air.

"Hey!" he sputtered, "Jerry Springer just called. He said 'thanks for the great material!'" and burst into laughter so loud he was scaring the seagulls.

"Very funny," I deadpanned to his giggling, hooting, and hollering. But, he was right. If my life was a reality show, right now *The Worst News Ever* would be headlining on Jerry Springer. Honestly, I like the ESPN channel better. (*Sorry, Jerry*)

I had cried intermittently the entire five hundred miles from my driveway to the beach, alternately joyful that I was on my way to the beach to write, and then flipping again to feeling miserable, wiping my tears while adjusting the windshield wipers. *The Worst News Ever* hung over my car like a purple storm cloud persistently following me from Ohio to the Jersey shore.

Dad had been suggesting for some time that I go away and devote myself to the book, offering to put me up in a hotel or the cabin for a week or two so I could focus. I had resisted the temptation up to now only because of the responsibilities that glued me to Ohio. But, after learning of *The Worst News Ever*, I ran.

I knew I had to get away, let things develop on their own at home without my help or intervention, and I had eagerly accepted his offer, upping the ante from two weeks to a five-week sabbatical in Ocean City, our family's favorite Hometown Beach. I'll be honest, though, my intention was as much to hide from the world as it was to write, and I was eternally grateful I could combine them both in one exercise.

Considering the fact that I was a first-time, as yet unpublished author, I was still breathlessly waiting for my million-dollar advance to travel around the world for a year and write a book about what I experienced. Come to think of it, I was also still waiting for my Brazilian businessman/lover to sweep me off my feet and sail me away in his yacht, and I kept looking for him in the bottom of every Crackerjack box.

It would have been a truly divine experience to deposit a bloated check with lots of zeroes before retreating to write Dad's book on the beach, but let's be honest, I was no Elizabeth Gilbert and this was no *Eat. Pray. Love.* This was me, an imposter, and my reality ran along the lines of Eat. Cry. Cry Some More.

Really, who has time to travel around the world for a year anyway, what with soccer and everything else on the Mom Schedule? And honestly, Liz, Bali and India may be nice, but you haven't truly lived until you've scraped baby poop from under your fingernails and *were happy to do it!*

I had exactly five weeks' *Zip Time* to be as productive as possible during this trip, and I wasn't going to squander a moment, making full use of the *Zip Time Zone Change*. I deliberately pushed aside the commercials for *The Worst News Ever Show* and saved them to replay on solo walks on the beach, which I planned to do as soon as I unloaded the car and picked up supplies.

After stopping for groceries at the Acme, I headed to Hoy's Five and Dime to stock up on little postcards and small gifts I planned to mail home to Gage every single day.

My first eleven days were spent in near isolation, with only daily trips to WaWa for newspapers, and the Post Office to mail a postcard, letter or small package, providing my only adult conversation, brief as it was. The postal clerk smiled at me and offered, "I know your name because you're in here every day, but by the way you fill out the return address on your packages to your little boy, I just want to call you *Mom*." I laughed with him.

Every day was exactly the same: After breakfast and coffee, I headed out for a walk on the beach north, then came back to write. At the end of the day, I repeated my walk, this time heading toward the south end of the island. Some days were brilliantly sunny, though freezing, and other days were windy and rainy and even more freezing. Bundling up in galoshes, parka, scarf, and hat, I adjusted my iPod and bravely faced the weather, sometimes head-on for those walks.

Ocean City has about 20,000 year-round residents, which swells to 150,000 on busy holiday weekends. These days, it didn't even seem as if the residents were in residence. It was utterly deserted, a scene I had never encountered in all my years of visiting the island. I was in Ocean City for days before I even saw another person on the beach in either direction, and it suited me just fine, thank you very much.

By day, I organized Dad's material and wrote page after page of text outlining his history, *The Preacher's* words, and family miracles. I described settings and wrote family member descriptions. But, on those long walks on the beach, I instead let my imagination float to every book I had ever read and loved, and wistfully wondered if it was in me to write something half as good. Seriously, every morning newspaper I read lately featured articles that suddenly seemed profoundly Pulitzer to my first time author status.

From the time I picked up my first book, *Are You My Mother?*, I have relentlessly devoured any and all reading materials, scarfing down newspapers and periodicals, business magazines and trade journals, gorging myself on novels and biographies, and consequently filling my home bookshelves ten times over. I will read absolutely anything put in front of me, and have been known, in a literary crunch, to studiously devour the side of a cereal box.

A literary snob I am not, preferring to learn instead from ev-ery-th-ing, not just what others deem appropriate or acceptable, hence my addiction to crime mysteries, beach books and trashy cheesy novels featuring strong heroines.

About five years ago, on a two-week driving tour through California, I came across the Scripps Research Institute outside La Jolla that was being described in the beach book I was reading at that same moment. What are the odds of that happening? I thought. Then it happened again. On a trip through Boston, I read for the first time in another crime and mystery novel what a "duck boat" was and looked up from my book to see a "duck boat" with my very own eyes. I've never seen another one since. What are the odds of that happening *twice*? I wondered. I believe you can learn from *eve-ry-thing*.

I want to write books like that, I thought. I want to research an area (like Greece, and Barcelona, and the beach!) and describe the scenery in compelling details. Wouldn't it be great if I could create a storyline out of thin air, craft a cast of characters from scratch, and watch them develop on paper? I want to see something grow from nothing but an idea, an inspiration, or an epiphany.

I *Zipped* back to the *time* when I had excitedly purchased *The Shining* in paperback, eager to devour it while soaking up the sun by the backyard pool. In chapter after chapter I read about the isolation of the deserted hotel in the frozen wilderness. I grew alarmed reading about the building anxiety of the dad as he roamed about the mysterious hotel mumbling, growing crazier by the page. I cringed when I deciphered the mirrored REDRUM and fearfully kept reading, frightened of the scene that threatened to leap off the next page.

I shivered as I read of the mom and son's escape from their deadly hotel/prison out the upstairs bathroom window, sliding down the frozen ice-encrusted roof, and then running for their lives through the barren wintry landscape. I had goosebumps from fear and was shivering from the icy cold described in the climax, even though the thermometer in the real world was surpassing ninety-four degrees, and the bright sunlight was causing me to squint to read the words.

I want to write books like that! I thought fiercely. Books that make you *feel* things. Wouldn't it be great if I could I do that? I wondered. Could I write a *really* good story that caused the reader to *feel* things? I honestly didn't know. I was relatively certain I could quickly draw up a mighty fine contract or a resume, but a *book*? Who knew? I sure didn't. I asked Dad that very question the next morning when he called.

"Do you think I can write a good story, one that makes you *feel* things?" I asked tentatively and hopefully.

"I don't know, but I know you can *tell* a great story. Did you forget you hold the award for Best Ghost Story Ever with my grandsons?" he asked, laughing, immediately stirring my memory of the night the kids had camped out in the tent in our backyard, and after surprising them by making them move over and make room so I could join them, I gave in to their begging and made up a ghost story.

"But *they* made that story up!" I exclaimed, and it was hilariously true. I started the ghost story with a setting of a haunted house (ours) and six little cousins (them) that had brazenly dared to enter through the creaky, creepy front door. From that moment on, every time I hit a roadblock in the story, I would turn to the kids and ask, "So what do you think happened next?"

The kids would venture a few scenarios, and I would just pick one and run with it.

"That's exactly right! That's exactly what happened!" I would exclaim, clapping my hands, and then I would embellish.

"Joseph opened the bedroom door and everywhere you looked it was sky, and beyond that, outer space!" I would laugh and continue on, noting their large round eyes and mesmerized stares, inserting their ideas at every juncture, making them all heroes after a bone-chilling climax that involved spaceships and oversized spiders. I laughed with Dad at the memory, but since I couldn't take any of the credit for The Best Ghost Story Ever, I couldn't exactly take consolation in it, either.

After eleven days of solid beach isolation therapy, I was ready to venture out to the rest of the island, and from the moment I started driving north on Asbury toward the downtown and boardwalk, déjà vu engulfed me and didn't leave me until I crossed the bridge to the mainland for home.

Ocean City, fondly referred to in our family as our "Hometown Beach," is a quaint island of colorful cottage style beach houses and rentals lining its "village-feel" streets. Situated in South Jersey, twenty minutes south of Atlantic City, and only an hour and a half from Philadelphia, my parents had adopted the Jersey shore as our vacation destination of choice long before I was born. From the time I was a toddler, my parents would stuff the VW Beetle with all of our gear and head to the shore for a weekend of camping (all we could afford at the time) in Sea Isle City or Avalon, in campgrounds a nine-minute drive from the beach.

For a few years before Tawni was born, we rented a motel room in Brigantine, another island north of Ocean City, and Sandi and I would play in the surf and search for shells with Mom and Dad near the pier. Perched perilously on the end of the ancient fishing pier stood The Brigantine Castle, a monstrous imposing four-story creepy haunted house made entirely of weathered wood that both thrilled and terrified Sandi and me as it beckoned us to wind our way through its maze of scary castle rooms.

We were enthralled with the horror potential, and we both pleaded tearfully and relentlessly with our parents to take us to the Brigantine

Castle until finally we wore them down. Come to think of it, Dad is *always* up for something fun, so I think we might have been had.

Four of us walked into the castle that terrifying night, but only two of us walked out. That's because as soon as we reached "The Rat Room" a pitch-dark corridor with the screeching sounds of mice and rats blasting from the tinny speakers, and started to feel our way blindly through the black hallway, the fake rat tails sticking out from the walls, which we couldn't *see*, but could *feel*, began to poke us and brush up against our ankles and legs.

Sandi and I stood frozen to the spot screaming bloody murder while Mom and Dad were forced to carry us both through the rest of the haunted house whimpering. We laugh about the memory now, but we never did ask to go there again. Oddly, we were both saddened several years later when the Brigantine Castle burned down and fell into the sea.

Year after year, we would creep closer and closer to the beach (as the family finances fluctuated between sometimes having a little extra, or sometimes, a little less), graduating from a deep-discount room at the White Deer Motel in Marmora, over the bridge, to finally renting a motel room right on the island of Ocean City. We promptly adopted this quaint island beach town as our own, visiting over and over again, and Ocean City generously reciprocated by providing us with oodles and oodles of happily delicious memories.

We enjoyed breakfast at Flanderers on the boardwalk, and picked up Mallon's cinnamon buns (Author's note: Go early, they sell out quickly) for Sunday mornings. We devoured Mack & Manco's award-winning pizza *all the time*, Mack's being the only pizza to rival the world-renowned Grimaldi's in Brooklyn. And then, we happily stocked up on nightly family game-time supplies including Johnson's famous caramel popcorn, Steel's mouth-watering fudge, and Fralinger's sticky sweet salt water taffy.

Yesterday's, directly over the 34th Street bridge, was quickly deemed our dinner venue of choice, with their freshly steamed clams, pierogies, and eclectic mix of music, locals, and weekend residents known as "shoebies" like us. Ocean City being a dry, family town, Yesterday's is also the closest place to the island to purchase alcohol, a fact that would years later become a vital *puzzle piece* of my mind when I retreated to the beach for my sabbatical writing.

My sisters and I would spend endless sunny hours playing paddleball on the beach, while Mom read a book on the beach blanket. As teenagers, Sandi and I modified the rules a teensy bit to now compete for *"Boy Points."* If a boy ran after one of our missed balls, it was a point. If two boys scurried after one of our balls, heading dangerously for the surf, then it was a double! We laughed and laughed until we were in danger of wetting our bikinis, with Mom looking up from her book and smiling at our teenage hormonal creativity.

When we eventually tired of watching boys run heroically around the beach, we would join Mom on the blanket to read books, eventually dozing to the happy background noises of Tawni singing while digging happily in the sand, kids playing and giggling, distant radios playing, an energetic volleyball game, random conversations, laughter, and the soothing surf sounds lulling us into a restful and peaceful nap.

Together, we would take long leisurely walks up the beach searching for shells, heading north with the skyline of Atlantic City in the hazy distance, Mom and Dad consistently and sincerely reminding us of our good fortune to be enjoying time together as a family at the ocean, and they would graciously and verbally give thanks for eve-ry-thing. *Thank you, God.*

Later, as we walked the boardwalk, with the seagulls greedily chasing our dropped french fries, our praises turned into playing the fun little game we as a family like to call *"Wouldn't it be great if...?"* Playing the *"Wouldn't it be great if...?"* game is much like playing the *"How will I spend my money when I win the lottery?"* game, only apparently with better odds of winning.

We would take turns filling in the blank with wishes like, "Wouldn't it be great if we could stay here at the beach for a whole week instead of just the weekend?" during the times we only had enough finances to fund a quick trip. And then, years later, a Miracle happened, we saved up and then *did* have enough money for a whole week at the beach! *It was a miracle! Thank you, God.*

"Wouldn't it be great if we could afford to rent a house right on the beach at the south end of the island?" somebody asked. The south end of the island was our favorite neighborhood, with only three blocks separating the ocean from the bay, and delightfully plastered with colorful and architecturally appealing homes. Then, one day, another miracle happened, we pooled our resources and *together*, we could afford it. *It was a miracle. Thank you, God.*

"Wouldn't it be great if we could live at the beach for an entire summer?" somebody else asked. Another miracle. When Tawni was a teenager, and Sandi home from college for the summer, Mom bought a little home in Bayberry Cove over the bridge in Marmora, and my sisters both lived with Mom at the beach for two whole summers – Sandi and Tawni's already tanned bodies darkening to ebony working as lifeguards at Bayberry's pool and lake those summers, and I was insanely jealous. Still am, a little bit. *It was a miracle. Thank you, God.*

And every single time another miracle happened, we repeated the joyful tradition of heaping praises onto God for ev-ery-th-ing. Mom and Dad never let us forget that living joyfully in the moment, appreciating ev-ery-th-ing you have, means you have to *live joyfully in the moment appreciating ev-ery-th-ing you have*. We were continually uttering praises of thanks, echoing their gratitude and adding to it with our own. And, then we would happily play another round of *"Wouldn't it be great if…?"*

As my sisters and I grew older and began to multiply, our whole family would often travel and meet up in Ocean City, sharing a beach house for a week of fun, sun, and more fun. We have been bringing our kids to Ocean City since they were born, and they wasted no time racking up boatloads of their own happy memories.

Like the year the cousins all paddled out into the Atlantic on their surf boards only to discover that the water was chock full of jellyfish, so they hysterically spent the next hour giggling while paddling back to shore with only their fingertips in the water. I think the fact that these kids cared enough to bank their happy memories for the future contributed to their strong mental health.

Then we continued the yearly tradition of digging a hole to China in the sand. Two separate teams would dig furiously on their respective holes all day, building reinforcements out of sand on the tide-side of the hole. Even the adults got in on the action, providing most of the heavy lifting. The winner was the team whose hole was breached last by the incoming high tide.

Or, the year that teenage Tyler spent four days ogling the cute college girls that were staying in the beach house next door to our family before announcing one day to the room, "Here's the deal. If I can get five dollars from each one of you, I will go next door and ask one of those girls to kiss me, *and* (he paused for dramatic effect) I'll get a picture of it!" he finished triumphantly, holding up his disposable camera. We all burst out laughing and Dad was the first to eagerly jump on board accepting Tyler's offer.

"I'm in. Here's five dollars, buddy," he said, laughing and reaching into his pocket to hand over the cash.

In all, Tyler collected twenty-five dollars in Lincoln's from us, but we got the better end of the deal because the priceless Kodak moment of a blushing Tyler being kissed by that flattered and graciously obliging cute college girl still hangs in our living room today. Now, that's the way to earn spending money, I thought cheerfully.

And, those kids spent their money like it's going out of style, I laughed to myself, Ocean City providing an endless array of "Shoppertunities" to cheerfully separate the kids from their spending money. They happily spent hours (when we would let them) examining every single knick-knack in Hoy's Five and Dime store on 34th and West. Crammed to the rafters with every imaginable beach chair, t-shirt, toiletry, kite, and beach toy ever invented, they scrutinized *every* single item, painstakingly deliberating its merits before finally reaching a decision.

Then, they happily carted their purchases home, and delighted in them for approximately nine minutes before begging to go to the boardwalk for even more creative ways to spend their hard-earned vacation cash. They ran from Jilly's Arcade to Kohr's Frozen Custard, from the boardwalk mall to the mini golf course. They religiously shopped in *every single* t-shirt and gift shop, and joyfully purchased tickets to Gillian's Wonderland Pier at the end of the boardwalk. Or, wait a minute, maybe that was me who did those things. I smiled and wondered if *Zip Time* was scrambling my memories, intermixing mine with my kids'.

I love this town, I thought. I love that my parents introduced my sisters and me to this quaint city, and I love that we all bring our kids here. I love that they are as fiercely devoted to the charming island as I am, as my parents were, and I easily imagined how our future fourth generation of kids would be on their inaugural tour of Ocean City.

Some *Zip Times*, we would travel off the island for even more family entertainment, heading south to the Wildwood boardwalk, dancing to Jerry Blabbitt at *Memories* in nearby Margate, catching a late comedy show at *Comedy Stop at the Trop*, or visiting the casinos on the boardwalk in Atlantic City. Zipping back five years to celebrate Mom's, birthday after she had "moved," Sandi and I drove out to Allentown and then continued on to Atlantic City with Dad, Tawni, and Ron. As we were cruise-controlling down the Atlantic City Expressway, Dad laid out the ground rules for the Gladstone Family Pledge.

To fully understand The Gladstone Family Pledge, you need to first understand Gladstone. Gladstone Gander was the cousin (uncle?) of Donald Duck, and his claim to fame was that he was "the luckiest duck in the world." Gladstone Gander didn't have to work, because he had the unfailing ability to just turn a corner and find a winning lottery ticket in the gutter.

Dad so fiercely believed in the Great Luck qualities of Gladstone, that he seriously offered me $10,000 to name Tyler "Gladstone" while Tyler was still in utero awaiting his entry into the world. Dad even went so far as to bring the money to the hospital *in cash* not even an hour after we met Tyler for the first time. Mom was aghast, and although I was tempted for a moment, I seriously couldn't see saddling a kid, any kid, MY kid, with a name like Gladstone. Think of the schoolyard bullies! So, I went for second best.

"Do I still get the money if I use Gladstone as his *middle* name?" I asked expectantly and not a little woozy from having just given birth.

"Negative," Dad answered firmly, reverting to Pilot-Speak, dashing my hopes of an instant college fund for my newborn.

Funny thing is, even though Gladstone doesn't show up on Tyler's birth certificate or passport, he is still an amazingly lucky kid, a Gladstone by default. Like the time he was hit by a car riding his bike to school, and walked away with barely a scratch. On the drive to the hospital to get checked out, he confided, "Mom, I always wondered what it would feel like to get hit by a car."

I kept my eyes glued to the road, replying dryly, "Tyler, please don't tell me you've ever wondered what it would feel like to get hit by a bus," and we both laughed. *It was a miracle. Thank you, God.*

Unlike my padre or offspring, Gladstone Gander of comic book lore had an exasperating quality – he was stingy and lazy, knowing it full well, and exploiting it everywhere that he did not have to do *anything* in life, yet good fortune would still always come magically his way. But, Dad isn't a duck, so instead of hoarding his good luck, he *gives it away.* That's right. Dad firmly believes that he *receives* his good luck for the sake of *sharing* it with others. He believes that the fastest way to create happiness for yourself is to create it for others first, and he also believes he has been blessed with great luck, which he happily and enthusiastically *shares* with eve-ry-one.

So, it is a common sight to see Dad in the elevator on the way down to the casino, or at the slot machines, handing out Gladstone stickers to random passersby, and telling them, "I'm the luckiest guy around, and I share that great luck with others. Here, now you have it too. Great luck to you, tonight," he concludes happily, wishing them well.

The amazing thing to me is that people *love* it and *believe* it! Who doesn't want to be told they have just been gifted great luck on their way into a casino? But, Dad is careful to never use the word gambling in his Gladstone Gifting.

"Why would you want to go in and gamble?" he asks logically, and then explains.

"With gambling, only three things can happen: you could win; you could lose; or you could break even. Walk into that casino *believing* that you have already won, and now you're just going in there to *collect* your money!"

"Repeat after me," he shares enthusiastically, "I am a member of the Gladstone Family. All my good luck is tripled, and all my bad luck is behind me. So shall it be." People respond to his enthusiasm and his unfailing belief in equal measure; it is truly fun to watch him in action.

Now, there's a little twist to The Gladstone Pledge, and it is The Numbers Game. Not numbers, like *Dialing For Dollars*, or counting cards, or anything like that, but, as in the numbers of people who are gathered together with the same purpose in mind. The power of numbers transcends traditional arithmetic, multiplying exponentially with each person added to the same focused equation.

On this weekend, for instance, the five of us were gathered together to celebrate Mom's memory and have fun, sharing with others along the way. *The Preacher* explains it this way:

> *The Power of One person to co-create their*
> *own reality is in itself, phenomenal.*
>
> *"So God created man in his own image."*
> *– Gen 1:27*
>
> *But the Power of Two who come together to*
> *create is exponential.*
>
> *"For where two or more come together in*
> *My Name, there I am with them."*
> *– Matthew 18:20*

"It's the new math! *One plus one equals three,*" Dad giggles. "It's the same concept in business. You, by yourself can only *do* so much. But, when you add other people to the equation, who are all focused on the same purpose, the growth is exponential!" he stated logically, and then leaned forward with a gleam in his eye. "It's the exact same principle as with the loaves and fishes, or creating a baby. Imagine you want to make a baby with your husband," he offers, explaining with a wink. "Both of you come together with a common purpose. Add God into that equation and Presto! Nine months later, you have produced a giggling, burping, pooping, bouncing baby!" He giggled. "One plus one equals three!" he concludes happily.

On this particular weekend, we had *five* people with a common purpose. The exponential possibilites gave me Googlebumps. The Gladstone Family Pledge was an oath the five of us took to share any and all winnings over five hundred bucks that we received throughout the weekend with each other in equal measure. No matter who won or who lost, we would split it.

From the moment we checked into the *Borgata*, we felt Mom with us, blinking room lights mysteriously on and off around us, as if her energy was delighted that we were dedicating a weekend of fun together in her memory, and it was too much for the wires in the room to handle, so the lights sparkled on and off repeatedly that weekend as I hummed to myself, Do-Do-Do-Do.

We set off for the casino with Dad joyfully and generously handing out Gladstone stickers as we walked along, waiting for the winning machines to call our names and playful Mom making weird things happen around us, like the Wheel of Fortune slot machine suddenly going on the blink. And, Dad enthusiastically shared The Gladstone Pledge with eve-ry-one he encountered. By the *Zip Time* Sandi grew tired and headed up to our room for some Ben & Jerry's TV Therapy, we had won over $4,000. But, the electric Mom feeling was still in the air, so the rest of us stayed in the casino.

Two *Zip Hours* later, we giddily burst into Sandi's room and threw another pile of cash onto her bed, watching hysterically as she laid comfortably reclining, with her feet up on a pillow, Ben & Jerry's spoon dangling in awe from her lips.

Then, it was my turn to grow tired and head to the room, but before I could even brush my teeth, Tawni, Ron, and Dad were back giggling deliriously with even more winnings – Tawni had won a $5,000 Wheel of Fortune Jackpot.

In all, we won over $14,000 that weekend, and true to our

Gladstone Pledge, we split it equally among us. Wow, I thought dreamily. Wouldn't it be great to celebrate Mom's birthday with her *every year*?

Thinking back to those fond, fun-filled memories, I was suddenly reminded of the loneliness of my beach isolation. I hopped on my *Zip Board* back to the present beach house, where I was cheerfully writing on the deck, and looking forward to Sandi driving out with the kids for a long weekend to break up the silence. The cousins enjoyed the beach and boardwalk while I kept writing outside in my fingerless mittens, and when they came back to the beach house later that day, laden with souvenirs from their boardwalk "shoppertunity," I noticed Mitchell staring for an inordinate amount of time at a photo of Gage that I had brought from home and had placed on the hall table.

"What's up, kiddo?" I asked, walking over to stand with him to look at Gage's picture.

"The kid in the picture," Mitch sounded worried and he looked over at me perplexed, "Look," he said pointing, "the kid in that picture looks *exactly* like Gage." He whispered, sounding spooked.

"Cutie, that *is Gage*," I laughed.

He looked at me obviously relieved, "It is?"

"Yeah, I brought that photo from home."

"Oh. I thought that picture belonged to the owner of the beach house, and I thought Gage had a double." I laughed with him.

"No, there's only one Gage, and I brought him from home." I laughed again, lessening his anxiety.

On their last night in town, Sandi and I shared memories, laughter, potato skins, pierogies, and Corona (Sandi doesn't drink alcohol, so I drank a Corona for her) at Yesterday's, just over the bridge. The next morning, they packed up to head home to Ohio via Allentown for another quick peek at Mia.

"Whose *Axe* deodorant is this?" I questioned my nephews, holding the bathroom product up in the air for somebody to claim, as they got ready to load the car with their numerous suitcases and backpacks.

"Oh, that's mine," Mitchell answered, "We used it to get the stink off the dead horseshoe crab we found on the beach."

Ewwwww. Then Sandi's minivan packed with kids and gear was gone, and I was alone again with the manuscript.

On another weekend, Dad car-pooled to the beach house with four of his good friends (and dancing party-animals) for a weekend of boardwalking by day and dancing by night at the casino dance clubs in nearby Atlantic City.

"Are you going dancing with us?" Dad asked expectantly, knowing that the last ninety-nine times of a hundred he had posed the same question, I had said yes.

"No, I have a date," I answered not daring to look up from my manuscript, knowing the response my words would illicit, and I was right.

"*What?*" Five people asked simultaneously and in varying stages of incredulity.

"What?" I answered innocently back in two drawn-out syllables, flopping my hands out in surrender, struggling to keep the laughter from erupting as I let their concerns frenzy around me, knowing it was coming, but letting it flow right through me.

"A date with *whom?* Where did you meet him? What's his name? What does he do? Are you sure about this? What happens when you go home to Ohio? What is your intention? Where are you going with this?"

"My intention?" I asked, barely suppressing giggles. Honestly, their questions made me feel like I was sixteen and I was lovin' it! It was like Mom, only five of her.

"Look. I know I haven't dated in over five years, but I met this guy, he's a nice guy, and we have a nice time together. We both know and accept that I have an *expiration date* when I go home to Ohio and nobody has any expectations beyond that."

"My intention is to just enjoy each other's company in the meantime, until the *expiration date*." I concluded confidently while my five newly adopted mother/father hens clucked around me protectively. I love my life, and I love my Dad's friends, I thought proudly. I don't want to change a thing.

Zippity Do Dah Time. "Uh-oh, it's ten to five in the morning!" my date exclaimed as my heart started racing.

"Oh, my God, I am so busted!" I blurted, feeling the adrenaline rush of being sixteen, missing curfew and conjuring up weird visions of chickens clucking around a baby chick.

He drove me the six blocks home, both of us quiet until we pulled up to the curb of the beach house and he asked hesitantly, "So, can I see you again tonight?"

"I don't know," I answered honestly, "I might be grounded." We both laughed as I hopped out of the car and ran up the steps, sneaking back to my bedroom to catch a few hours of shut-eye before the early morning games.

"You got in *after us* last night," My Dad's good friend Jake threw out the opening pitch while walking down the hall only moments after waking, judging by his bed head. I nodded, accepting my fate. And so my treacherous trail down the morning gauntlet of mother/father hens, otherwise known as Dad's four friends, began. Luckily for me, I got up early and made coffee.

"You go, girl." Boasted Felicia, Massage Therapist, the second hen.

Base Hit.

"Did you have a good time last night, sweetie?" Asked Jane, school board member, with a wink.

"W*ait*! Let me get a picture of the *morning after*!" playfully mocked Kathryn, newspaper photographer.

It's a Triple! The crowd roars!

So it continued until the ninth inning when Dad pulled out all the stops, "You know you forgot your phone last night. I thought it was mine on the kitchen counter, and when I slid the bar over, up popped all these messages and I blushed."

He added hysterically, "That phone was so hot, it didn't even need to be plugged into the wall to charge the battery!" He laughed uproariously, as did the peanut gallery.

"*What?*" I squealed, "You read my *Sext* messages?" OMG! I was instantly mortified and immediately grabbed for my phone to check last night's incriminating evidence, feeling like a teenage criminal caught with my pants down.

"Oh, don't worry about erasing them," Dad laughed out loud. "I already posted them to your FaceBook page," He finished with a side-holding, face-reddening, cringe-inducing guffaw that threatened to send the hermit crabs scurrying back under the sand, and I longed to join them.

Foul Ball!

Oh...My...God...I just wanna die, I thought. After some time, when the hens had cleared the henhouse, and Dad and I were alone on the deck, I said gratefully, "Dad, I'm glad I can laugh with you like this. Thank you."

"Hey, the way I look at it, you're forty years old (*Author's note: I'm older than that, but who's counting besides Sandi?*), have two kids, and own your own business. As far as I'm concerned, you can stay out as late as you want." He laughed, making me feel still sixteen, but utterly loved and accepted. "Besides, *thank you!*" he started chuckling and that should have been my first clue.

Bases loaded. Here's the pitch.

"Thank you for what?" I asked breathlessly blonde, Polish, and clueless, salt and sand clogging my ESPN reception.

"For the great material, of course! He burst out, "We're gonna laugh about this for *years!*" He laughed alone maniacally on the deck, while I blushed, smiled flatly, and then left to bundle up for a walk on the beach.

Home Run! The crowd goes wild.
Thank you, God.

My friend, Jack, called the next week, bringing me up to date on the status of the non-profit on which we both serve, and I brought him up to date with my progress on the book, then confided, "I had a date. Are you shocked?"

"Good for you, you should date," he replied instantly, and then turned serious for just a moment, "So, did you learn anything during your sabbatical?"

"Yeah. I learned there are a million fish in the sea," I answered, laughing.

He returned with his powerful, booming, and infectious laugh and countered, "Honey, let me tell you something. Men are like busses. Just go stand out on the corner and another one will come by *every* hour." I laughed with him and he ended the call with, "Now, hurry up and get home."

I laughed as I disconnected and prepared to get back to work, considering my friend's words, because although it was nice to go on a date, I honestly possessed no desire whatsoever to meet any more busses or fish. The way I looked at it was this: The only common denominator in both my failed marriages was, well, *me*. I was in no hurry to seek out any relationship that didn't already exist inside my carefully constructed hermit shell. I had already mucked things up enough in that department, I reasoned.

I put all my feelings regarding relationships on my mental back burner and got back to work. All the material is here, I realized gratefully, as I sat down at the table to review my progress. All of Dad's history, from where he was born, to where he went to school, to the businesses he opened, all the way up to his present day public speaking role. All the details, facts, and humorous family stories were here, too, neatly organized into ten units or chapters that would take the reader through Dad's step-by-step, boots-on-the-ground process for co-creating your own reality.

But, every time I read what I had already written for the manuscript, I cried. This wasn't a story that I want to read by the pool or on a beach blanket, I thought miserably, this was a *seminar*. This book didn't give me goosebumps – it gave me boring bumps. This was a book I wanted to burn in the fireplace.

So, I set out to craft a plot to wrap up all of Dad's philosophies into a story. I attempted a few pages of text creating scenes where a reporter was interviewing Dad about his life, but there was no *oomph*, so I started over. Then I began a section that read like a bedtime story that I could read to my kids, but since I didn't *really* want to write a book that puts people to sleep, I started over.

The story I started with Dad as Mayor Gladstone of a fictional town held promise for a little while, but when I introduced *The Preacher*, he came across on paper as a homeless crazy person, so I started over. The adventure story wasn't much better, I thought miserably, considering that I wasn't Ian Fleming, and Dad wasn't 007.

Dad's dancing form suddenly jumped from my imagination to the living room floor singing, *"I think I better think it out again."*

He continued to dance, happily humming the tune sung by Fagen in Oliver, until I dragged myself back to Real Life.

Everything I wrote was as stale as last week's Mack & Manco's pizza, wholly without flair or pizzazz. I didn't want to write a dry boring textbook that makes unsupportable claims and preaches to the choir, I thought shakily, but that was exactly what I seemed to be producing and I was scared shitless. My writing lacked personality; reading it sounded like a "how-to" book, like *Life for Dummies*, only not as funny.

Too bad those thousands of PowerPoints and standard operating procedures I've written over the years couldn't somehow converge and become a book, I thought, because everything I was cranking out now was about as titillating as a legal contract.

Eat. Pray. Love? Not for me, it was only Eat. Pray. And Pray some more. But I kept at it, writing on the deck, or at the kitchen table, from morning to evening. Every once in a while, I would read back over what I wrote and be pleasantly surprised at a clever phrase or creative play on words. Wow, I would think, who wrote *that*? *Thank you, God.*

I thought about every book I had ever read and considered riffing off their plot lines. I remembered the Neale Donald Walsch's book, *Conversations With God.* Wouldn't it be great if I could write a *Conversations With Dad*? Nah.

I considered the amazing book I read last summer on my Kindle, *The Help*, by Kathryn Stockett, and wondered if I could write a book whose subplot is well, *writing a book*. Nah, already been done.

Then I suddenly remembered that practically every benefit our company has offered to our employees over the past eleven years had been unceremoniously borrowed from a famous dot.com or blue-chip Fortune 500. Zipping back in time, I would read in my business journals with growing envy of those perks and bennies that those billion dollar companies would lavish on their employees, and think, *wouldn't it be great if* we could do that too, despite being a mom and pop shop? Wait a minute, why can't we?

We ignored the dictum that states you must have over 1,000 employees housed on a multi-million dollar campus in order to treat them like valued members of the family. Instead, relying on the DNA and environment provided by Dad and his Fun Workplace, we set out to *spoil nurses silly* with programs that included free roadside assistance if their car broke down on the way to work, Daily Instant Pay to a PayCard, and Free PayDay Loan Advances, thwarting the *loan sharks* in the payday lending traps.

After Gage had starting ordering our beloved nanny, Linda, around the house, making full use of his newly acquired toddler authority, we hired Ashley, a certified preschool teacher, and installed an on-site preschool in the third-floor attic for our office and field staff. We only had five kids upstairs, but the joyful noises of the preschool would float downstairs while we were working and it felt like a zillion bucks to be able to experience it on a daily basis. It was even better than working at home because now there were more of us to enjoy it. Eventually, all the kids grew older and graduated from the preschool to real school. We leaked sentimental tears as they headed off to kindergarten on their first bus ride ever, but remained resolutely *thankful* that we were able to enjoy our time working/playing/living while it lasted.

Once a month, we host an Open House party for employees and clients, (really, the whole town is invited) with tons of food, usually set to a holiday theme like Mardi Gras, or our Thanksgiving Feast or the Christmas Celebration complete with Santa Claus and gifts for kids who visit. We even celebrate Halloween, the divisive issue, the pagan holiday, the non-PC celebration. But, we give it our own twist, re-naming it "No Tricks, Only Treats" complete with free treats to every person (kids and moms included) who visit each office's desk.

It would often hurt my feelings how professionals in the business community looked down on employees of staffing companies, derisively referring to a long-term employee as a "temp," the four-letter word in our office that nobody is allowed to say, and I wanted to shout out loud, "These aren't *temps*, these are *people!*" I wanted to tell eve-ry-one that it wasn't like they thought. Do you even *know* these people? I would think incredulously.

I *knew* these employees like they were members of my own family, watching their kids grow up over my head these past eleven years (not a difficult feat, really), and hugging them or holding their hands when life came at them too fast. I watched them drag themselves to work while their loved ones were sick, or worse, dying. I watched them live paycheck to paycheck and yet painstakingly whittle down a wage garnishment, then drive cautiously through five inches of Ohio snow to get to the nursing home on time in order to provide compassionate care for the elderly. I *love* these people!

The first page of our employment application asks each applicant, "What is your American dream? What makes you go to work every day, besides paying your bills? What's holding you back from that dream?" And, do you know what? In all the years I've been asking those questions, the answers are amazingly similar: "I want to have a stable job so I can pay my bills on time. I want to own my own home. I want to save for my kid's education. I want to travel. I want to open my own business someday." What's holding them back? The Big Three: time, money, and responsibility. *They are me*, I thought resolutely.

For three years, to share our appreciation and show off our employees, we hosted *Agency Awards*, an Academy Awards style show complete with red-carpet and limo pictures. We hired the Junior Staff, (our employees' kids) as paparazzi to scream and beg for autographs from our staff, and cheerfully handed out Star Statues for numerous awards including Best RN and Best Hair Day. (Note to self: This is certainly one way to make nurses cry.)

We're not Microsoft. Our family business doesn't have a café on site, (we don't even have a kitchen!) but we *do* have an Otis Spunkmeyer cookie machine that bakes delicious cookies every morning in sixteen minutes flat, filling the floors of our home office with their mouth-watering gooey aroma. One of the favorite parts of my job is asking little kids who come into the office, "Hey, cutie, do you want a cookie?" and watching their smiles as I hand them a still-warm chocolate-chip confection. "Want another one for the other hand?" I always ask, and they always say yes.

We may not work in a GooglePlex, or own a company jet, or lavish stock options and checks with lots of zeroes on our CEO's, but we treat everyone like family, we care about them, and we have fun when and where we can. In our home, *everyone* is welcome, and *everyone* is family. *It is what it is. It is what you make it.*

For a moment, I felt a smidgen of guilt for stealing all those great benefit ideas from other companies before I remembered Ben Stiller and his newly founded non-profit charity whose mission statement includes "stealing all the great ideas of other charities," and I laughed out loud.

Feeling less guilty, but no closer to a plot solution, I plodded on, this time attempting a *Travel Guide Through Life* with Dad as the travel guide, but it still wasn't workin' for me, and I shivered, unsure whether it was from the cold or fear.

Dad came out that next weekend, and he sat at the kitchen table reading newspapers and magazines for most of the day while the sound of my fingers tapping the keyboard were drowned out by the storm currently pummeling the coast. It had been raining for days and the weather forecast held dire warnings of flooding and high winds overnight to allow the storm rushing in from offshore time to deliver her damage.

We sat together at the table later that evening with the rain battering against the glass doors to the deck, and even the blazing fireplace couldn't keep me from shivering. Dad looked up from my fourth or fifth attempt (who's counting?) at wrapping up his life history and philosophies into an actual plot that had a beginning, a middle, and an end – something that told, you know, *a story*.

"You know, Daughter, we don't *really need* a book," he commented gently. The gales of wind outside battering against the house sucked my breath away as it raged violently around us. Oh. My. God.

Dad continued softly while I died a little tiny bit inside with each truthful syllable, "We don't need a book because, honestly, it's the *speaking* that gets people excited." He was right. The book *sucked*.

I sat quietly, not trusting my voice, not trusting myself to even breathe. After some Zip Time, I asked quietly, "What about 'the platform'? The book is supposed to be a platform."

"Look, Daughter, I love my life. I don't want to change a thing. I don't want to travel around speaking." He smiled tenderly and added, "I love my life just the way it is, and I love you too, so don't worry about it."

I drew a shallow breath wondering, what am I doing? Why am I here in this beach house wasting Dad's time and money when he could have hired a ghost writer to whip out a book about his history and philosophies in six weeks' time. Who do I think I am?

Great. Add the book to the end of the long list of things I've mucked up in my life. Another dead-end that rides the fast-track to nowhere, another failure, another time I thought I *knew* something, but was unceremoniously and cruelly reminded by the "forces that be" that I was naively full of shit.

The storm continued to ravage our coastal city, and they were forced to close the only two bridges off the island by mid-evening due to severe flooding. I posted the island underwater crisis and bridge closing on Facebook, candidly omitting my failure in life as a writer, and my friend Jack responded, horrified, "The bridge to the *bar*????"

Same one, I thought to myself. Luckily I had stocked up yesterday, and rose from the kitchen table to open a bottle of Italian *vino*.

It was *that time*, I thought. time to lose myself in my favorite dark trilogy, *Wine. Whine. Why?*

Funny how drinking spirits can deplete your spirit. When both the bottle and my reserves were nearly empty, I went to bed praying not for wisdom or guidance, or even for strength, but for my alcohol induced drowsiness to hold steady so I could escape my devastating reality at least until morning.

The wind rocked the beach house all throughout that long night, shaking it violently while the shoreline crept ominously closer to the houses lining the dunes, threatening to test the strength of their moored pilings. The raging storm outside my room, combined with my dreams of ghosts milling about inside my room, prevented my pressed grape comatose calm, and I woke repeatedly.

I hugged Dad tight the next morning as he readied to depart for the drive home to Allentown, my dejection at having disappointing him *again* weighing heavily on my slumped, sleep deprived shoulders. "I love you, Dad, and I'm sorry."

"Don't be sorry. I love you too," he responded sincerely. "Just keep at it. Keep writing something every day. It will come to you."

What, the Apocalypse? I wondered. "Okay, I will Dad."

"*Will* is in the future. Be a writer *now*," he said playfully, and I envied his carefree spirit, but, was also eternally grateful he wasn't adding to my self-induced misery.

"Besides, you're living your dream, are you not? You're writing books at the beach!" he said happily, kissing my cheek, and after a few more bear hugs set off for home, navigating his way through the lingering half-flooded streets to the bridge, thankfully now open, and I set off for the beach.

I walked the sixteen blocks through the sand heading toward the fifty-ninth street beach, the sun shining brilliantly overhead in direct contrast to the storm's memory and my mood, reluctantly realizing that it is often darkest right before it turns pitch black. But, I bravely donned my shields and faced my fears head-on. I looked at my dread of Bear dying, who at sixteen years of age, had survived much longer than I had expected, but was failing quickly and gave it the name *Heartbreaking*.

Before I had left for the beach, I had held Bear's face in my hands, The Best Dog Ever, my third "child" who had been with me through two divorces and both my other kids growing up, and made her promise that she wouldn't leave us until I returned, and I swear she had tiredly nodded her assent.

Passing the gorgeous mansion on the 49th Street beach that boasts wrap-around porches, a widow's walk lookout tower on the roof, and jutted way out onto the sand was closer to the ocean than its neighbors, I quickly played a round of *"Wouldn't it be great if I could write books on the beach in a house like that?"* and then looked at my fear of writing the book and gave it the label Panic, then put that feeling on hold for a moment. Whew. I examined my plot problems and labeled them *Polish Cluelessness*. How could I write a book with a beginning, a middle, and an end, when Dad's story, our family's story, is ongoing? We're still living it! It's happening right at this moment all around me.

I was experiencing all of the cycles that Dad talks about on a daily basis and feeling all the positive and negative energies just like he described. Unfortunately for me, at this moment I was experiencing mostly negative energies, I thought as I walked along the shoreline, only two other people on the beach adding to my loneliness. Each step I took on the sand was another step further from the comfort of the beach house and another step further inside myself, further from the safety of my carefully constructed and faithfully maintained emotional boundaries.

Issue by issue, step by step, I peeked into every corner of my consciousness *Recognizing* what I felt, and *Expressing* each emotion by giving it a name. Then, I *Dismissed* them to the wind one scattered ash at a time.

I reached the end of the island, the ocean cutting inland at Corson's Inlet, where Dad had scattered Mom's ashes all those years ago, and turned for home.

It was that time again – time for another journey to face *The Worst News Ever*. It's time to look at what frightens me to death to *Recognize*, let alone *Express*. How many times have I walked this path along this shoreline? How many times have I cried my eyes out since learning the truth? How many times will I have to? As many times as it takes, I realized, and set off for the walk home. Please, God, I prayed, won't you at least meet me halfway?

I stood at the edge of the shore, the edge of the abyss, alert for the *Zip Tide* I sensed was lurking just below the surface. My shields are up. I'm ready for this, I thought. Bring it on.

The water at first holds nothing but suddenly
a ripple hints with the vast potential of eve-ry-thing.

I know nothing. Absolutely nothing.

The ripple grows into a swell.

Okay, there were some clues of the *The Worst News Ever*,
that the two of them were now together as a couple,
but I didn't want to believe it was true.

The swell grows, carves edges, it's a wave.

When did it start?
When did they first look at each other "that way"?
It's too terrifying even for *me* to imagine.

The wave swallows smaller waves, gathering force.

She's so young. We've both known her forever.

It has grown into an unstoppable tidal wave;
the entire ocean's power behind the wave that threatens
to overwhelm me and sweep me away.

Kissing? Having future kids? Push it down!
It's too far off my Jerry Springer Richter scale.
What kind of protection are shields against the ocean anyway?

The wave crashes onto shore,
sacrificing broken shells, or more, in its wake.
Woman loves Man. Man is best friends with Woman's Ex.
Woman's Ex sleeps with Man's nineteen-year old Daughter.
Man's Daughter sleeps with Woman's Son.
Woman can *NEVER* be with Man, *The Worst News Ever.*
Oh, my God. I feel so betrayed. By eve-ry-one.

The ocean recedes backward, falling into itself.
I am alone. Again.

The wave promptly joins another group of waves
on the same enthusiastic journey to shore.
I am not alone?

The waves conjoin, thrusting forth generations of gurgling,
giggling new waves to take their hastily abandoned places.
You were never alone.

The ocean disappears, swallowing
back into the wave, back into the drop.
I was never alone.

There was nothing left to do but cry, and I wanted to, really I did. But, there was *nothing* left inside of me to Rinse and Repeat. I was empty. There was just, well, nothing. All the ashes, remnants of my emotions, had been sacrificed to the waves. And then suddenly, in a miraculous moment, there was Eve-ry-thing. *Oh. My. God. Thank, you, God.*

I rushed for the beach house, fully expecting to see another set of footprints alongside mine as I raced for my laptop and frantically began to write down ev-ery-th-ing I could remember. It was already all there, floating along merrily in my imagination, and I just needed to write it down. All I needed to do was tell Dad's story, our family's story. And the *Zip Time* was *now*. I could see the light at the end of the tunnel, and this time, it *wasn't* a freight train.

When my expiration date arrived, and it was time, I said goodbye to Ocean City and drove home to Ohio by myself, but I wasn't really alone. The car was packed with every vibrant character from The Book, and everyone was talking at once. Their excited and passionate voices competed for my attention as I desperately attempted to focus on both their words and the road signs. *I was never alone.*

The scenery up the Atlantic City Expressway blurred with the scenes from Dad's colorful stories, and I missed my exit twice, precipitating two extra trips across the Ben Franklin Bridge in center city rush hour traffic in the City of Brotherly Love. It is what it is. *It is what you make it. It is bigger than all of us. One plus one equals three.*

The trip west on Route 80 was a study in *Zip Time Travel* ripe for the science textbooks. I visited every setting in each chapter, traveling timelessly from North Canton to Allentown, from Ocean City to the city dump, taking as much time as I needed to mentally record every detail, then sent my observations wirelessly over the ESPN network to my laptop.

I had enough *Zip Time* to converse endlessly with each character, chatting lazily over coffee, interviewing them on the deck, asking questions at our favorite restaurants, laughing at their jokes on vacation and noting their timeless wisdoms that appeared seemingly out of nowhere at *Just the Right Time. I was never alone.*

My job description at Dad, Inc. had been modified from *writer to typer.* Honestly, I do absolutely nothing but tap the keyboard while the book meanwhile seems to be miraculously writing itself, the words coming mysteriously and gratefully from *above and beyond.* I'm just along for the ride. What a fun ride this is, I thought as I pulled into the driveway. I love being a *writer/typer,* and, I love coming home. *Thank you, God.*

And then, just as Dad's friend Daisy predicted, it got even funner and funner as I squeezed Gage tight in a hug (I missed you so much, cutie!) and he froze, so I wrote it down. When he pleaded with me, eyes big and round, not four minutes after I stepped through the door (after being gone for five weeks!) to go to Benji's to play, I laughed and wrote it down. When I almost tripped over Bear lying in the center of the living room floor, I smiled, stepped gently over her, and wrote it down. When Tyler asked to borrow ten dollars because he was low on gas, I cheerfully handed over the cash and wrote it down.

When later that night I threw in a load of laundry because I needed clean clothes for work the next morning, and that little niggling feeling of responsibility started to grow, I pushed it down and wrote it down. When Dad called to check that I was home safely, he boasted that he had politely relayed the "my daughter missing her curfew" story to *every single one of his friends.* We laughed, and then I wrote it down.

When I got my late night text from Sandi that read, "Night Maw," I smiled, texted back "Night Paw," and wrote it down. Before I went to sleep every night, I remembered to "save as" that which is my internal programming, and when I awoke every morning, I instantly gave thanks to God for eve-ry-th-ing. While making coffee, I promptly rebooted my spiritual hard drive, eager to embrace another glorious day, and then, I wrote it down.

I handed out LightBuck$ like they were free (Oh wait, that's right, they are!), and happily watched my investment pay amazing returns with smiles, hugs, patience, and ongoing Zen, and I wrote it down. When sometimes, just for a moment, I forgot and handed out DarkBuck$ by forcefully closing cabinet doors, I immediately recognized the "*Sideways*" and wrote it down.

When I thought about calling Dad to check in with him, and instead his picture popped up on my iPhone with him calling me, I laughed out loud, and wrote it down.

The fun and productive being/living/writing days were multiplying exponentially while *Zip Time* slowed everything else to a crawl, opening the time portal I needed to repeatedly go to a scene, meet the characters for a tasty lunch, and record what I saw – and I wrote it all down. Every single day mirrored the last: Live. Life. Write. Over and over again. Every day it was the same thing, only this time, I was lovin' it!

After some *Zip Time* had passed, I found that when I struggled with wanting to remain nestled under the covers instead of hopping onto the treadmill, *again*, I grabbed my laptop and re-read Chapter Seven about Do. Did. Deed. Then I remembered that the only way to lose ten pounds is to get on the treadmill over and over again, day after day. When I found myself at the end of a long line at the bank drive-through, I re-read Dad's words about flying in Chapter Six, and remembered I could fly to my own Happy Place, the beach. When I reached a roadblock with the story, I promptly pulled up Chapter Three and made a plan (actually a to-do list), then I picked something, anything, off the list and *just did it*. When somebody hurt my feelings with a random put-down, intentional or not, I went back to Chapter Five and re-read Captain Kirk's instructions on how to properly engage my shields. When all the decisions in my life seemed to be being made *for me* instead of *by me* and I felt cornered, I dug out *The Preacher's* words and remembered that I'm the *CEO of My Own Life*, too.

When I found myself missing my mom, and wishing I could just call her and talk to her on the phone, I revisited Chapter Four and re-lived the radiantly soothing feeling of her holding me close, and then I happily chatted with her anyway, even though she communicates only through the ESPN channel. When I felt regret for something I had said, I re-read Chapter Four, *again*, so I could learn how to forgive *myself* after I've already apologized.

When things went wrong, as they sometimes will, and the road I was trudging seemed all uphill, and I was ready to give up my last vestige of hope, I picked up the book and read *everyone's* Miracles, and I felt better.

Every single day I woke up giving thanks for another beautiful day, no matter the weather, paid attention to every thought so I could live my life in the moment, and *wrote it all down*. Then, I would spend hours upon hours of *Zip Time* reading and re-reading, refining and fine-tuning, working and re-working, writing and re-writing.

I was an active, attentive student in my newest class, *Creative Writing* at Life University. I wasn't just thinking about writing, I wasn't just talking about writing, I wasn't just reading what other people wrote, instead, I was *being* a writer. I was *living* writing. I was *living* this book, proving it to myself over and over again, day after day, that I could, indeed, write this story. If I was *being* a writer, and I was *living* writing, then I *believe* that I am a writer, and I like that. I like it a lot. *Be + Live = Believe. Thank you, God.*

Chapter Ten

"Be Yourself!"

"I can't believe it," I confessed to Dad as we were sitting together on the back deck.

"Believe it, it's real. It's right there!" he laughed, pointing to the binder stuffed full of pages on the table between us.

"Although," Dad stated with a wink, "I can't for the life of me figure out why you named it "Six Senior Care Services," and burst out laughing.

"Very funny," I deadpanned. "I needed a bigger binder, so I re-cycled an old one," I explained unnecessarily, and smiled, feeling not at all like I expected I would feel at this juncture. Instead of giddiness and cloud dancing, I was outwardly and oddly calm, even though my insides were sparkling like multi-colored Christmas tree lights. I didn't feel the need to jump around because in my imagination, I already was.

"It's a great story, and it's *our* story," Dad beamed. "Every time I read it I laugh and then I get tears in my eyes." He laughed out loud, his eyes crinkling and his body shaking merrily.

"And the best part is, *This story is REAL. We're living it right NOW!*" he proclaimed emphatically, leaning forward and making his point on his knee, and he was right. *Be it + Live it = Believe it. Thank you, God.*

"It's like a series of reality shows, only not just starring Jerry Springer!" he laughed uproariously, and then attempting to mimic a floozy with a hand on her hips and big, batting eyelashes (me?), squeaked, "Hi. I went to the beach to write a book about my Dad's life, and I had a *frantastic time*." he finished his impersonation with a flip of his imaginary skirt.

Me, I thought, he's talking about me. I let him have his fun, ignoring his slip of the tongue, and even laughed along because, seriously, I didn't care – I'm writing a book! All I have to do now is finish it, I thought.

The Jerry Springer Show broke to a commercial I had seen years ago (when I still watched TV) of a successful businesswoman who confidently proclaimed, "We're going global!" and then her shoulders slumped, and she instantly appeared more human, "Just as soon as we go national."

"I'm not quite finished with the book, yet, I need just a little more time," I said calmly, changing the channel to ESPN, knowing what he would say next, and I was right.

"Take all the time you need. But remember, the deadline for the editor is in twenty days," Dad answered easily.

"I know," I laughed, "Thank you, Dad. Thank you for eve-ry-thing. Thank you for letting me do this for you, *with* you. Even though it is absolutely the hardest thing I have ever set out to do, I *truly love* doing it. I am having so much fun! It's like heaven only with page numbers. Thank you," I said, all my inner Christmas tree lights buzzing on and staying on.

"And we're *still* having fun, are we not? How many times have we had the opportunity to spend time together laughing and working on the book these past months? It's like Christmas every day!" he exclaimed, leaning in for a hug, and I graciously returned my gratitude with a tight bear hug of my own, no longer spooked or even surprised at how tuned in to my thoughts my Dad has grown. Or maybe it was I who was tuned in to *him*, I wondered. Who knows? Do- do-do-do.

"The important thing is that you are aware of it as it is happening in the moment. It's about celebrating the joys along the journey in every moment, not just the feeling you experience when you reach your destination."

Before I could respond, Gage came running out to where we were sitting, and asked breathlessly, "Quick, Mom, what can I do to earn two dollars?"

"What for?"

He answered in a rush, "Tyler is going to Target and I have ten bucks. What I want to buy costs eleven bucks and I need another dollar for tax. Hurry, what can I do? He's getting ready to leave!" he pleaded desperately.

I laughed and responded instantly, "Take out the kitchen trash and take your dirty clothes down to the laundry room, and I'll give you two bucks." There's always something to be done, I thought, grateful for the offer.

"Thanks, Mom," he smiled, and took off running.

Dad laughed and said, "Now, that's the spirit."

I laughed along, "Might as well teach them young that the only way to get money is to earn it. It's a life lesson."

Dad suddenly turned enthusiastic, "Don't you see, Daughter? My *children* and my *grandchildren* are living this too! Right now! Look at you girls. You live this because you grew up with it. Now your kids are living it as well, because they are learning it from you!" He sat back contented.

"How can they be learning it from me when *I'm still learning it myself*" I pleaded, believing he was extending me far too much credit.

"By osmosis! By example," he giggled. "Look, just like Tyler always says, 'Life isn't all rainbows and butterflies.' There are no answers, only more questions to be asked; no guarantees, just more opportunities. Your kids are watching you navigate your way on your path and learning when you learn. They are either learning things *because* of you, or *in spite* of you."

"Gee, thanks, Dad," I said, immediately *Zipping* through every single misstep, random curse word, or inappropriate behavior I've exhibited over the past twenty years in front of my children's watchful, Sponge Bob-full eyes.

"Hey, kids bounce," he laughed. "You kids survived our parenting, and they survived your parenting, did they not?" he asked plaintively, and I had to agree.

I smiled and asked, "Did you hear about Nick and his post-Thanksgiving enterprise? He went with Sandi to Target on Black Friday before the stores opened and sold hot chocolate to the people waiting outside in line. He made ninety bucks!" I exclaimed, in awe of his teenage ingenuity and spunk.

Dad put his arms behind his head and said, "Like I said, it's in their DNA. They are living this too."

"DNA *and* environment," I corrected.

"Yes, it does take both, but, like I said before, you learn *because* of your circumstances, or *in spite* of them. You could be born with a silver spoon in your mouth and frivolously squander every opportunity that comes your way; or you could be born into poverty and accept every opportunity that comes along to make your own way.

"But, opportunities don't come along every day. Some opportunities are once-in-a-lifetime," I countered, feeling confident for the moment.

"Oh, *really?*" Dad smiled and threw up that one eyebrow. Grrrrr, I *really* need to learn that facial maneuver.

"Is that right?" Dad queried. "So, you believe that *miracles* happen every day, but *opportunities* only come along once in a lifetime?" he asked incredulously, and he was right.

"I could have easily given up in that State Home for Boys, or when I only had two bucks to my name. *You* could have said 'no, thank you' to my offer to make a placement, or train for a new job as a headhunter, or start your own business, but you didn't say no, you said yes.

"You have to be aware of the opportunities that present themselves seemingly magically in the moment, and then you have to do all the things necessary in order to bring your creation about. *Do, Did, Deed!*" Dad emphatically stated and then stood, pointing to where Gage had just run past lugging the trash bag behind him.

"And, now *your* kids are living this too!" He placed both hands on his knees and leaned forward, locking his eyes with mine.

Gage came running back out of breath, "I'm done. Can I have the two dollars? Hurry!" he pleaded urgently.

"*Buen trabajo. Gracias,*" I said smiling, handing over the money.

"De nada." I watched as Gage pivoted and ran from the deck.

"Gage could have easily just *asked* for two dollars, but he didn't! He *asked* for the *opportunity* to *earn* two dollars. Just like you *asked* for the opportunity to *write* this book." Dad stood standing, eyes still in a laser lock with my own, but then promptly turned the floor over to *The Preacher*.

> *"Once you have mastered the art of Paying Attention to your surroundings, you not only possess the ability to spot Opportunities everywhere in the Moment, you now possess the Power to create your own Opportunities in the Moment."*

Dad resumed command and announced, "These kids are living this every single day! It's in their DNA. Gage asks for a job, Nick opens an impromptu hot chocolate stand, and Tyler started a chocolate business! This is my *dream*, Daughter!"

It was true. I *Zipped* back to the day after I came home from Ocean City to Tyler handing me a brochure for his new confection business, Hometown-Chocolates.com, that he had launched while I was hiding among the waves of pages at the beach. He did this *without* me? I wondered incredulously. Me? His mother? Entrepreneur? Business owner? *Oh, my God! Thank you, God!*

"Tyler, I am so proud of you guys! This is amazing!" I beamed.

"We have a web site," he beamed back, electrifying the room.

"You *do*?" I was *more* stunned, realizing with a pang that it took me five years of being in business before I got around to building a web site. OMG! Kids today are TechniGurus!

Tyler was on a roll. "We have a business plan, too. It's fourteen pages."

"Oh, my God! *You do? Can I read it*?" I exclaimed breathlessly, enveloping my firstborn into a hug so tight it would rival Dad's. "I am so proud of you! You are amazing! You did all this on your own! I *love* being your Mom!" I gushed.

Wow, I thought as he left to retrieve his business plan, it took me seven years in business, *and* I had to hire an MBA to write it for me before I had a business plan. I was in awe. I instantly recalled the day he had claimed, "Maybe I'll start my own company and sell it for a million dollars." *Wouldn't it be great if...*?

He did all this while I was at the beach? He's just twenty years old, a baby bird still living in his mother's nest. Isn't he of the generation that is supposed to do *nothing at all*? Who thinks young people today are slackers? I should get out of this kid's way more often, I thought, and then just as quickly realized, I can learn from him! So, I promptly added Tyler to my list of mentors and gurus that I emulate in life. Wrap your mind around that!

Dad pleaded with me, dragging me from my *Zip Memory*, "Don't you see, Daughter? My goal was not just to live these truths for myself, but to have my daughters and grandchildren live them too, and they are! That was my intention for writing the book. I am whole. I am complete." He clasped his hands together in prayer.

"If my life ended right now, I would be satisfied," he finished softly, sitting back down contentedly, allowing the vibrations of his words to dance around the deck and bounce off the furniture.

"You're not going anywhere, Dad, we still have work to do," I laughed softly.

After some *Zip Time*, we walked back into the house and into the living room to find Gage kneeling on the floor desperately attempting to open the carved wooden box holding Bear's remains. She had heartbreakingly "moved" after I returned from my beach sabbatical, just as she had promised.

She had declined rapidly that March, and by April, we knew in our hearts that she wouldn't be with us much longer, which didn't make it any easier to call our friend and veterinarian, Dr. Wayne, for Bear's "last" appointment. I agonized over the decision for over two weeks before Gage finally cornered me in the living room and whispered, "Mom, don't you think it's time to…you know."

"Know what?" I returned softly, knowing exactly what he was referring to, but not allowing myself to admit it.

"You know," he said just as softly, and then drew his finger across his throat in the universal sign of kicking the bucket.

"*What?*" I asked alarmed, clearly not expecting his ready acceptance of our beloved Bear's imminent demise.

He answered readily, "She's old, mom. She lived a good life. It's time to let her go." I stared in awe at Gage, my timeless wizard disguised in a basketball jersey, and then silently nodded, knowing he was right. Then I called Dr. Wayne. *Thank you, Bear. Thank you, God.*

"Gage, what are you doing?" I asked, alarmed, zipping back to my present living room.

"Mom, I almost have it open," He answered immediately, referring to the "secret" latch opening on the bottom of the box.

"Don't do that, cutie," I laughed. "We don't want to *open* it. It was nice when Bear would sleep on the living room floor, but we don't want her *all over* the living room," I said, taking the box from him and placing it gently on the bookshelves lining one wall of the room.

"Okay." He shrugged, and left to scope out another adventure that hopefully wouldn't involve me vacuuming up cremated remains around the house. Aaahhhh, the joys of motherhood, I though tenderly. If I'm not careful to enjoy every moment, I'll blink and Gage will turn eighteen.

Dad, who had been laughing at Gage's attempted misadventure, commented, "I love your bookshelves and how you decorate your house, it's so homely."

"*What?*" I laughed, stunned.

"Your house. I love it," he repeated, "It's homely."

"Dad, you *have* to stop saying that." I was close to losing it.

"Why? I'm giving you a compliment."

I did lose it, and burst out laughing, then noting Dad's confusion, explained, "Dad, homely means ugly. I think what you mean to say is "homey.""

"Oops." He giggled and made a funny face, crossing his eyes at me.

"You are sooooo goofy, Dad. I love you." I smiled, reaching for a hug, which he returned with vigor. I gazed at my collection of used household items collected from years of haunting garage sales and auctions, and smiled. Homey? Maybe, but most definitely lived-in.

"Besides, Dad, the house wouldn't be like this if it weren't for you. You gave me the money to hire somebody to build those bookshelves, among other things, like my windows, the fireplace, and my bathroom sink. Thank you for all that," I gratefully responded.

"We did it together!" he cried gleefully. "We created it together! You had a sincere desire to improve your home because you love it, and I had a sincere desire to help you achieve that, because I love you.

Sprinkle a few two dollar bills on there and then step back and give the Creator a little time and space to do the rest, and presto! Look around," he finished, waving his arms across the bookshelves, laughing. I joined him, and then added,

"Hey, that reminds me. I have a question for you about the book."

"Shoot."

"Well," I began, "throughout the whole book, I refer to God as 'God' and you refer to God as 'Creator.' Why? Is there a reason?"

He answered immediately, "You say tomato and I say tomahto," then shrugged and offered, "I just like the word Creator rather than God because of all the dogma associated with the word God. But they both mean the same thing, the *eve-ry-thing* that is our world. You could just as easily insert the term 'Yahweh,' 'Mother Earth,' 'Energy,' 'Life Force,' 'Eywah' or 'The Matrix,' depending on what you believe.

"The Matrix?" I repeated skeptically, attempting to arch one eyebrow. Hmmm, I think I felt something move.

"Sure! You never know." He laughed and I joined him.

"Okay, Dad. I'm going to leave it the way it is. You say Creator, I say God. You say tomato and I say tomahto, and we'll agree to leave The Matrix out of it." I laughed again with Dad, and just as suddenly wondered why he calls me "Daughter." I suspected that if he didn't, he would probably call me VickiSandiTawni, running our names together as he had when my sisters and I were little, and in his excitement, forgot who was whom. Now, he's never wrong.

Taking a quick *Zip Trip* to a few months after the divorce was final, I had thought it would be a good idea to change my last name back to my maiden name, but when I broached the subject with Gage he burst into tears.

"You can't change your name," he pleaded. "We have to have the same last name," he cried, and that was the end of that.

Come to think of it, what's in a name anyway? I've already had three last names so far in my life (four if you count the adoption), so maybe the next time around, I should just request a blank line as a last name with the words *Insert Name Here* printed underneath it.

Dad brought me forcefully back to earth when he emphatically stated, "With every thought, word, and deed, you create your own reality. So order it up! But, choose your words very carefully because you get *exactly* what you ask for. Eliminate expectations and desires and instead *choose* your creation. Don't say, 'I want this' or 'I want that.' Instead, replace it with, 'I choose this' or 'I choose that,' 'I prefer this' or 'I prefer that.'

"Every word you speak is a prayer already answered. The universe literally takes your words and manifests them into reality. So, if a person says they *want* something, they are never going to get it. If they say they *need* something, they are never going to get it." Dad was bouncing around, delighting in his own words.

"The reason is very simple. You get exactly what you ask for. So when you say you want something, the universe is going to manifest the experience of *wanting*. If you say you need something, the universe will manifest your experience of *needing*. It's never going to fulfill it because you didn't say you choose it or prefer it. Instead, you will experience wanting or needing. You literally get what you ask for." He paused, looking thoughtful for a moment, then continued confidently, "And, then there are your deeds, your actions. Your actions of the day must back up your thoughts and words. As you change the balance from destructive to constructive, your outside world will change to back up the new reality of who and what you are.

"If your thoughts are aligned with the Creator, and your words are aligned with your thoughts, and your deeds are in alignment with your thoughts and words, then the amount of time to manifest your reality becomes shorter and shorter because you are now aware and focused on what you are thinking, saying and doing. We are accountable for every thought, word and deed. So choose carefully," he finished, pointing at me.

Always the contrarian, I countered, "But some people believe that we don't really have any free choice or free will. They believe that everything in the universe is predetermined and predestined, that we don't really have any choices. We're just clever animals who invented knowledge."

"Well, whether it boils down to free will or destiny doesn't really matter when you're standing in the grocery store trying to decide between chips or pretzels, now does it?" he laughed.

"Or choosing between the beaches of Jamaica and Mexico!" I laughed back, agreeing.

"As human beings, our intellect allows us to *think* we're choosing, whether we are or we aren't, so why not pick *something*? The Pastabilities are endless," he laughed.

"I know several people who *never* choose anything, instead preferring to let the fates dictate their lives," I stated, picturing them in my mind, ignoring Dad's reference to lunch.

"Is that right?" he smiled. "Let me ask you something: Isn't the act of not *choosing* technically choosing to *not choose*?"

"I guess it is," I admitted.

"So, really, *not choosing*, is really just choosing to let somebody *else* make the choice for you," he concluded.

"Life is change. Growth is optional. Choose wisely."
– Karen Kaiser Clark

"Why would people do that?" I asked perplexed, but not from blondeness.

"Lots of reasons," Dad answered instantly. "One reason is

they might be fearful of making the wrong choice, so they choose to do nothing."

"But there are no mistakes," I interrupted, "Only more opportunities to make more choices," I blurted, recalling chapter three.

"That's what I believe, and you believe, but they might believe differently," Dad smiled. "Another reason is fear. Fear of failure often keeps people glued to the mundane, or they don't want to assume responsibility for a decision, so they let somebody else make it for them."

"Or money. That's always a big obstacle," I supplied. "I'm broke."

"People believe that money is an obstacle, but I don't. Look what two bucks can grow to!" he laughed and reached into his pocket.

"Here." He offered me a two-dollar bill and I smiled. "Now you have as much money as I did starting out," he laughed.

"Thank you, Dad." I laughed, taking the bill, planning to add it to the piles of two-dollar bills Dad has handed out to my family over the years. I have amassed quite a collection due to the fact that I always buy my kids' two-dollar bills from them for five dollars and save them.

"Hey Dad, do you still want to include two-dollar bills in our book?" I asked.

"Absolutely!" he replied enthusiastically. *"Wouldn't it be great if* we could create a job for somebody to stuff a two-dollar bill inside each book and then shrink-wrap it?" he laughed, and I agreed. Hey, every little bit helps.

"Yeah, that would be great," I laughed. "Okay, so money is only a perceived obstacle, what about time?"

"The only time is now."

"Right."

"What about difficulty? Lots of people quit because it's too hard."

"If it was easy, everyone would do it," he returned. "Honestly, Daughter, if people were truly honest with themselves, they *know* what needs to be done, they just don't do it because they think it's too hard. But, if they looked closely, they would see that *not doing* something is much harder in the long run because it leads to regret and self-remorse."

He thought for a moment, then added, "Or it could be that they don't really *believe* they can do it, so they don't even try, or there could be a million other reasons."

"That's kinda sad," I said, thinking to myself, I've felt *all* those things.

"I agree," he immediately replied, "but, people have lost hope. Look around. They're worn down by external events. They don't believe that things will get any better, and they don't believe that they have the power to change *anything*. They believe that the world is happening to them, but really *they* are happening to *it*."

"Why shouldn't they lose hope?" I asked, suddenly feeling defensive. "'Look around' is right. It sucks out there, Dad. Every single person in this country has the potential to be productive beyond just providing for themselves, yet the system that exists leaves the many working for the benefit of a few. It pisses me off."

Dad chuckled, nodding his head. "I know. You're right. It is what it is. And, what can you do about that?"

Before I could answer he jumped in with, "Nothing. It is what it is. You only have the power to change you and nothing else. And, do you know how I know that?"

"No, how?" I asked. I really should have seen this coming. ESPN must be on commercial break.

"Because I read your book!" He laughed uproariously, and I had to join in. "Seriously, Daughter, I hear where you're coming from and I agree with you. But, things are changing and they are changing fast. The circumstances outside are such that it is forcing people to retreat, take cover and *go inside*, and that's a good thing. Every single moment is beautiful, just, and perfect in the Creator's eyes, don't you see? The only thing lacking is our understanding of the moment."

"I don't understand *this* moment. Why does it have to be this way?"

"You're giving yourself too much credit, clever animal," Dad laughed and locked his gaze on mine.

"Did you forget that you are the size of a hair follicle on a gnat's ass compared to the size of the universe, cosmos and infinity?" he asked evenly. "Think about it, Daughter, this 'Moment in Time' that you speak of, this economic crisis, how does that compare to the amount of time that the earth has been here? The amount of time that life has roamed our planet and will in the future?" he asked logically.

He was right. I laughed out loud and added, "I saw this t-shirt once, I think it was Ron's t-shirt, it had a picture of the cosmos, with a tiny little sign that pointed You are Here. We both laughed.

Dad said softly, "You know, it's easy for us mere human beings to forget that absolutely eve-ry-thing is beautiful, just, and perfect in every single moment; it was created that way for us to experience and enjoy. And, as people endure this crisis, they will turn inward and focus on what is really important. And that is....?" he queried, then immediately answered his own question,

"Their love for their children and their families. What did we do when we didn't have enough money to go on vacation at the beach?" he asked playfully, slapping the table.

"We still had fun!" I enthused, and we did.

"That's right!" He stood up spiritedly. "We *always* made it fun!" He was right.

Sometimes we had a little extra, sometimes we had a little less, and sometimes *a lot* less. But we always had fun, playing hide-and-seek in the dark and playing board games by flashlight when the storm knocked out the power, raking the leaves to completely cover Mom's VW Beetle, camping in the backyard, or competing in Rummy 500 competitions. We made our own fun, because we loved our family, and we loved having fun.

"You know what, Daughter, that's what brought our forefathers, my grandparents, to Ellis Island all those years ago."

"What, fun?" I asked, going for the Blonde Trophy.

"No, the love for their families," he replied automatically. Maybe the Polish in him appreciates the Polish in me.

"People who immigrated here loved their families and sought the opportunity to provide a better life for them. They didn't come here expecting handouts. They came here expecting to work hard, love their families, and enjoy the freedom of worshiping their God. And, because those opportunities were encouraged, they loved their country. They loved their families, their God, and their country, and they worked hard to prove it. And do you know what happened? As a nation, we prospered."

We both thought for a moment and then I offered, "Not much has changed, yet ev-ery-thing has changed." *One plus one equals three.*

"How right you are," he replied, chuckling.

"So what do we do?" I asked obviously, for eve-ry-one.

"Who knows?" Dad laughed. "I don't have all the answers. But, I do know this, whatever we do, our intention must be born of love, not chaos. Our thoughts, words and deeds must originate from that same place: love. If our intention is constructive, then the outcome will be constructive." He grew more animated.

> *"The entire law is summed up in a single command:*
> *'Love your neighbor as yourself.'"*
> *– Galations 5:14 (NIV)*

"And then, we need to go back to the time and place when we joyfully took responsibility for ourselves and our families. That's as good a place as any to start," and I had to agree.

"That's where I believe that this is already happening! People are looking around at their families, their neighbors and their community and saying to themselves, "We don't need or want another 9/11 to hug our kids and hang out our flag. We don't need or want to pollute our waters with tea, oil, or anything else. We don't need or want a revolution. We prefer a transfornation," he finished triumphantly.

"What did you say?" I asked, jumping up, stunned at what I had just heard, "Oh, my God, do you know what you just said?"

"What?" Dad's perplexed look had me giggling inside before it bubbled over into the room.

"Dad, Oh, my God. Do you know what you just said?"

"Uhhhh, no," he replied slowly.

"You said 'transforNation'! I think you meant to say transformation, but you didn't, you said transforNation!" I giggled again.

"I did? Oh, I did!" he happily exclaimed, bouncing around a little, laughing along with me.

"That is funny, Dad. The whole time we've been working on this book, it bothered me that it would seem like just another how-to-book to 'change.' But it's not about *changing*."

Dad grabbed the remote to flip to the ESPN channel and jumped up, "Oh, my God, you're absolutely right!" I watched him dance around the room, glued to his performance on ESPN.

"This isn't about *change*. This is about becoming *whole*," he laughed.

"Yes, yes," I agreed, laughing and nodding.

"This isn't about 'change,' a transforMation. This is about 'being,' a transforNation."

I watched Dad giggle and dance merrily with his arms in the air, smiling inside and out, growing more excited by the moment.

"TransforNation is a foundation for becoming more of your greater self in the moment. Every moment. Every day. Being aware of every moment as they are unfolding, enjoying them, and then sharing that joy with others. It's doing your part for the world by being yourself. I love it!

"Our natural state of being is joyfulness and happiness. Being yourself is being joyful and happy in the moment! Sharing that joy and happiness with others is our purpose! TransforNation! I love it!"

I watched as he whipped out his iPhone and asked, "Are you writing it down as a miracle?"

"No. I'm logging onto GoDaddy to buy the domain name," and I laughed even harder.

"'itransforNation.com' is the best I could get. I love it!" he exclaimed a few minutes later.

"Me, too, Dad, me, too." And I smiled.

"Wow, Daughter, that the second time that happened!" he boasted.

"What do you mean the second time?" I wondered what he was thinking.

"I mean the second time a misspoken word turned out to be *perfect*, remember?" He giggled, body dancing in laughter, obviously still tuned into ESPN.

"Oh, my God, you're right," I said in awe, instantly *Zipping* back to when Gage was three years old playing on the back deck with his books and papers. All at once, he had gathered up his supplies and turned to leave.

"Where are you going, cutie?" I had asked, looking up from my own book.

"I'm going to work," Gage replied with the complete certainty that comes from being a toddler and *knowing everything*.

I laughed out loud at my adorable cherub, "Really? Great! Where do you work?" I asked the obvious question.

"At New Work City," he answered authoritatively, and made again as if to leave.

"*What?*" I jumped up, unsure if I had heard correctly. "What did you say, cutie?" But, his attention span was already focused on turning the doorknob to go inside.

I turned to Dave, "Did you hear that? Did you hear what Gage said? New Work City! It's perfect!" I laughed and began dancing my happy dance around the deck. "Oh, my God, I can't believe it! It's so perfect!"

And, it was. For years, I had been searching for a new name for our company. Although I loved the name American Personnel, it really didn't convey the fun character and playful mission I wanted to exhibit. It was a great name in the beginning when we first opened, but by now, we had implemented so many *New* policies for our employees revolving around Work that we practically needed a *City* to house them.

"New Work City! Oh, my God!" I said aloud, racing to log onto GoDaddy. www.NewWorkCity.Jobs. Perfect! *It was a miracle! Thank you, God! Thank you, Gage!*

Years later, after we had secured the federal trademark, we presented Gage with a certificate and a check for fifty dollars. Thinking ahead, I saved the certificate for posterity, while Gage happily blew his newfound wealth within hours. I smiled tenderly recalling how he periodically will ask, "Mom, tell me again how I named your company." And I do, every single time. Wow.

"Now there's a New Work City in New York City!" Dad enthused, and he was right.

Years later surfing the internet, I came across NWCNYC.com, a small start-up run by the "Mayor of New Work City" that provides "co-working" space to computer programmers in a Manhattan loft. In the process of forming their own non-profit charity to provide educational computer classes to women and kids, their spirit and policies line right up with ours!

We promptly jumped on a plane to New York City to meet this other New Work City and talk legalities, and so enjoyed our tour and our impression of the "Mayor" that we agreed to lease our trademark so that they could continue their good works provided we were allowed to visit them once a year! Yippee! A great reason to visit the Big Apple and walk over the Brooklyn Bridge for Grimaldi's pizza over and over again! I love it when we all win!

I *Zipped* back to our present sad state of affairs or, should I say, Nation of Despair.

"So, Dad, how do we do it? What do the people do? How do we become a transforNation? We all know it doesn't pay to buck the system," I said solemnly.

"Nor would you want to, Daughter. It is what it is. So what's the next question? *Wouldn't it be great if...?*" he laughed merrily and then sang with tears in his eyes, "Do you know how I knew that? I read your book!" and laughter danced through his body.

"Okay, fine then, let's play 'what if?'" I could allow myself to get fired up if I wanted to, so I stood up to walk off some of my pent up frustration, put on my game face and began, "Wouldn't it be great if a certain number of greedy people hadn't risked our retirement funds with their creative hanky-panky financing and cooked books, melting our 401Ks into 201Ks, and nearly collapsing our very economic foundation?"

"You're absolutely right, Daughter."

"I know I am," I replied hotly. "And, I also know what you're going to say; *it is what it is*, but what can we *do* about it? The *last* thing we need is more committees and overhead. Our nation is tapped out. We're broke. We can't afford to police an increasingly corrupt system. We don't just feel hopeless, we feel helpless too," I pleaded, instantly defusing my anger and replacing it with despair for eve-ry-one that had been adversely affected in our nation.

Dad remained calm and replied, "I don't remember the exact words, but Buckminster Fuller said something like this: Don't fight the system. Create a new system that makes the old system obsolete."

"How *exactly* do you do that, create a new system?" Inquiring minds want to know.

"I don't know what anyone else should do, but here's what I did," he began.

"This happened to me in the eighties with $50,000 I had painstakingly saved in a mutual fund for our retirement. Every month I would receive a statement detailing the fund's performance and how many investors had joined or departed the fund. Well, one month the statement showed that nearly one third of the investors had opted out of the fund. 'That's weird' I said to myself."

Dad immediately shot up at attention and thundered, "Within thirty days the entire stock market had tanked. Along with everyone else, I had instantly lost over a third of my invested money. I was furious." He stormed around the room.

"Ughh, I seem to remember that time, Dad," I said quietly, sitting safely out of range.

Dad laughed and expounded, "I learned two things that day: One, some people knew ahead of time that the stock market was in for a correction, and two, I wasn't one of those people." He suddenly got quiet, *Zipping* back to the hair-band era. "So do you know what I did?"

"What?" I asked.

"Nothing for a few days but stomp around the house and grumble," Dad laughed, "But then I gave the problem over to my intuitive mind, over to the Creator that is ev-ery-th-ing, and I kept playing the, *'wouldn't it be great if...?'* game over and over again."

He started to bounce around in his seat, growing louder, "Then, one night a few weeks later, I jumped out of bed at three in the morning to finish the game as I shouted, '*wouldn't it be great if* we could create our own *family bank?*'"

"A bank?" I thought, immediately picturing my bank in the triangle shaped building on the corner of Main and Maple.

"Not your typical bricks and mortar bank on the street corner," Dad said into the ESPN amplifier, "but a Family Circle Bank that each family member could invest into and borrow from," he enthused. "So I cashed in my investments and deposited them into federally guaranteed savings accounts. In the beginning, that's all they amounted to, savings accounts.

"Eventually, the first opportunity arrived, and The Family Circle Bank lent Tawni the start-up funds to open her employment agency. And, it grew from there, eventually doing the same thing and lending the start-up funds for your business. Then, for other family members, we loaned two home mortgages, credit card refinancing, and auto loans.

"Now, after some time, we got serious and formed a corporation. But, most people don't have to be that structured. Retirees can purchase their kids' mortgages, and the payments and interest function much like a traditional reverse mortgage, providing instant income. Only this time, you're the bank and your kids are your customers," Dad said with a flourish and then sat back, thinking, then suddenly started chuckling.

"And, the best part is, we take care of our own," he said proudly. "This economy hit everyone hard. But, did any of our family members lose their homes? No. Because if somebody would happen to lose their job, we would simply rewrite the terms of the loan and then work together to help them find a job! Nobody's going to kick *family* into the street especially when they're down on their luck. Since it's our bank, we can do what we want. We're making it up as we go along," he announced happily.

"My bank only offered me a toaster and a chance to opt in or out, but either way it cost me money," I retorted dryly.

"Exactly!" Dad exclaimed, pointing at me. "Don't buck the system. Create a new system that makes the old system obsolete. Every person I tell that story to is encouraged by it. Even if they don't choose that way for themselves, it comforts us to know we have other options, that we aren't stuck in a system that controls us." He sat back for a moment, and I gave him time to collect his thoughts. It didn't take long.

"*Wouldn't it be great if* we could offer all the forms, documents and instructions on our website to make it easier for people to get started on their own family bank?" Dad asked, taking his turn in the game.

I love playing this game, I thought as I quickly added, "*Wouldn't it be great if* eve-ry-one had a family bank that invested in their families' mortgages and businesses? What would happen to bankers' bonuses then?"

"Don't you see, Daughter? That's not bucking the system, like the people who try to manipulate it, that's creating a *new* system that makes the *old* system obsolete." But, I wasn't finished playing, I was having fun.

"*Wouldn't it be great if* the bankers and investors could still play their greedy games, but the next time their Ponzi scheme implodes, the only money lost would be their own?" I asked giddily. Okay, I was getting carried away, but a girl can dream, can't she?

"Exactly," he agreed. "Invest in yourself and your family. There will always be people out there who try to beat the system, find a shortcut, or try to profit from the stock tip of the century. They're in it for themselves, and woe to the uninformed. But, for those of us who aren't privy to that information, it's an unbalanced system."

"So, I guess you won the *wouldn't be great if...* game, right?" I asked playfully.

Dad stood up triumphantly and pronounced, "No daughter, we *all* won! Don't you see? Investing in yourself and your family is a win-win-win situation. You win, your kids win and the economy wins because it can continue growing. You're *adding* to the system, not taking away from it. It's win-win-win."

"Yippee!" I clapped and cheered, "I Love it when eve-ry-one wins!"

"Me too, Daugher, me too." Dad smiled serenely and then continued, "And I believe that more and more people are reaching that point, and saying to themselves, 'Hey, wait a minute. It is what it is, but it doesn't have to be that way. I may not be able to change the system, nor do I want to buck the system, but I do have the power to create my own system that works for our family.' Then they play the *'wouldn't it be great if'* game." He smiled broadly. "And, I think people are playing that game more and more, faster and faster" he spoke slowly, growing quieter.

"It is what it is, and it is what you make it, but, from where I'm sitting, the physical manifestation of conscious creation is happening faster and faster. The amount of people who are reaching an awareness of their reality is growing quickly. The growth is exponential," Dad said soflty.

I wondered if it was true, if it was growing exponentially like he claimed, remembering that Abraham Maslow's Hierarchy of Needs considered only two percent of the population to be self-actualized.

"You know, Dad, people complain that twenty percent of the people do eighty percent of the work, but that's certainly more than Maslow's two percent. Maybe it is growing faster and faster."

"I believe it is," he mused.

"Like happened on Tawni's porch with the tree?" I asked, referring to the story Dad told at Neale Donald Walsch's conference.

Dad immediately and enthusiastically agreed. "Yes, exactly like the tree! It was a miracle! That's physical manifestation of conscious creation in five hours. *Five hours!*" he repeated solemnly, holding up five fingers.

"That's how it works, Daughter, don't you see? Thoughts are things. Now, Tawni did something most people wouldn't think to do."

Like me, I thought to myself as Dad continued.

"She told Darnell to move his car. She *made room* for the miracle to happen. She did her part. Darnell did his part. The Creator did the rest!"

"Wow," I replied. I never thought of it that way before, wondering how *The Preacher* could stay so far removed from a discussion that had Dad so exhilarated. But suddenly, *The Preacher* snuck up behind me and announced live from the ESPN channel.

"She made room for the Miracle because she Believes in Miracles. And, because she Believed it, it was Real. She did her part, small as it was, Darnell did his part, small as it was, then they stepped aside and let the Creator perform a Miracle, causing the city do the rest.

Because Tawni stepped out of the way to allow the Miracle to happen, it manifested itself even better than she had wished. That's because the city hauled away the bundles for her, and she didn't have to. It was a Miracle and it happens every day."

"Is that true? Do you really believe that's how it works? You say it and it is so? That sounds like magic." I wasn't being skeptical. Okay, I was.

"Who knows? Prove it to yourself. Was there ever a time in your life that you didn't experience something you truly believed?"

"Well, I haven't won the lottery yet," I flipped back.

"Daughter, do you even *buy* lottery tickets?" He smirked in return. Oh, my God. Did he just arch the *other* eyebrow?

"You must not believe you are going to win the lottery very much if you're not even willing to invest a dollar in a ticket." He laughed, and then sang, "You can't *win* if you don't *play*."

I laughed along, but honestly, all this ESPN and SCI-FI stuff is sometimes difficult to fathom. Where's the science? Where's the proof?

"You know, Daughter, you say it seems like magic, but isn't magic merely science we don't understand yet?" *Oh. My. God.*

Dad chuckled, ignoring my absolute incredulity of his extra-sensory perception, and stated, "There was a time we thought electricity was magic, or radio waves, or the internet, or flying to the moon. Impossible! People claimed, it can't be done. There was a time when we thought it would be a Miracle to protect our children from polio, or the Cold War to end, or the government to be run *by* the people *for* the people," he burst out laughing and admitted. "Oh, yeah, we're still working on that last one. I forgot!" And, I laughed out loud with him.

"But, do you know what, Daughter?" Dad leaned forward with a fiery, yet serene look in his eyes (is that even possible?), his gaze fixed on me, and then both he and *The Preacher* stood up confidently as One in front of the bookshelves and struck a Professor's pose and demeanor.

In the beginning
There was nothing
And yet there was everything

It was a light
It was a lightbulb
It was a thought
It was a word
It was a deed
It was a Miracle
It was Real.

"But in the beginning, while it was still magical and unbelievable, somebody, anybody, one body, had an idea! And, that may be because we are clever animals, but nevertheless, that intention: that spark, that lightbulb, that Big Bang of ingenuity, that little self who was thinking to its bigger self, 'It is what it is, but it doesn't have to be that way. *Wouldn't it be great if...? Wouldn't it be great if* it was a different way? That intention was born of love."

I couldn't help it, I raised my hand.

"Yessss?" *The Preacher/Dad/One/Professor* asked, smiling patiently and looking down at me as if he had bifocals, which he did, but wasn't currently wearing. At least there were no eyebrows involved.

"I have a question," I stated the obvious, while Dad waited, rocking on his feet, hands in pockets.

"*Who* had the idea? *What* was the idea? And *why* did he/she/it *want* to do it? *What* was the intention?" I asked carefully, modulating my vowels.

"You are such a sensor," he laughed knowingly, but infinitely kindly.

"*What*?" I asked laughing.

"You see the trees where I see the forest. Details. Details. Details. Okay, let me think a moment." He assumed a pondering stance.

Suddenly, he turned to me, locked his gaze on mine and said merrily, "Pick something!"

"*What*?" I asked. "What do you mean, pick something?" I asked, maybe from blondeness, maybe from my Polish heritage, maybe from my youth and inexperience?

"You're the teacher, I'm just a student," I shot back, giggling.

"Don't you see, Daughter? You call Gage *the Bouncing Ball of Happiness*, but you have your very own Bouncing Ball of Happiness right before your very eyes! Pick one thing to focus on!"

"It's just like choosing a topic for a book report, or a term paper, or a business plan, or a book, you just have to choose to focus on something! Just like the bank robbers and the dynamite, everyone's perspective is different, so just pick one!"

"Okay," I laughed, tuning into Dad's channel. "How about flying?"

"Perfect!" The Professor replied happily, making me feel taller. Then, he stated matter of factly, "Leonardo DaVinci drew a sketch of a helicopter over four hundred years before it was actually invented. Out of thin air, a magical thought comes to a mere human being, who believes that it is possible, so he writes it down. Is he just a clever animal? Is he crazy?"

"Now it took over four hundred years for the world to evolve to the point where the science could catch up with the magic, and the helicopter became real. You could fly in it. If Leonardo Da-Vinci had built that helicopter the very night he drew it, then he *would* have been deemed crazy. It would have seemed magical because people's awareness of technology had not evolved to the point where they could absorb and accept the seemingly impossible overnight."

"But, this evolution of consciousness is speeding up! It's getting faster and faster. Just as advances in technology are developing at exponential rates, so is the science of the mind. Physical manifestation from conscious creation is speeding up to the point that it almost seems magical. And, the more we understand the magic, the faster it becomes science."

The Professor/Dad/*The Preacher* stood back for a moment, then waved an arm in the air, "Right now, even though we can't see it, there exist all around us invisible radio waves, sound waves, microwaves and light waves, which were each a new discovery at one time." He pointed to me and proclaimed, "Now, can you imagine if someday, maybe in our lifetime, maybe not, that there was a *new* discovery, and it was called the ESPN wave?" He laughed out loud and I joined him, imagining my favorite channel's future mind blowing IPO.

"Miraculously one day, all around us, people might suddenly *understand* how to tune into the ESPN network's invisible waves, or maybe there will even be an app for it on your iPhone." We both took a few moments to dreamily picture using the newest technological wonder yet to be invented.

He concluded happily, "Once people understand this seemingly impossible technology, now the merely possible has turned into probable. It is real. Science catches up with the magic, and we get to experience it on a daily basis. And, the funny thing is, future generations who are born into these amazing leaps of technology take for granted what we currently can't even comprehend during our time.

"Remember the first fax machine? The first Apple Macintosh? The first video game? The first cell phone? The first PDA? Your kids were born into this! Imagine what future generations will get to experience.

"And, all because people have the freedom, the inalienable right, to go inside themselves, into their Mind Field, conceive of an idea, believe it is possible, and then do everything important and necessary to make it a reality. It's the ultimate pursuit of happiness – the American Dream.

"More important than *what* they do, is *why* they do it. They do it because they *believe* it! Add to that the love for their families, the love for their God, and the love for their country." He seemed to get misty for a moment, but then giggled, giving me a clue to what was coming next.

"Somebody, somewhere in the world, could be working on the ESPN app right now!" he sputtered, and we both broke into gales of laughter.

After we calmed some (relatively speaking), he continued in the same scholarly tone, "Maslow puts forth that only two percent of the population is self-actualized, maybe it's more than that, but I see a new era being ushered in before our eyes. It is the new epoch of the mind. The times we are facing are forcing people to come to terms with themselves.

"The hopelessness and despair they are experiencing leave them no choice but to confront head-on their own personal responsibility for how they conduct their lives. Nobody else is going to do it for us, nor should they. This is the time and space for the human consciousness to evolve. That inside journey is something no person, no government, no stock market can ever take away from us."

He grew quiet for a moment, thinking a far-away thought, and then said softly, "You know, Daughter, there was another time in my life that intuition saved me from accepting a ride in a buddy's airplane that crashed to the ground a mere one hour later." He stopped talking and devoted a moment's silence to his friend's memory.

"The pilot in the second plane who also died that day, Mr. Wooten, would repeatedly boast at the bar, 'When I die, I'm gonna spin it into the ground.' Even though we all laughed at the time with him, that is *exactly* how he died. And, that scares me, don't you see? People don't pay attention to the words they speak, and when they don't, they have nobody to blame for the circumstances of their lives but themselves. When they run around every single day telling everyone around them how miserable their life is, wouldn't you expect their life to be well, *miserable*? Yeah, Spit Happens and Life Comes at You Past, but it is what it is. I don't want people to be miserable, I prefer for people to be *joyful*, because it also is what you make it," he said softly.

"We all experience misfortune and tragedy. God knows, our family has, haven't we?" he turned to me questioningly with sadness spilling from his eyes, and I had to agree.

"Mom dying, illness, disease, the house fire, the office fire, divorces, betrayals, people we trusted stealing money, lost loves, business failures, bankruptcies, starting over from scratch and two dollars, Tawni's infertility, although that one turned into a miracle," he said wistfully.

"The sinkhole," I added. "That was a tragedy," I commented, remembering the thirty foot sinkhole that had opened up overnight in front of my parent's Happy House the day before the public auction to sell it so they could downsize anticipating their pending retirement. I cringed, recalling the headline the next morning, "Who Would Buy This House?" it accused. And, they were right.

"That wasn't a tragedy, that was a miracle," Dad immediately countered.

"*What*?" I was amazed.

"Absolutely! The sinkhole was a miracle. If we had sold the Happy House at that auction all those years ago, we wouldn't have eventually sold it to Tawni and Ron, and our family wouldn't still be enjoying it today. The sinkhole was a miracle, all that was lacking was our understanding in the moment!" he enthused. "It is what it is. But, it is also what we make it. We are co-creating our reality according to our thoughts, words, and deeds." He was right. Wow, I thought to myself. Wow. *Thank you, God! Yes. Yes. Thank you, God! Wow.*

"This new technology of self is the old technology of self merely reinvented, because nothing is new in the universe, it is simply repackaged. I see a stampede of people rushing to go inside to learn about themselves, to discover themselves.

"Once people prove to themselves their own formula for personal independence, their co-creation power, and practice it, and prove to themselves that what they believe is indeed true, then they will truly never again be surprised by external events. But for this to happen, individuals must be sincere in their motivations and take responsibility for themselves and their families in the most profound of ways. Once you are *aware* of this and *know* this, you have no choice but to be deeply accountable for every thought, word and deed to ensure that they are constructive because human nature is basically good; it is constructive."

Dad looked over at me merrily, "Do you know what I'd like to construct at this very moment?"

"What?" I asked.

"Lunch," he laughed, and I agreed, so we set off for the short commute, Dad looking around, appreciating the picturesque view of my neighborhood. He turned to me, bouncing to attention and exclaimed, "The human consciousness has already evolved beyond our basic survival instincts, like food and shelter. Now is the time for us to take responsibility for our thoughts, words, and deeds. We are indeed making it up as we go along."

"Think about that, Daughter. You wouldn't even be here in North Canton if you hadn't chosen to create your own reality. You made it up!"

And, he was right, I surmised, hopping on the *Zip Train* back to the circumstances leading up to my move from Pennsylvania to Ohio over eighteen years ago.

Okay, I'll admit it. At that time, I was materialistic and superficial, but I wanted a bigger house, darn it. The skyrocketing home prices in and around Allentown due to the influx of North Jersey and New Yorkers, was making my search for a larger home in the area that I could afford agonizingly difficult.

So, I set out on a search for a more affordable city in which to live and raise my family. I scoured the bookshelves in the reference section of the library (in the days before Al Gore invented the internet), researching cost of living indexes and scrutinizing quality of life surveys for cities within an eight-hour drive from my family in Allentown.

Since I worked from home as a headhunter, and my then-husband was a car salesman, we could realistically move anywhere in the country and still be able to work, I reasoned. It was an adventure!

After narrowing down our choices to five cities, I contacted the Chambers of Commerce in each and requested relocation information on their respective towns, devouring the packets chock full of statistics on education, crime and healthcare (more stuff to read, yippee!) as they arrived one by one in the snail mail.

And then one day, there it was in black and white in the Harmon Homes magazine – the house I was born to live in. Nestled on brick paved streets in the Historic Ridgewood neighborhood of Canton, Ohio, this beautiful Tudor mansion was my dream house, and they were practically *giving* it away! The next weekend, we drove out to see the house and promptly bought it on the spot, rushing home to Allentown to place our own home on the market and begin preparations to move four hundred miles from our families.

We excitedly shared the news of our relocation adventure with everyone when suddenly Dad stopped me cold in my tracks with, "*Stark* County? Why the hell would you want to move to place named *Stark*? Doesn't that mean empty and barren?"

My heart sank. He was right. Why was I moving to a place that spelled isolation and desolation in its very name? But, I was already committed, so I put on my brave face and moved, first to my dream house, and later after the divorce, to North Canton with my sister and her family as our neighbors. *It was a Miracle! Thank you, God.*

Eleven years later I called Dad, and when he answered, asked giddily, "Dad! Guess what I just found!"

"What? Your car keys?" he guessed, playing the good sport.

"No! I found a Star!" I couldn't help it, I started laughing out loud at what was obvious the whole time, but I had never seen before.

"What?" he asked, obviously having no clue what I was about to reveal.

"A Star! There's a STAR in STARk County! I can't believe I never saw it before!" I cried.

"What are you talking about?" He sounded worried, probably questioning my sobriety.

"S-T-A-R-K!" I practically shouted, spelling the word slowly. "There's a Star in the *word* Stark!" I giggled and waited. One one-thousand, two one-thousand.

"Oh, my God!" Dad yelled, "You're right! There's a Star in Stark County!"

"I know, I know! I can't believe we never saw it before. It took me *eleven years* living in Stark County to see that!" I exclaimed.

"I didn't see it, either. Wow." Dad laughed along with me for a while and then asked, "So, who's the star?"

"North Canton. North Canton is the 'Star' in Stark County," I replied instantly, and I meant it. I *seriously* love this town! Take the best parts of Mayberry, and add in the neighborly spirit of Bedford Falls, and you still wouldn't come close to picturesque North Canton.

With just under 16,000 residents, North Canton is a small bedroom community of the larger Canton, home of the Pro Football Hall of Fame, and this area takes their football *very seriously*. Situated in northeast Ohio, it is only ten miles south of Akron (Akron *Zips!*) and fifty miles from Cleveland (Cleveland *Rocks!*) The only down side? The beach is five hundred miles away. Boo-hoo. Unless you count the northern shore of Lake Erie, then it's only an hour away.

Years ago, a client had laughed at me, "You were born in New Jersey? Why, that's the armpit of the United States!" he had accused good-naturedly.

"Oh really?" I playfully countered, "You're from Texas, so what part of the anatomy does that make you?" We had laughed, but truly, if Ohio is *the heart of it all*, then North Canton is a vital artery.

North Canton itself is surely your destination if you are seeking a quiet community in which to raise your family with affordable housing, an "Excellent" rated school district for ten years running, numerous parks, and the glorious Belden Village shopping and restaurant district a short five minute commute away.

On the other hand, if you're looking for outrageously overpriced homes, rampant crime or exorbitant property taxes, keep looking, because North Canton is none of those things. Honestly, my property taxes in North Canton are the same today as they were in the house I had moved from in Allentown, *eighteen years ago*! Don't believe me? Look it up.

I love this town! It's like heaven with a Zip Code. I wish I had the ability to extend an open invitation to everyone to relocate to North Canton to build a family, to start over, to open a business, or to just exist peacefully *every single day* knowing that their kids are safe and receiving a fantastic education.

It might sound corny, but this town adds *value* to our lives, infusing each day with a quiet confidence in the strength of our leadership, an enthusiastic support system for the kids in our schools, and the sincerity of its residents to gather together to celebrate our small town heritage.

Don't get me wrong, we sometimes have our semi-tabloid dramas, including a fired-up antagonist/zealot who routinely interrupts city council meetings with flaming rhetoric and acid-toned accusations. But, that just makes it more interesting. It is what it is, and I couldn't love it more!

I *Zipped* back to the driver's seat and excitedly pointed out the sites while mentally introducing Dad to all the great people I had met since moving here. I pointed out the corner on West Maple where Aunty Zoom Zoom stands sentry as crossing guard. A part-time clown when off-duty, she uses her crossing-guard flag as a magic wand to point to the stoplight and change it (with unfailingly perfect timing from years of practice) so the kids can safely cross the street.

Turning right at the town square, I headed south on Main passing Bitzer Park and the YMCA, the social hub of our community, and then pointed out the town newspaper, owned by Jeff, the most dedicated and selfless volunteer in our quaint city with the wickedest sense of humor I have ever encountered. This guy *never* says no, and he *always* says it in a funny way. I pointed out Gino's Foreign Auto Service, where its competent owner has been maintaining our cars for eighteen years with an honesty and integrity that lead me to pay thirty-two dollar car repair bills. Seriously.

Further south on Main sat our favorite Café, whose proprietor Steve, provides enthusiastic support for the young entrepreneurs in our family enabling Tyler to sell his chocolate from his café. And, they have the *best* hamburgers in town. I explained to Dad how I had *Zipped* by one day to pick up my lunch order and thanked Steve again for helping the kids.

"They are so quiet, I don't even know they're here," Steve had laughed, and then grew serious, nearly whispering, "Do you have any idea how much it hurts me to take their money?"

I had smiled and agreed, "I know it does, Steve. Thank you for that. But, keep taking it! They want to own their own company, and they need to learn how to pay expenses." I laughed and added, "But, I know how you feel, though. I feel the same way. Thank you again for helping them."

After turning around in the Café's parking lot, I headed north, picking up our lunch order, scrumptious quiche, at Hantzel Bakery, and then continuing my enthusiastically guided tour. I pointed out El

Rico, who's dedicated employees begin baking tortillas as early as nine, and with the mouth watering aroma snaking out of the vents and wafting across the street to our front door, you can't help but salivate waiting impatiently for lunch.

On the northeast corner sat the magestic Hoover District, so renamed after Maytag, the parent company of Hoover, had moved out of town, turning the Hoover Building, a once vibrant and active part of our community, into a ghost of its former grandness. I cringed describing to Dad the mass depression and pall that settled over our fair city when the closing was announced. It sucked the life right out of us, but only for a *Zip Time* for those of us in this amazingly resilient community.

The historic landmark was purchased by a developer from California, with the brilliant idea of turning the old worn-down factory into a mixed-use office/retail/restaurant/business district, and slowly but surely, it is miraculously coming back to life. With over nine businesses, large and small, now housed comfortably among the hallowed Hoover halls, it is attracting the young, the professional, the artistic and the family-owned businesses that will help our community thrive, while still maintaining the charming integrity of our town square's iconic building.

But, there is plenty of room to grow and a number of economic development and community groups are working diligently to attract new tenants to our bustling city. I told Dad about the Rotary, *again*, whose motto is "Service Above Self." Seriously, does it get any better than that?

I *Zip Tripped* back to the day that Dad had picked up a copy of the *Rotarian* magazine, and had loudly exclaimed to the room, "Listen to this!" repeatedly as he read of their global good works cover to cover. I'm still trying to get him to join our club that meets here, instead of Allentown's, since he spends so much time here visiting our family, and volunteers as much in town as anyone else. He would fit right in!

Heading north, we passed Brightly's Restaurant, which hosts the Monday Morning Meetings held every week at 7:45 am, where local owners and business people meet for lively business discussions, offer friendly and professional advice to entrepreneurs, and generally work to improve the local economic community. I have never failed to enjoy a tasty breakfast, laugh out loud, or learn something valuable at one of those meetings. Everyone is invited, and while the meeting is free, buying a cup of coffee or breakfast helps stimulate our local economy because every little bit helps. Go enough times, and Mindi will remember your order and bring you an extra iced-tea to go without even asking.

I *Zip Timed* it back to the day that my friend Jack had shared his idea of forming the group as a way to help the business community.

"I think it's a great idea!" I had enthused, "I think you should do it."

And, he did, just like that. For some people, you just have to get out of their way, and they make great things happen, and North Canton is *filled* with people like that. Seriously, what's not to love about our Mayberry/Bedford Falls/North Canton? Don't believe me? Come visit and prove it to yourself, and if you do, and enjoy it as much as I do, then tell everyone else you know so they can enjoy it as well. Visit enough times, and you might as well put down roots, purchase an affordable home in a quiet neighborhood, or launch a family business. Trust me, you'll have plenty of support and encouragement from the folks in this town, just like I did when I moved here from out of state so many years ago.

"I love this town!" I continued to enthuse to Dad on our drive as he just laughed, bouncing in his seat and agreeing. He is as much at home here in North Canton as I am, I thought merrily, and he lives *four hundred* miles away!

"Tell me how you *really* feel," Dad teased, "Do you know what I love?" He asked back.

"You love our town too?" I giggled back.

"Yes, I love your town, too," he agreed. "I also love how you found a way to give back to this town you love by being yourself." He turned half serious. "You have taken this feeling of love and joy that you receive from the people in your city and you've found ways to share it with others. You give back in your own way.

"The fastest way to experience joy for yourself is to create it for others first. That's exactly what you are doing with these Fun Raisers. Don't you see? It's in your DNA. You organize these events so that people can have fun, and then you experience joy watching them. You're doing it, and you're not even aware of it." He laughed some more.

"I never looked at it that way before," I said, meaning it. It hadn't started out that way. It had actually started with the same devastation and hopelessness that everyone in town experienced when Hoover closed their doors.

Seriously, this is happening *again*? I had thought incredulously. Zipping back to being a teenager in Allentown, I had watched sadly as Mack Trucks moved out and then Bethlehem Steel slowly decayed over time into a post-apocalypse ghost town. Living and breathing the employment business on a daily basis only allowed the news to impact us on a more personal basis. And now it was happening *again*? Here? *In my town*? It was high time for Billy Joel to pen a new tune.

So, we organized a group of volunteers and founded a non-profit charity, NewWorkCityFoundation.org whose mission is to create jobs. The premise is simple: Have Fun. Raise Money. Give it Back. Our all-volunteer board hosts a fun event and all proceeds raised from our Fun Raisers are offered back to a company or the community in the form of a matching grant to hire somebody.

Grant recipients can't use the money to buy a sign or a copier, they can only pay wages for somebody to work for them. We don't raise millions, in fact, we just recently enjoyed our first comma. You know, we raised enough money to have a dollar sign, a number, a comma, then a zero, zero, zero. It may not seem like much, but to someone trying to make this month's mortgage payment, every little bit helps.

We hosted two parking lot parties with live music and good food and raised enough money to hire somebody to work at the North Canton Theatre Company to sell tickets and run the concession stand for three months. We threw a "Taste of North Canton" spotlighting local restaurants at the city-owned golf course, and raised enough money to hire somebody to work part-time in their kitchen for five months and counting.

As an extension of their Junior Achievement program, we sponsored "You're Hired!" in two elementary schools, where we "hired" one hundred and fifteen fifth graders to "work" in over twenty-five local businesses for one hour on one day. The kids' exuberance for "working" in the real world was overwhelming, encouraging the town's business owners and reminding them of their own youthful enthusiasm. When they were finished "working," they were "paid" with a PayDay candy bar ('cause Pay Day is the best part of working), a Hundred Grand ('cause sometimes you get a great job), and a bag of peanuts ('cause sometimes you work for peanuts.) It was like heaven, only with mini Donald Trumps.

"Don't you see, Daughter," Dad exclaimed from beside me, pulling me from my *Zip Bus Trip* with the fifth graders, "that's how it starts. One person starts digging a hole. Then another person joins in, then another and another. After awhile, do you know what happens? That hole, that took 1,000 shovelfuls to dig, now has 1,000 people each shoveling one scoop. The hole gets dug instantly!"

"*Wouldn't it be great if* 1,000 people actually started digging at the same time?" I asked gleefully. "Like, next week, for example?" Thinking of our teeny tiny group of dedicated tireless volunteers, who would love some help.

"Yeah, that would be great," Dad agreed, laughing.

"*Wouldn't it be great* if eve-ry-one who had a great idea to help their community, and there are lots of those great people and great ideas floating around, told another person, and then they worked together to make it happen?" I asked wondrously, barely pausing for breath. I love this game!

"*Wouldn't it be great if* enough new people moved into North Canton so that all the empty storefronts were transforNed into bustling family businesses, and all the homes "For Sale" were filled with happy families with lots of kids?" I was on a roll.

"Yeah, that would be great." Dad was laughing so hard he was straining his seatbelt.

"*Wouldn't it be great if* every company in North Canton was able to offer cool benefits like flexible hours, free PayDay loans and free Roadside Assistance. That way, just working in North Canton would be a part of your bonus package!" I laughed and played another round out of turn.

"*Wouldn't it be great if* every-one donated two bucks to NewWorkCityFoundation.org to create jobs? Think how many people we could hire and all the good we could do!" I dreamed, thinking of Stark County winning the jobs lottery, where for less than the cost of a latte, we could put people to work where they are needed. Okay, maybe I was getting carried away.

"Here's one for you," he practically shouted. "*Wouldn't it be great if* eve-ry-one in town was assured food, shelter and clothing just because, as a community, we *care*, and we all work together to make it happen?"

"Yep," I enthused, "that would be great!" It was Dad's turn to roll.

"Wouldn't it be great if the 'New Healthcare' was actually based on people taking individual responsibility for *being* healthy? That way, they could fill their prescriptions for exercise and healthy eating plans, instead of overpriced pharmaceuticals." He laughed, "Of course, that means you would have to give up smoking, Daughter."

I shot him a look and then replied with the obvious, "Yeah, that would be great," and smiled, knowing he was right.

"I have one," I changed the subject quickly. *"Wouldn't it be great if* employment agencies became talent agencies and people had 'talent agents' representing them to companies, negotiating their projects and contracts, treating them like movie stars or sports heroes?"

"Oh, here's another one," I sputtered. *"Wouldn't it be great if* unemployment was transforNed into re-employment? Where people could be *paid to work* hands-on learning a new skill or opening their own business?" I asked, eyes shining with the audacity of hope. Now, there's a shovel-ready project, I thought.

Dad jumped in, *"Wouldn't it be great if* Oprah taped one of her shows here in North Canton as a Fun Raiser? Think of the jobs we could create just from that! Especially if she gave away gifts, but shopped only in Stark County for them!" We laughed together, dreaming, until Dad took another turn in the game.

"Wouldn't it be great if eve-ry-one loved what they did for a living, had fun doing it, and got paid for it too? They could experience the feeling of going to life, have fun and get paid all at the same time!" He giggled and bounced in his seat.

Oooohhh, that's a good one, I thought, then jumped in with, *"Wouldn't it be great if* our educational system was such that kids could travel around the country to physically see our great nation and *experience* geography and history, and great teachers were paid on the scale of corporate CEO's?"

"Oooohhh, that's a good one," Dad said soberly, and I laughed out loud at his ESPN tracking system. *This is Fun. Thank you, God.*

> *"Where there is no vision, the people will perish."*
> *– Proverbs 29:18*

"Don't you see, Daughter, it *could* be that way! That way of life is not only possible, it is probable!" he laughed. "Once people go inside and transforN their perceptions, they have no choice but to then spread that happiness and joy to others. First, they start with their families and their kids, then they spread that good news to their friends and neighbors, turning every house on the block into a sanctuary. Soon, those people are reaching out to their communities, and then to the world. You can indeed change the world by changing yourself.

He continued exuberantly, "Being yourself is a state-of-the-art way of being that you take with you from city to city. It's ev-ery-where you go. TransforNation is a virtual city, a feeling, a way of being in the moment that spreads from yourself, from your home, to others, to your neighborhood, to your city, to your world. It's eve-ery-where. It's in the cities, the villages, and in the 'burbs, on the tops of the mountains, and in bottom of the valleys, it stretches across the purple mountain plains and spreads from sea to shining sea, because it's in eve-ry-one. It's the ocean back into the drop. As more and more people decide to be themselves by being aware of their thoughts, words, and deeds, then you will see the magic of numbers grow exponentially. One plus One equals Three."

His voice grew softer, "And then one day, people will look back and ask, 'How did they do that? How did they improve their nation?' Do you know what the answer will be?" He paused dramatically before continuing, "The answer is that ev-ery-one did it! Each and every person each did their own part, small as it was, then they stepped aside and allowed the Creator to perform a miracle! And it was indeed a miracle, but it got done, at *Just the Right Time*, one shovel full at a *Time*. Do. Did. Deed. It was a transforNation."

* * * * *

Dad and I returned to the house and sat at the table, devouring the sausage and cheddar quiche, each of us lost in our own thoughts, our own worlds and our own *Zip Time Zones*, looking at the book, only pages from completion, on the table between us. I still couldn't believe it was real. It had been there all this time, waiting for me, waiting for us. All I had to do was write it down. And now I'm almost done. It was so close I could *taste* it. *It is already there, waiting for us.*

After some *Zip Time*, Dad brought us both back to earth, "You know, Daughter, I still get teary thinking about that day in our dream house when I had the epiphany that not only do I create my own reality, but that it was already there waiting for me the moment I conceived of it. At that moment, I just wanted to shout from the rooftops what I had discovered. I wanted to share it with the world."

I knew exactly how he felt, *Zip-Sticking* it back to my own epiphany the week I had spent blissfully considering the myriad possibilities. Could I do it again? Did I *want* to do it again? Back and forth I went, over and over again, delighting in the limitless possibilities.

By the time that long-ago, exciting week ended, I knew what I wanted. I chose to prove it to myself again, but this time, I chose not to do it for myself, but to do it for eve-ry-one, starting with my kids. I remembered a comment I had once heard, "Don't let go of your dreams." Hah! I thought, they won't let go of *me*!

I think I knew *exactly* how Dad felt, and he proved me right by dialing into the same ESPN wavelength, saying, "I had proven it to myself that I could create *something* out of *nothing* and from that point on, I wouldn't rest until eve-ry-one had proven it to themselves as well. My ideal choice would be for eve-ry-one to feel this way, and I'm starting with my daughters and grandkids. But, I could easily imagine ev-ery single person experiencing the same exhilarating rush of excitement and *belief* in themselves that I felt at that very moment. I prefer for eve-ry-one to live their creation. To be it and experience it in all its glory and wonder. To view every moment as an opportunity to celebrate and experience the joyful magnificence that is our life. It is our birthright to create, maintain, and experience our own heaven on earth."

"Whatever anyone chooses for themselves, I choose those things for them as well, and I make the obvious choice to serve them in any way that I can to assist them in realizing their dreams. This isn't about me. This is bigger than me, this is bigger than *all of us*."

And yet, oddly at the same time, I thought, it is us. It's the ocean back into the drop. *It is what it is. It is what you make it.*

"Where two or more are gathered
in My Name, I am there."

Dad continued, "The greatest gift you could ever bestow on another is to give themselves back to themselves. Neale Donald Walsch writes, 'The purpose of the process of personal creation is to create a happy, peaceful, joyous life for everyone whose life you touch, and for you, in that order.' And that's what I do, every single day!" Dad rejoiced. "I search for ways to bring joy and happiness to others so that if they are feeling low or miserable, they might say to themselves, "It is what it is, but maybe it doesn't have to be that way. *Wouldn't it be great if...?*" He laughed out loud.

"I want everyone to feel that way!" He beamed, glowing from the inside out. "The fastest way to experience happiness for yourself, is to create it for others *first*! I'm creating it and making it up as I go along. In the reality of the moment, I am affecting every energy field around me. I am in awe of what is being created one moment at a time right before my very eyes. Don't you see, Daughter, all these cycles of creation we talk about are happening every single moment." Dad paused to breathe deeply before continuing.

"Coffee takes six minutes to brew, this book has taken roughly eighteen months up to now, you've been in business for eleven years. Why, with a joyous act and nine months, you can do your part to make a baby! These are all cycles of co-creation that are happening every single moment of every single day, but every moment is at the *same time.* Wrap your mind around that!"

The Preacher jumped in quickly before retreating again,

"There is a new creation every Moment,
yet every Moment exists at once.

All that ever was, is, and ever
shall be is happening Now.

Enjoy the Moment.

Be Yourself.

Live in the Moment."

"Believing is 'Being it' and 'Living it' in the moment." Dad laughed. "Wouldn't it be great if eve-ry-one was being real in the moment, every single moment? Wouldn't it be great if eve-ry-one could experience this joy received from creating happiness for another? We would have nothing to fear from anyone we encountered. We would be safe. We would be Home."

Dad went on with a flourish, "It starts with the hope that things *could* be that way, which gives way to a belief, and eventually TransForns into a knowing that it is indeed that way in our world. It is a primary law within infinity that nothing ever truly dies. Energy is neither created nor destroyed, it merely changes form. As people TransForN themselves from a person of *wanting* and *needing* into persons of *being*, they can make room for their greater self to emerge and shine." Dad turned the floor over to *The Preacher*.

> *"This psychological state of Being is not an illusion, it is a dimension for experience. As you TransForN yourself from a state of wanting to a state of Being, you will look back and evaluate the life you are leaving behind."*

> *"TransForNation is alchemy of the soul, building upon your Greater Self and TransForNing it for the Greater Good of eve-ry-one. It's a State-of-the-Art Way of Being. Wouldn't it be great if we could TransForN the "Me" generation into the "We" generation?"*

Dad interrupted *The Preacher* with, "If people can do it once, they can do it a thousand times. If they can bring peace, joy, and happiness to themselves and their families, they can do it for others as well. Prove it to yourself. As long as the world has people, people will have needs. We can indeed change the world if we just focus on *being* ourselves. So, dream bigger dreams. Be the change you want to see in the world, *now*. As our forefathers promised, our country is once again becoming a nation "By the People and For the People. We *are* indeed a transforNation."

And, I believe him. But everyone believes differently.

Dad turned and focused his laser gaze on me picking up my ESPN signal, "As for what we *believe*?, every person still needs to decide for themselves what they believe, according to their perceptions. They have to prove to themselves what's true for them. Every single person has the inalienable right to believe what they believe to be true, and I respect their right to believe it."

"We can't tell anybody else how it is. We can only tell how it is for us. We can only speak for ourselves and describe our perception of what it feels like to be *us* in the world we live in today. We can only describe what it is like to be *us*, in our family, at this time."

"Everyone has his or her own story to tell," Dad mused, "his own beliefs to state, his own dreams to prove. All I can share with my grandchildren is what we did, what we lived, and what we still live today – the good, the bad, and the ugly. I would share with my grandchildren: Be yourself joyfully in the moment, give thanks continually, and share that joy with ev-ery-one, at *every* opportunity. Write it all down, and prove it to yourself that what you believe is true. It is what it is, and it is what you make it. All roads lead to Rome, so choose your own path and stick to it."

"You co-create your own Reality
according to your thoughts, words and deeds.
Imagination and feeling follow that Belief."

I thought about his words, and although this book has transforNed from something I was scared to write to something I was eager to read, I'm not even finished yet, and who knows what will happen after that?

At the very least, I'll have a book about our family's history and my Dad's beliefs that I can put on my bookshelf and read to my kids of their starring roles in our lives (hopefully not putting them to sleep). It's like a family tree or a scrapbook, but instead of pasting photos of fond memories, I've described what it felt like for us to be there and to live it, moment by moment.

As for you holding this book? You have to prove it to yourself. Write your own story. Write your family's story. Describe what it feels like to be a daughter or a son, a dad or a mom, a brother or a sister, to have a dream that miraculously came true, or a dream that was squashed like a dropped watermelon during a secret game of Pass the Potato at Girl Scout camp. (Author's note: I'm innocent on that one, too.)

Wherever you are in your life, right now at this moment, turn to a clean blank page and write the end in the beginning. Your story will meet you right where you are, and will unfold miraculously at *just the right time.*

It's already all there, waiting for you. Just write it down. Write down what you believe, or think you believe, and prove it to yourself. Write down what it feels like to be you as you grow stronger through the trials and sacrifices that you alone face.

When you get to a point in the story that you don't like, turn to a new page and continue on. Don't erase it or tear out the page, just build upon what you've already written. Write of the relationships that fulfill you, and share your story with others to ease their transforNation. Be yourself, and write it all down.

It's already all there, waiting for you. Count your miracles and write them all down. And when the circumstances dictate, go back and re-read what you wrote, and then rinse and repeat as many times as necessary.

Tyler, you once bemoaned to me, "there is nothing *new.*" I disagree. There is nothing *but* new! This is the story of the moment and each moment is a new story. Wrap your mind around that!

If I had a dollar for every single time somebody said to me, "I always wanted to write a book. I have *great* stories," I would be a bill-ion-aire, complete with my pinky on my lip. If you are at all receiving the ESPN channel, then you would know what my response is: "That's a great idea! You should do it! Because I believe in you." Please, *share* your story. I'll read it. (I hope at the beach) I love to read!

One thing I do know: this is my Dad's story and our family's story wrapped in a Tale of Three Cities: Allentown, Ocean City, and North Canton. It's the story of our lives, the story of our times, and the story of the moment. The best part is, we're still living this reality show.

Is it true? As Dad would say, question everything, especially a five-foot tall, blonde, Polish, uneducated single mother, a woman in a man's world with a pronounced fear of public speaking, who lacks the ability to raise one eyebrow at a time but holds the Olympic record for breaking out into goosebumps at the slightest provocation. (Author's note: That's my story, and I'm sticking to it.) Prove it to yourself.

In the meantime, I am a *writer/typer* because I write and type. I'm having a fantabulous time and although blood, sweat and cheers have gone into it, I wrote a book…almost! *This is a miracle! Thank you, God!*

I turned to hug Dad, and with a twinkle in my eye, Googlebumps and laughter erupting from my body, exclaimed, "This is Fun, Dad! Wanna do it again?"

About the Authors

Richard Grudzinski

Richard Grudzinski has enjoyed a successful career as an entrepreneur for over forty years, opening his first employment agency in Allentown, PA 1966, and later transitioning the company into an executive recruiting firm and career counseling practice. For the past ten years, he has been recognized by the "Learning for Life" program sponsored by the Boy Scouts of America and serves the community as an energetic and often requested public speaking expert in Strategic Career Planning, enthusiastically presenting his program to thousands of students.

As part of his program, he gives each student a two dollar bill telling them, "now you have just as much as I did when I started out," enthusiastically giving away thousands of dollars over the years. His passion for sharing his message through public speaking oozes from his pores and electrifies his audience. He giggles with a wink and laughs with his whole body, infusing people with his positive energy that instills not just hope, but belief. People walk away from his seminars yearning for more of his philosophy, more of his funny stories, more of his passion...and a book.

Richard is committed to devoting the next twenty-five years to serving as an enthusiastic messenger for Two Buck$, sharing with others how to create their own personal happiness... not only because it is an ongoing testimony proving that he creates his own reality, but because it makes him and others, well, happy!

Vicki Stanley

Following in her father's footsteps, Vicki Stanley has over twenty-five years in the employment industry, and with a grateful start-up loan provided by her dad, founded her own medical staffing agency, in North Canton, Ohio in 1999. Apparently finding people jobs isn't the only DNA she inherited from her father, and her entrepreneurial spirit led her to open a home-improvement service for seniors, and to launch the New Work City Foundation, a 501c3 non-profit to create jobs. She spends her days raising her two delightful boys, running the nursing agency, volunteering, and devoting her spare (!) time to her newest passion, writing.

Two Buck$
to Happiness

Visit www.TwoBucksToHappiness.com
for more information, free resources and
additional products and materials.

Coming Soon

Man of Spiel

Men. If there's a million fish in the sea, why did she have
to catch a shark? Three women looking for love meet a
dashing archeologist with a heart-melting British accent
on the same online dating website. But behind his sweet
talking façade is an international con artist with things on
his mind other than Cupid. Within thirty days one person
has lost their innocence, one has lost their life savings, and
one has lost a life. How these women react and overreact
to their new Romeo will have you jumping out of your seat
yelling, "You go girl!" as they race the clock toward a cata-
clysmic showdown of revenge and the ultimate payback.

Available summer 2012.